Sustainable Tourism in Protected Areas

Guidelines for Planning and Management

Sustainable Tourism in Protected Areas

Guidelines for Planning and Management

Paul F. J. Eagles, Stephen F. McCool and Christopher D. Haynes
Prepared for the
United Nations Environment Programme, World Tourism Organization
and IUCN – The World Conservation Union

Adrian Phillips, Series Editor

World Commission on Protected Areas (WCPA)

Best Practice Protected Area Guidelines Series No. 8

IUCN – The World Conservation Union
2002

This publication has been made possible in large part by funding from Cardiff University, Environment Australia, United Nations Environment Programme, World Tourism Organization and IUCN.

Published by: IUCN, Gland, Switzerland, and Cambridge, UK, the United Nations Environment Programme and the World Tourism Organization

Citation: Eagles, Paul F.J., McCool, Stephen F. and Haynes, Christopher D.A. (2002). *Sustainable Tourism in Protected Areas: Guidelines for Planning and Management*. IUCN Gland, Switzerland and Cambridge, UK. xv + 183pp.

ISBN: 2-8317-0648-3

Cover design: IUCN Publications Services Unit

Cover photos: Front: Cheetah in Masai Mara Game Reserve, Kenya, ©*Robert Bernard*

Back: Ferry at Heron Island, Great Barrier Reef Marine Park, Australia, ©*Paul F. J. Eagles*; Birding in Monteverde Cloud Forest Reserve, Costa Rica, ©*Jim Boissoneault* and Banff Springs Hotel, Banff National Park, Canada, ©*Paul F. J. Eagles*

Layout by: IUCN Publications Services Unit

Produced by: IUCN Publications Services Unit

Printed by: Thanet Press Limited, UK

Available from: IUCN Publications Services Unit
219c Huntingdon Road, Cambridge CB3 0DL,
United Kingdom
Tel: +44 1223 277894
Fax: +44 1223 277175
E-mail: info@books.iucn.org
www: http://www.iucn.org/bookstore
A catalogue of IUCN publications is also available

The text of this book is printed on 115gsm Fineblade Smooth made from low-chlorine pulp.

Table of Contents

Foreword by the United Nations Environment Programme

Tourism is good business, as it produces 4.4% of the world's GDP, and employs around 200 million people globally. It can also help the sustainable management of protected areas, as a market-based alternative catering to the growing number of discriminating travellers trying to find, understand and enjoy a natural environment. Tourism can support the protection of natural resources, as local residents realise the value of their asset and want to preserve it.

At the same time, our global heritage of living species is threatened as never before, as the protected areas that harbour so much of our biodiversity are exposed to the pressures of unsustainable development. The precautionary approach urges us to be especially concerned about tourism in protected areas, given the risk of damage and destruction to this unique natural resource.

Visitor impact management is ever more important as the number of tourists increases, and their distribution is often concentrated in major tourism destinations in ecologically vulnerable areas. The United Nations Environment Programme (UNEP) has been actively supporting protected area managers, working with WTO, UNESCO and IUCN, for over 12 years, through technical assistance to key stakeholders, and capacity building in projects and publications. This publication is the latest in this series, and UNEP is proud to be a partner in this milestone reference work.

Ensuring that tourism follows a truly sustainable path, and that it contributes to the sustainable management of protected areas, whether public or private, will require enhanced cooperation and concrete partnerships among the tourism industry, governments at all levels, local communities, protected area managers and planners, and the tourists themselves. This book describes how this can be done, and UNEP is happy to present it to all interested parties, especially protected area managers, on the occasion of the International Year of Ecotourism 2002.

Jacqueline Aloisi de Larderel
Assistant Executive Director
Division of Technology, Industry and Economics
United Nations Environment Programme

April 2002

Foreword by the World Tourism Organization

The World Tourism Organization (WTO) is pleased to present to the international community, and especially to public administrations and private sector businesses directly involved in tourism activities, this new publication containing guidelines for the sustainable development and management of tourism in protected areas.

Tourism has become a major sector of economic activity since the latter part of the twentieth century and all indications are that it will continue growing in the years to come. With this growth, a diversification of tourism products and destinations is taking place, with increased demand for nature-related tourism, including ecotourism, visitation to national and natural parks, rural-based tourism, and the like. The tourists themselves are becoming increasingly sophisticated in their demands; this is not only in terms of luxury at the various establishments they use, but especially in terms of having a meaningful travel experience, including such aspects as cultural authenticity, contacts with local communities, and learning about flora, fauna, special ecosystems and natural life in general, and its conservation.

The expected growth and the new trends observed put tourism in a strategic position to make a positive contribution to, or to negatively affect, the sustainability of natural protected areas and the development potential of surrounding areas and their communities. Tourism can in fact be a major tool for the conservation of such areas and for raising the environmental awareness of residents and visitors. These objectives can be achieved through the generation of financial resources from tourism that can be dedicated to conservation measures, and through appropriate information, interpretation and education programmes for visitors and residents. Additionally, tourism operations within protected areas need to be carefully planned, managed and monitored in order to ensure their long-term sustainability. Otherwise, negative impacts will be generated and tourism will instead contribute to the further deterioration of these areas.

WTO has been producing know-how and specific guidelines for the sustainable development and management of tourism in different types of destinations. It has also been disseminating good practices observed throughout the world, and supporting governments and the private sector with the necessary tools and technical advice to continuously raise the level of sustainability of the industry.

In presenting this publication to all types of users, WTO would like to emphasise the need for tourism managers, be they public or private, to work closely with those responsible for nature conservation and protected areas. Their joint cooperation should ensure that the twin objectives of conservation and development are suitably balanced and that tourism effectively contributes to safeguard the planet's precious resources. This book, coming out during the International Year of Ecotourism, can be a useful instrument for achieving this goal.

World Tourism Organization
Madrid, March 2002

Acknowledgements

Special thanks must go to Jeffrey A. McNeely, James W. Thorsell and Hector Ceballos-Lascurain who prepared the first version of these Guidelines. Peter Shackleford, former Chief of Environment and Planning of the World Tourism Organization (WTO) initiated a new version of this publication and Eugenio Yunis of WTO continued his work. Helene Genot, Senior Consultant with the United Nations Environment Programme (UNEP), encouraged a co-operative effort in the development of this new, expanded publication supported by Giulia Carbone. David Sheppard, Head of the Programme on Protected Areas of IUCN – The World Conservation Union, was a strong supporter of multi-agency co-operation in the preparation of these Guidelines.

As a result, these new Guidelines are the product of the co-operative effort of many people in UNEP, WTO and the IUCN. The funding for the project came from UNEP, WTO and Environment Australia. The authors and other content contributors came from the World Commission on Protected Areas (WCPA) of IUCN.

Thanks to the Universities of Waterloo and Montana, which supported Dr Eagles and Dr McCool respectively in this work, and to the Department of Conservation and Land Management in Western Australia which similarly supported Mr Haynes.

A special debt is owed to Pam Wight, a tourism consultant, who undertook a full review of a draft of the Guidelines. She provided thorough and very helpful editorial changes and comments, and substantial additional material. Her suggested revisions and document reorganisation were very influential in the final version, and the result was much improved through her contribution.

In addition, Dick Stanley of the Department of Canadian Heritage, Ross Constable of the New South Wales National Parks and Wildlife Service in Australia, Lee Thomas of Environment Australia and Derek Wade of Parks Canada contributed significantly to the economic benefits section of the Guidelines. Per Nilsen of Parks Canada provided a key section of the Guidelines dealing with risk management, and commented extensively on the chapter dealing with infrastructure and services. Rob Black of Parks Victoria provided important comments on the concession management component of the Guidelines. Oliver Hillel of UNEP provided critically important editorial advice and publication guidance.

Thanks also go to Ross Constable, a Ranger with the New South Wales National Parks and Wildlife Service, for providing assistance with the Montague Island Case Study. Richard Davies of the Northwest Parks Board of South Africa helped with the Madikwe Wildlife Reserve Case Study. Information on Chumbe Island came from Eleanor Carter in Tanzania. Chuck Hutchison of Conservation International provided current information on the Kakum National Park project in Ghana.

A number of the case studies were taken from winners of the Protected Areas category of British Airways Tourism for Tomorrow Awards. This category is organised jointly with IUCN and we applaud the airline company for this encouragement for environmentally sound tourism.

IUCN gave permission for the use of case study material originally published in the *Guidelines for Tourism in Parks and Protected Areas of East Asia* (Eagles *et al.*, 2001).

Dawn Culverson and Elizabeth Halpenny, both graduate students in the Department of Recreation and Leisure Studies at the University of Waterloo, were the research and editorial assistants on the project to prepare these Guidelines. Ms Halpenny undertook a complete editorial review of a late version of the draft. Ms Culverson wrote the Human Resource section of the Guidelines. The Department of Recreation and Leisure Studies at the University of Waterloo provided office and support services to the project. Catherine Eagles provided detailed comments on the copy proof version of the document.

The reproduction of the photographs used in this book was made possible by a contribution from Environment Australia. The photographers include Paul Eagles, Jim Boissoneault and Robert Bernard. Thanks are due to the photographers for the use of their images.

The authors thank their wives and children for years of patience and assistance.

About the authors

Paul F. J. Eagles was originally trained as a biologist, then went on to receive M.Sc. and Ph.D. degrees in resource development and planning. He is a Registered Professional Planner in Canada. As a Professor at the University of Waterloo in Canada, he has published over 270 publications. He started working in Ontario Provincial Parks in 1970, first as a summer student employee, then later as a full time parks planner.

From left to right: Paul Eagles, Chris Haynes and Steve McCool.

He went on to work as a planner in many areas, with planning projects in parks, tourism, highway design, electrical power line placement, subdivision design, environmentally sensitive areas, mine and pit opening, wetland creation, urban design, watershed planning and government policy development. He has worked in over 20 countries, with substantial experience in North America, Africa and Central America. Since 1996 Dr Eagles has been the Chair of the Task Force on Tourism and Protected Areas of IUCN's WCPA.

Stephen F. McCool is Professor of Wildland Recreation Management at the School of Forestry, The University of Montana in Missoula, Montana, USA. Dr McCool was initially trained as a forester, and then went on to receive M.Sc. and Ph.D. degrees in outdoor recreation management. He has been professionally involved in management and planning of protected areas for over 30 years, and has authored over 200 publications. His work emphasizes sustainability, public participation and natural resource planning processes, particularly the Limits of Acceptable Change. He is a member of WCPA and serves on its Task Force on Tourism and Protected Areas.

Chris Haynes has had a career in natural area management for over 36 years. Having trained in forestry, he worked in different aspects of that field in South Australia and the Northern Territory of Australia before becoming the first superintendent of Kakadu National Park, one of the largest and most biologically diverse protected areas in the world. He was Director of National Parks in Western Australia between 1985 and 1994, and Director of Regional Services in the Department of Conservation and Land Management in the same state before spending four years working as a consultant. During this time he also lectured in environmental management at the University of Notre Dame, Australia. He has just returned to Kakadu National Park, as Park Manager. Mr Haynes has published papers on Aboriginal use of fire and on visitor use in natural areas, and was co-editor of *Monsoonal Australia*, a book about the biogeography of Australia's north. He is also a member of the World Commission on Protected Areas and its Tourism Task Force.

Preface

The link between protected areas and tourism is as old as the history of protected areas. Protected areas need tourism, and tourism needs protected areas. Though the relationship is complex and sometimes adversarial, tourism is always a critical component to consider in the establishment and management of protected areas.

These guidelines aim to build an understanding of protected area tourism, and its management. They provide a theoretical structure, but are also intended to help managers in practical ways. The underlying aim is to ensure that tourism contributes to the purposes of protected areas and does not undermine them.

While protected area planners and managers can do much to build a more constructive relationship with the tourism sector, they operate within legal, political, economic and cultural contexts that greatly limit their freedom. Moreover tourism itself is driven by many forces that are beyond the influence of park managers. Therefore the success of these Guidelines depends in part on action taken by governments and others, for example in updating legislation relating to protected areas and tourism, or introducing economic incentives to encourage sustainable forms of tourism.

Nonetheless, managers can and do play a critical role. By working with a broad range of stakeholders, and notably the industry and local communities, they can do much to ensure that tourism works for their park and for the people living in it or nearby. These Guidelines contain numerous practical suggestions about how this can be done, based not only on sound theory but also on practice from around the world. In order to draw out practical advice, a number of sections are highlighted thus: *Guidelines*.

1. Introduction

1.1 Purpose of the Guidelines

The main purpose of these Guidelines is to assist protected area managers and other stakeholders in the planning and management of protected areas, visitor recreation and the tourism industry, so that tourism can develop in a sustainable fashion, while respecting local conditions and local communities. A key message is the importance of managing resources and visitors today, so that tomorrow's visitors can also experience quality sites, and the conservation values that these places represent.

The Guidelines also have a number of more detailed objectives:

■ To discuss the role of visitor management, including techniques that control and limit impacts of use, while allowing maximum enjoyment of as many visitors as can be accommodated within the limits set by environmental and social conditions;

■ To outline approaches to the planning and development of tourism infrastructure and services in protected areas;

■ To provide guidance on the definition, measurement, management and use of park tourism data;

■ To outline ways of enhancing the quality of the tourism experience;

■ To describe positive examples, through a variety of case studies, of how tourism can effectively contribute to the conservation of natural and cultural diversity; and

■ To give positive examples, again through the use of case studies, of how tourism can contribute to the development of local communities.

This is a handbook, not a cookbook. The major questions and issues involved in managing tourism in protected areas are developed for the reader, but the publication does not set out to provide all the detailed answers. Thus a framework is provided to establish principles and guide decisions. There is no "one-size-fits-all" answer to the challenge of tourism in

Cave and Basin Hot Springs in Banff National Park, Canada

Many of North America's earliest national parks contained hot springs and health-related tourism
©*Paul F. J. Eagles*

1

Campsite in Bon Echo Provincial Park, Ontario, Canada

Throughout much of the world the provision of camping opportunities is a fundamental aspect of park tourism. ©*Paul F. J. Eagles*

protected areas – indeed an attraction of visiting protected areas is to see how each park manager has developed his or her local situation in a way that projects its uniqueness, while contributing to the common endeavour of conservation. To a large extent, management must be responsive to local conditions.

It may appear that protected area managers have a relatively simple job in achieving the task of conservation and visitor use, but in fact it is not easy at all. Managers have the challenging responsibility of balancing the many competing pressures thrust upon them. This challenge grows and becomes more complicated with increasing numbers of visitors, changes in patterns of visitor use, and the emergence of an ever more critical public demanding higher standards in conservation management.

The challenge of protected area management, especially that of dealing with the pressures of recreation and tourism, will only be met effectively through building partnerships between all the interested parties. It is hoped that this document, by being available to protected area managers as well as other important stakeholders, such as local communities, tour operators and conservation groups, will help build such partnerships.

1.2 Tourism terms and definitions

All tourism is measured and described by statistics on volume and impact. It is important for measurement, statistics and reporting, that standardized definitions of tourism be used. Appendix A contains the World Tourism Organization definitions for tourism.

A programme for the measurement of public use of a protected area should meet the requirements of park managers for reliable data for management, natural resource protection, maintenance operations and visitor services. Moreover, public use data of protected areas are important to all stakeholders. But this requires standardised terminology and approaches to the measurement of tourism. Only in this way will we be

Environmental Education with School Children, Kruger National Park, South Africa

Environmental education with children is very important to the development of a supportive local and regional community in the future. ©*Paul F. J. Eagles*

Figure 1.1   Annual public use of the national parks of Costa Rica

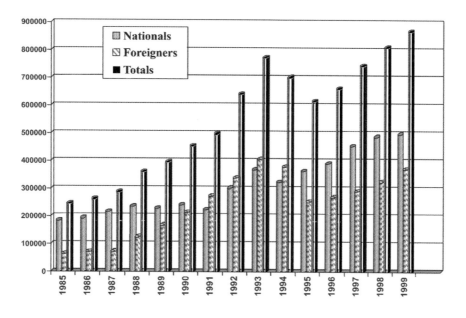

Adapted from Baez, 2001

assured of comparable data between protected areas, over time, across a protected area system and amongst countries. WCPA has published standardised terms for park visitation and tourism (Hornback and Eagles, 1999), some of which are reproduced in Appendix B.

Figure 1.1 illustrates the importance of reliable data based on consistent methods of collection. Like thousands of other tables of its kind, it shows park usage figures over

3

time, in this case for the national parks of Costa Rica. These figures reveal a nearly fourfold increase between 1985 and 1999 (despite a downturn in the early 1990's). In this case, we know that the data show meaningful trends because they have been carefully collected, with an eye to truthfulness and reliability. It is very important that all protected area management agencies collect and provide data that are accurate, consistent and up-to-date.

2. Protected areas, biodiversity and conservation

2.1 A short history of protected areas

Protected areas are a cultural artefact, and have a long history. For example, some historians claim that areas were specifically set aside in India for the protection of natural resources over two millennia ago (Holdgate, 1999). In Europe, some areas were protected as hunting grounds for the rich and powerful nearly 1,000 years ago. Moreover, the idea of protection of special places is universal: it occurs among the traditions of communities in the Pacific ("tapu" areas) and parts of Africa (sacred groves), for example.

While many societies set aside special areas for cultural and resource uses, protected areas were first set aside by kings and other national rulers in Europe early in the Renaissance, typically as royal hunting reserves. Slowly these sites became open for public use, providing the basis for community involvement and tourism. The English poet, William Wordsworth, wrote in 1810 of his vision of the Lake District as "a sort of national property". And in 1832, the American poet, explorer, and artist George Catlin pointed to the need for "...a nation's park, containing man and beast, in all the wild and freshness of their nature's beauty". Catlin was responding to the destruction of aboriginal peoples and cultures in the rapidly developing eastern part of this expanding

Great Plaza of Temple I in Tikal National Park, Guatemala

Many countries have national park systems that protect both natural and cultural heritage.
©*Paul F. J. Eagles*

5

country; in contrast, he perceived a harmony between the native peoples and their environment on the Great Plains. In 1864, with the Yosemite Grant, the US Congress gave a small but significant part of the present Yosemite National Park to the State of California for "public use, resort and recreation". The first true national park came in 1872 with the dedication of Yellowstone by United States law "as a public park or pleasuring ground for the benefit and enjoyment of the people". Interestingly, the creation of Yellowstone did not allow for the sympathetic treatment of native people and their environment as envisaged by Catlin.

These and other early United States national parks, such as Grand Canyon and Mount Rainier, were created in the west and covered extensive tracts of land with superb natural features. However, the idea of making the great natural areas of the US into national parks was most popular with large sections of the population that lived in the east of the country.

In 1866, the British Colony of New South Wales in Australia reserved 2,000ha (nearly 5,000 acres) of land, containing the Jenolan Caves west of Sydney, for protection and tourism. Later additions created a park complex now known as the Blue Mountains National Park. In 1879, Royal National Park was set up, also in New South Wales, in the wilds south of Sydney, so as to provide a natural recreation area for the burgeoning populations of this metropolitan area.

In 1885, Canada gave protection to hot springs in the Bow Valley of the Rocky Mountains, an area later named Banff National Park. The legislation passed in 1887 borrowed from the Yellowstone legislative wording: the park was "reserved and set aside as a public park and pleasure ground for the benefit, advantage and enjoyment of the people of Canada". The railway companies, whose lines were under development

Kit Fox in Tikal National Park, Guatemala

The conservation of the important cultural site of the Mayan City of Tikal also conserves the rare Kit Fox.
©*Paul F. J. Eagles*

Ocellated Turkey in Tikal National Park, Guatemala

The rare Ocellated Turkey is abundant in Tikal National Park due to effective biodiversity conservation management. ©*Paul F. J. Eagles*

across the country, saw the creation of a park as an excellent way to stimulate passenger growth through tourism (Marty, 1984).

Elsewhere, several forest reserves were set up in South Africa in the last years of the nineteenth century. In 1894, Tongariro National Park was established in New Zealand by agreement with the Maori people, a place that was, and still is, important to them for spiritual reasons.

There were common features to these emerging national parks. First, they were created by government action. Second, the areas set aside were generally large and contained relatively natural environments. Third, the parks were made available to all people. Thus, from the very beginning, park visitation and tourism were central pillars of the national parks movement.

In large, federated countries, such as Australia, Canada, South Africa and the USA, the provincial or state tier of governments also started to create protected areas. For example, the Province of Ontario in Canada created Queen Victoria Niagara Falls Park in 1885 and Algonquin National Park, later named Algonquin Provincial Park, in 1893.

As more and more parks were created, it became necessary to set up a coordinated management structure. In 1911, Canada created the world's first park agency, the Dominion Parks Bureau under its director, James B. Harkin. The US National Park Service (USNPS) was established in 1916. The management philosophy given to the USNPS involved both protection and use. The Act states that:

"the Service thus established shall promote and regulate the use of Federal areas known as national parks, monuments and reservations ... by such means and

measures as [to] conform to the fundamental purpose of the said parks, monuments and reservations, which purpose is to conserve the scenery and the natural and historic objects and the wild life therein and to provide for the enjoyment of the same in such manner and by such means as will leave them unimpaired for the enjoyment of future generations".

Both Stephen T. Mather, the first Director of the USNPS and James B. Harkin advocated getting people into the parks so that they could enjoy their benefits and support the parks financially. They also developed management principles and structures to handle such visitation, sometimes creating situations that were later widely regretted.

Thus, a theme that runs right through the early history of protected areas is of people and land together, of people being as much a part of the concept as the land and natural and cultural resources. It was also part of the message of John Muir, Scots émigré and founder of the Sierra Club, who, in his "make the mountains glad" appeal, invited people to get out of the cities and into his beloved Sierra Nevada mountains for the good of their souls. It was also apparent that, almost from the outset, different countries were ready to learn from each other about how to set up and run parks.

So the modern protected area movement has nineteenth century origins in the then "new" nations of Australia, Canada, New Zealand, South Africa and the USA, but during the twentieth century the idea spread around the world. The result was a remarkable expansion in the number of protected areas. Nearly every country passed protected area legislation and designated sites for protection. In all, by the year 2002 some 44,000 sites met the IUCN definition of a protected area (see below); together these covered nearly 10% of the land surface of the planet (data from UNEP-WCMC). The growth in the number and areal extent of protected areas is shown in Figure 2.1.

As the network grew, understanding of what is meant by a "protected area" evolved. Thus, the initial, relatively simple concept of large wild areas "set aside" for protection and enjoyment was complemented by other models more appropriate to different parts

Figure 2.1   Growth in protected areas – 1900 to the present

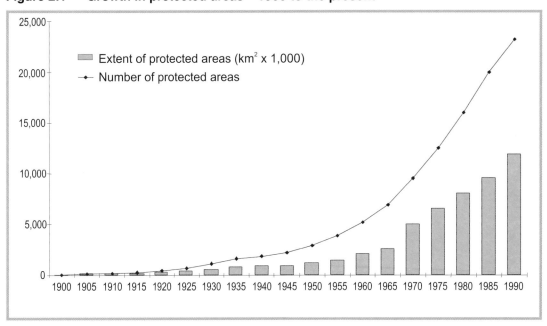

Peter Murrell Conservation Area, Tasmania, Australia

Even small parks can have important conservation roles. This small conservation area in Tasmania provides habitat for the endangered Forty-spotted Pardalote. ©*Paul F. J. Eagles*

of the world. Many countries placed more emphasis on cultural values than was initially the case with the early national parks. Protection of lived-in landscapes, for example, came initially from European experience. Also concern with the marine environment has grown markedly in recent years (Kelleher, 1999).

The thinking behind the establishment of protected areas developed rapidly too. For example, the development of the science of ecology led in the 1960s to a broader understanding of the need for a systematic approach to resource planning and management. This can be seen with the IUCN (1994) classification system for protected areas, which takes biodiversity conservation as its starting point, though it also recognises the importance of other protected area objectives such as recreation and tourism. Many park systems started to use ecology as the co-ordinating concept for the establishment of new parks. However, when the best and most interesting natural and cultural sites in a country are placed in a protected area framework, there is a natural tendency for people to want to experience these environments. Tourism grew in many parks and became a major element in the culture of society.

Economics was an important consideration in the development of many protected areas. In particular, the economic impact of tourism in protected areas emphasises their community, regional and national importance. It is probable that in the coming decades a developing understanding of the economic impact of park tourism will lead to a more systematic treatment of park tourism. The time may come when a park system is understood within the framework of a park tourism system as well as an ecological system.

Moreover, there is increasing appreciation of the economic importance that many protected areas play by providing environmental services, like water supply, flood

9

control and mitigation of the effects of climate change (IUCN, 1998; and IUCN, 2000). Furthermore, particularly since the adoption of the Convention on Biological Diversity (CBD) in 1992, and especially because of Article 8a, much more stress is now put upon the idea of developing national *systems* of protected areas as a means of conserving biodiversity *in situ* and for other purposes (Davey, 1998). Indeed many protected areas now form part of international networks, both global systems, notably World Heritage sites, Ramsar sites and Biosphere Reserves; and regional systems, such as the Europa 2000 network of nature conservation sites in Europe. There are also calls to recognise fully the role of indigenous peoples in respect of protected areas (Beltran, 2000), and to develop international co-operation in protected areas across national boundaries (Sandwith *et al.*, 2001).

2.2 The IUCN Protected Area Management Category System

So the notion of protected areas developed a great deal in recent years and now embodies many different ideas. Nonetheless, IUCN has agreed upon a single definition of a protected area as follows:

"An area of land and/or sea especially dedicated to the protection and main-tenance of biological diversity, and of natural and associated cultural resources, and managed through legal or other effective means" (IUCN, 1994)

Within this broad IUCN definition, protected areas are in fact managed for many different purposes. To help improve understanding and promote awareness of protected area purposes, IUCN has developed a six category system of protected areas identified by their primary management objective (IUCN 1994), as shown in Table 2.1.

Table 2.1 IUCN Management Categories of Protected Areas (IUCN, 1994)

Category	Description
I	Strict Nature Reserve/Wilderness Area: Protected area managed mainly for science or wilderness protection.
Ia	Strict Nature Reserve: Protected area managed mainly for science.
Ib	Wilderness Area: Protected area managed mainly for wilderness protection.
II	National Park: Protected area managed mainly for ecosystem protection and recreation.
III	Natural Monument: Protected area managed mainly for conservation of specific natural features.
IV	Habitat/Species Management Area: Protected area managed mainly for conservation through management intervention.
V	Protected Landscape/Seascape: Protected area managed mainly for landscape/seascape conservation and recreation.
VI	Managed Resource Protected Area: Protected area managed mainly for the sustainable use of natural ecosystems.

The IUCN protected area management categories system is based upon the primary objective of management. Table 2.2 shows how an analysis of management objectives can be used to identify the most appropriate category.

Table 2.2 Matrix of management objectives and IUCN protected area management categories (IUCN, 1994)

Management objective	Ia	Ib	II	III	IV	V	VI
Scientific research	1	3	2	2	2	2	3
Wilderness protection	2	1	2	3	3	–	2
Preservation of species and genetic diversity (biodiversity)	1	2	1	1	1	2	1
Maintenance of environmental services	2	1	1	–	1	2	1
Protection of specific natural/ cultural features	–	–	2	1	3	1	3
Tourism and recreation*	–	**2**	**1**	**1**	**3**	**1**	**3**
Education	–	–	2	2	2	2	3
Sustainable use of resources from natural ecosystems	–	3	3	–	2	2	1
Maintenance of cultural/traditional attributes	–	–	–	–	–	1	2

Key: 1 = Primary objective; 2 = Secondary objective; 3 = Potentially applicable objective;
        – = not applicable.
*** Emphasis added for this publication**

Table 2.2 shows that some kind of recreation and tourism is likely to occur as a management objective in every category of protected areas, save Category Ia (the strict nature reserve). It also shows that biodiversity protection, though a critically important function of many protected areas, is far from the only purpose and is often not the primary purpose of a protected area. It is, though, a requirement of the IUCN definition that any protected area should always have a special policy to protect and maintain biodiversity.

Many park systems have the commemoration of cultural and historic integrity as central elements of management. These systems are often very important tourism destinations. However, protected areas that are primarily established for cultural or historic reasons, such as those in the large historic national park systems of the USA and Canada, are not classified by the IUCN system shown in Tables 2.1 and 2.2.

Marine Protected Areas (MPAs) are covered by the IUCN definition and categories system. They recently gained prominence as the need for the protection of marine environments became more widely recognised. Green and Paine (1997) indicated that there are over 2,000 protected area sites with some marine element, covering approximately 2.5 million km^2. MPAs may include terrestrial lands as well as reefs, seagrass beds, shipwrecks, archaeological sites, tidal lagoons, mudflats, salt marshes, mangroves, and rock platforms. The growth of MPAs appears to rise dramatically in the 1970s. This was largely because Green and Paine included Greenland National Park in their calculations; at almost 1 million km^2, it is the largest protected area anywhere, but most of this park is in fact terrestrial. However, there has been a decline in the number of MPAs established in the 1990s. The trend seems to be to establish fewer, but larger sites. It is though clear that the number and extent of MPAs are inadequate to achieve even basic conservation objectives (Lawton, 2001). The factors suggested to account for this neglect include:

- Limited state of knowledge about marine ecosystems;
- Perceptions that marine resources are limitless and so do not require protection;
- The fact that most marine resources do not stay within imposed administrative boundaries; and
- Because only a small portion of marine space lies within the clear jurisdiction of States and dependencies.

Designation and the declaration of protected area objectives do not of themselves ensure the survival of the protected area values. Therefore, the listed statistics on number and size of protected areas can be misleading, since protected areas do not offer a single, homogenous level of 'protection', and, as noted, have many and different management objectives. Most importantly they are managed to widely varying levels of effectiveness. There is wide agreement that much more needs to be done to improve the effectiveness of protected area management (Hockings, 2000). It is important therefore that, when tourism takes place, management frameworks and strategies are put in place to ensure that it supports and maintains protected area natural and cultural values. Managers have a mandate and a responsibility to protect the natural and associated socio-cultural values of protected areas. They must also ensure adequate and appropriate access for tourism and recreation. This is a substantial challenge, involving difficult judgments on the trade-offs that occur between tourism development, the protection of the resource values for which protected areas are established and the interests of the local community. These Guidelines address this challenge by assisting park managers and others to be effective in their management of visitation and tourism.

3. Tourism in protected areas

3.1 Trends affecting the planning of tourism and protected areas

Planning is a process that involves selecting a desirable future out of a range of plausible alternatives, and implementing strategies and actions that will achieve the desired outcome. Thus, by definition, planning moves us from the present to the future. It is critical therefore that planners and tourism operatives understand social, political and economic trends, as these form the context for planning. Such understanding provides opportunities to capitalise on emerging markets, develop actions that are more efficient and effective, and ensure that strategies and actions can be adapted to changing conditions. Since the world is more dynamic than static, park planners and tourism operators need to understand how dynamic change, often non-linear in character, may affect their plans and aspirations.

The growth of interest in sustainable tourism and ecotourism reflects a rising tide of social concern about the quality of the natural environment and the effects of tourism. Activities closely associated with experiencing natural environments are very popular (Tourism Canada, 1995).

Sabi Sabi Private Game Reserve, South Africa

Conservation and ecotourism are effective partners in South Africa, both in national parks and private nature reserves.
©*Paul F. J. Eagles*

Some trends complement each other. Some operate at the global level, some at the local level. Many represent collisions in powerful, but countervailing values and attitudes. Thus, while the trends briefly discussed below are presented independently, one can expect them to interact in various ways, often with unanticipated consequences.

3.1.1 Rising educational levels and demand for travel

The average level of formal educational attainment is rising globally, for both males and females. Literacy is increasing too, particularly in less developed countries. Higher education levels are strongly correlated with demand for outdoor recreation activities, and lead to changes in the patterns of recreation and tourism.

As a result, there is a general trend towards appreciative activities, with more travellers seeking life-enriching travel experiences. There is growth in general interest tourism that involves learning-while-travelling (e.g. guided tours), in specific learning travel programmes (e.g. group educational tours), and generally in learning activities, such as wildlife viewing, attending festivals, cultural appreciation and nature study. The natural and cultural resources found in protected areas, lend themselves to such forms of tourism. And thus the groups most interested in visiting protected areas, such as eco-tourists, tend to be more highly educated than tourists in general (Wight, 2001).

Tourism of this kind requires explanatory materials (e.g. guides, booklets), interpretive facilities (e.g. in visitor centres) and interpretive guiding (e.g. ecotours). It increases the expectations of service quality in protected areas, and raises political pressure for greater protection of cultural and natural heritage. It can also help generate a greater personal commitment to park protection – something that protected area managers should foster and tap into.

3.1.2 Ageing population

Advances in health care mean that people are living longer. Over the last century, there has been a significant increase in the proportion of people over the age of 60 (6.9% in 1900, 8.1% in 1950, 10.0% in 2000). This proportion is expected to increase even more dramatically over the next century. UN predictions are for 22.1% of the global population to be over 60 in 2050, and 28.1% in 2100. "By mid-century, many industrial countries will have median ages of 50 or higher, including Spain (55.2), Italy (54.1), Japan (53.1), and Germany (50.9)" (Center for Strategic and International Studies, 2002). Therefore the proportion of the population which is available to visit protected areas will have an increasingly elderly profile in the future (Figure 3.1).

Older individuals are staying healthier longer. Although physical capacity decreases with age, older people are increasingly able to lead healthy, physically active lives. So, while the demand for such activities as downhill skiing or mountain climbing decreases with age, elderly people maintain, or even extend, their interest in other outdoor activities, such as walking, nature study, fly-fishing or wildlife observation. Or again, a reduced demand for camping is offset by a greater demand for more comfortable lodge accommodation.

In wealthy countries, the ageing population, early retirement and good savings create large numbers of able-bodied senior citizens with strong inclination to travel. The recreation vehicle industry in the US sells over US $6 billion worth of new vehicles each

Figure 3.1 Three centuries of world population ageing

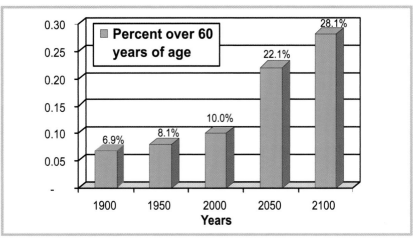

Source: Long-range World Population Projections: Based on the 1998 Revision. The Population Division, Department of Economic and Social Affairs, United Nations Secretariat.

year, much of it purchased by retirees. This kind of travel is expected to grow in North America, Europe and Australia in the coming decades of this new century.

Older visitors present some challenges for protected area planning and management. For example, there will be a need for more accessible toilets and for trails with lesser gradients; also for greater provision for people with disabilities. On the other hand, older visitors represent an opportunity. They tend to be more interested in the kinds of experience offered by protected areas, have more disposable income, and are thus more willing to pay for higher levels of interpretation, guiding and other services. Park managers must develop an understanding of the needs of this older population, or risk losing the involvement and support of an influential group.

3.1.3 Changing roles of women

In many countries, there has been a revolution in the role of women, and the process continues. More and more, men and women are adopting each other's characteristic role in the workplace and in the household. Women are becoming more prominent, even numerically dominant, in the paid workforce. Often their earnings are increasing more rapidly than those of men; and they make a greater demand for recreation and tourism opportunities. Indeed, it is often women who determine the choice of travel destination.

There are differences between the interests of men and women at the individual activity level. While there are, of course, many exceptions, men tend to be more interested in physically challenging activities, and women tend to be interested in more appreciative activities, such as nature and culture studies and ecotourism. Many women are interested in protected area recreation opportunities. Also, women are increasingly drawn to protected area and tourism management as a career. In many countries, they are moving into key positions in the development of economic, social, environmental and protected area policy.

It is important for protected area managers to understand that the role of women in park travel is strongly influenced by their life stage. Thus single, young women are not generally strong users of protected areas, but women with young children often choose parks as good places for child-centred leisure. Middle aged women often find work and family responsibilities very challenging, leaving them little time for park visitation, an activity requiring planning and considerable time commitment. Older, retired women, especially those travelling with their partners, show strong interest in the activities which involve visiting protected areas.

3.1.4 Changes in the distribution of leisure time

There are important and sometimes conflicting trends in the amounts, distribution and availability of leisure time, a very complex area to understand. For many people, leisure time is increasing due to a shorter working week, increases in the automation of housework and other factors. Yet leisure time is decreasing for others; for example working women who retain household responsibilities. Growth in single parent family numbers increases the leisure time of the absent parent, yet reduces that of the responsible parent. Often young people need to work to support their education, or expand their purchasing power, so they have less leisure time.

Of relevance to park visitation is the re-apportionment of time for vacations. In North America, there tend to be more frequent, shorter vacations, closer to home, rather than two or three week family vacations: short, fast trips (particularly 2 to 4 day weekend trips) now account for 80% of vacation travel in the USA. Therefore many parks now need to allow for short visits by tourists with limited time, which calls for higher quality

Pog Lake and Campground in Algonquin Provincial Park, Ontario, Canada.

This attractive lake is located within a high use car campground. Careful design, effective management and respectful park visitors ensure that the environmental quality of the lake and the surrounding forest remains high. ©*Paul F. J. Eagle*s

service, and specialized recreation opportunities. In much of Europe, by contrast, leisure time involves longer paid vacations and shorter working weeks. For example, Germany introduced a 6-week holiday with pay in the 1990s (Tiegland, 2000); and France has adopted a statutory 35-hour week. As a result, European countries, and those of the EU especially, are very important generators of park visitation all over the world. In some of the emerging economies of East Asia, notably China, the advent of paid holidays and greater freedom to travel are creating a fast growing mass market for tourism; as these new tourists become more discriminating, a significant proportion of them are likely to be drawn to protected areas.

3.1.5 Importance of service quality

Tourists are increasingly demanding high quality recreational opportunities and the services that support them. Those who receive quality service during their normal working week expect to be offered this by their leisure providers as well. They expect guides to be knowledgeable and good communicators. They want their hosts to make them feel welcome, comfortable and part of the communities they visit. Increased ecotourism means greater demand for specialised recreation and accommodation, all with a focus on *quality*. Most park agencies do not have service quality goals, or monitoring programmes, making their programmes appear unresponsive and primitive.

Protected area managers and the private sector need to deliver quality visitor services. The challenges for managers include ensuring they have service quality goals, programmes to deliver high quality service and monitoring programmes in place. Importantly these sophisticated consumers recognise quality service and are willing to pay handsomely for it.

3.1.6 Changing leisure patterns

At first sight, one might expect gains in leisure time to occur in all countries that experience economic development, increased income, ageing populations and the shifting roles of men and women. However, the experience of the more developed countries suggests that in fact some significant losses in leisure time may occur during the working period of life, particularly among white-collar occupations with very high workloads. But, by contrast, there are big increases in leisure time due to earlier retirement and longer life spans. Older, retired people are also able to travel for longer periods each year. Rising incomes in North America, Europe, Australia and some parts of Asia in particular are driving up the volume of domestic tourism, and of outbound traffic from these countries. If this continues, there is likely to be a further general increase in recreation pressures upon all protected areas, even remote ones, and of demands for higher quality service.

3.1.7 Advances in global communications and information technology

Among wealthier societies at any rate, many people are now getting access to a huge volume of information on protected areas and travel options through the Internet and other communication technologies. The Internet leads to increased demand for trips to a wider variety of locations, and enables park agencies to provide current, sophisticated information directly to visitors, at very low cost. Since images on the Internet can create expectations about a particular protected area, protected area managers and tourism operators need to be aware of what is being communicated, and to be ready to meet the expectations that have been raised.

These new technologies enable visitors to be well informed about everything, from management policies to the recreation experience. As a result, visitors may be more likely to support protected area policy. However, many protected area agencies, especially those in the developing world, are not yet able to maintain sophisticated Internet web sites. Instead, private interests, such as non-governmental organisations (NGOs), hotel and lodge providers, and tourism companies, provide most of the Internet information. This is particularly so in much of Eastern and Southern Africa, and in South America. When this happens, the protected area agency has little control over the accuracy of information, and cannot influence the kinds of visitor expectations that may be created. Nor can it build support for park management objectives.

Technology may have far-reaching consequences. For example, local hotels, resorts and so forth can cross-market their web sites with those of nearby protected areas, and so increase the number of short visits by business travellers. Private ecotourism resorts can utilise real time web cam experiences (e.g. of wildlife dramas) to draw visitors from around the world. And visitors themselves can help promote awareness of protected areas by providing web cam information about the park to the world while experiencing the park.

There may also be threats from the new technologies. For example, some lobby groups have designed web sites to look exactly like those of a protected area agency, and thus provide potential visitors with false management perspectives. Also park visitors could have access to sophisticated databases in the field, in real time, connected to geo-referenced mapping. This will give them immediate, accurate information on wildlife locations and distributions, along with maps and photos. They may have more information at their disposal than the local park manager has! This could put the manager at a disadvantage in controlling visitor behaviour. The long-term implications of the advances in global communication and information technology are profound and mostly unknown.

3.1.8 Proliferation of travel options

As the world's fleets of passenger aircraft and cruise ships expand, visitors can travel more efficiently, quickly and further afield. International travel has been growing rapidly in the last few decades (Figure 3.2 shows growth since 1980, and forecast growth to 2020).

The WTO predicts that international travel will grow at the rate of 4.1% annually between now and the year 2020, mostly from North America, Europe and East Asia (WTO, 1997). While this trend is likely to continue, it will be affected by such factors as the health of the global economy, security fears due to terrorist activities and regional instability, and the

Figure 3.2   International tourism arrivals (figures in millions)

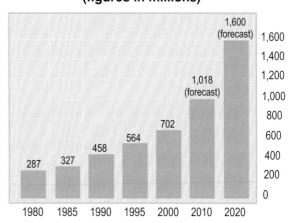

Source: WTO, 1997.

18

extremes of global climate change. Ultimately, the availability and cost of fuel oil will be an important limitation on long-term travel growth.

The proliferation of long-haul air travel has revolutionised global park visitation, with people seeking out World Heritage Sites, national parks and other protected areas. Indeed, the very existence of a protected area, particularly of a national park, is often a lure for tourists. This trend will continue and in general protected area managers should prepare for more visitors from around the globe. While they will present a challenge in terms of language, culture or knowledge and preconceptions of the protected area, they also represent a good source of income, employment, and a means to convey cultural and ecological values to a wider world.

Cruise ship travel can be particularly problematic. Because large cruise ships carry so many people, they can cause huge environmental and social impacts very quickly. For example, large numbers of people, many of whom are poorly prepared for a marine park experience, can overwhelm a marine protected area. The threats of cultural and eco-logical damage are very high if there are insufficient management resources. However, in some locations where smaller, expedition-type cruises visit and are expected (e.g. in Arctic Canada), protected area managers actually prefer cruise visitors, since staff can prepare to meet and guide the visitors, who come in manageable group sizes. These cruise ship visitors make fewer demands for onshore facilities, thereby reducing the eco-logical footprint of tourism infrastructure.

3.1.9 Personal security and safety

More than any other factor, threats to personal security and safety adversely affect tourism demand. The fear of terrorism can affect global travel trends. When regional wars, rebellions and terrorism occur, domestic and international travel falls, and fewer tourists visit protected areas. The effects are felt most in developing countries, where international visitors are often a significant proportion of all visitors. A sense of personal security is also affected by the prevalence of violent crime, petty theft, water quality, disease or bad sanitation.

Dramatic differences exist between countries in their ability to provide acceptable levels of security and safety. This is especially relevant to tourism, since people planning their trips will often compare destinations with such factors in mind. Once a destination achieves a negative reputation, it is very difficult to rebuild visitor confidence; and such negative perceptions of a country will also affect the appeal of its protected areas. Violent attacks on tourists themselves, as have recently taken place in Egypt and Uganda for example, can set back tourism by many years. Leisure travel is a luxury good, people have a wide range of opportunities and they will not travel to areas perceived as unsafe.

Indeed, the perception of safety is nearly as important as the reality. Many protected areas have been badly affected by unrealistic security concerns created by misleading media reports and poor geographical knowledge of potential consumers. Managers must expect some naïve visitors who are not prepared for the dangers that occur in many natural environments.

Protected area managers should be aware of safety expectations of visitors, explain the local situation to potential visitors, and respond to visitor safety demands. If possible, protected area managers need to have security management plans in place, including a public relations component. It is important both to take security seriously and to tell people exactly what the situation is. Failure to do so can lead to complicated and expensive results, since it is becoming more common for park visitors to take legal action against park management for safety-related injury, or damage to personal property.

3.1.10 Increasing social and environmental concerns

Across the globe, people express concern about social injustices and environmental problems. They are increasingly aware of the need for low impact tourism which does not harm the environment. They tend to want to support local conservation or community development initiatives. They are themselves moving from consumptive to less consumptive activities, often adopting "green consumer" life styles. The growth of interest in sustainable tourism and ecotourism is a response to such concerns. Protected areas are well placed to take advantage of this trend as they embody the values that such travellers hold.

Some tourists are "voting with their feet". They are attracted to destinations that have a positive reputation, and are actively avoiding destinations that have social or environmental problems. There are also international schemes for recognising the adoption of high environmental standards in tourism provision, such as the Green Globe 21 scheme (Box 3.1). Green Globe has recently joined with the Ecotourism Association of Australia to develop a new programme aimed at ecotourism, an activity that could provide important opportunities for park tourism managers. It is thus doubly important that managers work to preserve protected area values, seek high standards from their tourism

---

Box 3.1 Green Globe 21: an industry accreditation scheme to promote and market environmentally sound tourism

Under the Green Globe accreditation scheme, companies, communities, suppliers, professionals etc. can graduate through three categories to obtain higher levels of recognition for the sustainability of their operations, which they can then use for marketing purposes:

A: Affiliates. Affiliated companies etc. are those who wish to gain a foothold in sustainable tourism and access a whole range of support and information sources in order to be officially recognised as environmentally sound, and to support and spread eco-conscious values.

B: Benchmarking. Benchmarking companies and communities are on the second step of the pathway towards sustainable travel and tourism. They have access to the Green Globe 21 web site which provides them with information on benchmarking. They receive a sustainability assessment and are assisted in their progress towards the next step.

C: Certifying. Certified companies and communities have travelled further along the Green Globe 21 path to sustainable travel and tourism. Certified members have their performance independently assessed and audited. Audits take place regularly to ensure that performance levels are maintained or improved.

Web site: http//www.greenglobe21.com

partners, and so help ensure that the appeal of the area to visitors is maintained. Thus a high quality resource can sustain high quality tourism, thereby making, in effect, a virtuous circle.

3.1.11 Globalisation of the economy

In a globalised economy, individual countries and communities are influenced by decisions and economic conditions elsewhere. Thus political or corporate decisions in origin countries can influence overseas travel, which may in turn affect the viability of protected area tourism a continent away. This linkage between origin and destination communities makes achieving sustainable tourism difficult, since the host country often has a limited ability to influence tourist trends; it also leads to competition between destinations. However, protected area managers can take advantage of this global context through clever marketing, using the Internet and by promoting the distinctive niche which they offer as a tourist destination. To do this, protected area agencies should have knowledge of global tourism trends, so as to position themselves, develop the right messages, and respond through appropriate management measures.

3.2 Growth and diversification of market niches

3.2.1 Ecotourism and nature-based tourism

The number of people taking part in many outdoor activities is growing, especially in hiking, cycling and water-based activities such as sea kayaking or scuba diving. There has also been a huge growth in 'soft' adventure and ecotourism or nature-tourism types of trips. 'Soft' activities are those where a more casual, less dedicated approach is taken to the activity or natural attraction, and a desire to experience it with some basic degree of comfort; whereas 'hard' adventure or ecotourism involves specialist interest or dedicated activity, and a willingness to experience the outdoors or wilderness with few comforts. The tourism industry has responded to this range of interests by developing many types of niche market packages.

Protected areas are very attractive settings for the growing demand for outdoor, appreciative activities in natural environments. Challenges for protected area managers are to ensure that while visitors have opportunities to participate in desired activities, they are aware of and maintain the values. Opportunities are to tap into such market demand, through target market programming, perhaps in collaboration with the private sector, both to increase attractiveness as a destination, and manage the visitors appropriately.

3.2.2 Protected area visitors comprise many market segments

There is no such thing as the "average protected area visitor". In reality, markets comprise many *segments,* each of which has somewhat different characteristics, expectations, activity participation and spending patterns. Marketing exploits these visitor segments by comparing and matching them with the biophysical and cultural attributes of the park, and then sensitively promoting appropriate protected area attributes to the targeted segment. This reduces adverse impacts on the protected area, increases the economic benefits and makes it more likely that visitors are satisfied.

Ways to segment visitors include:

1) *By socio-demographic characteristics* (e.g. variables such as age, sex, occupation, origins, income level, ethnic association, religion, level of education or class): Thus, one segment might be those under 30, while another might be visitors of 65 and older. These segments would be expected to have different characteristics and activity participation.

2) *By geographic characteristics* (e.g. origins, distance from sites and modes of transport*)*: Thus one market may be local visitors, whereas another might be international travellers.

3) *By "psychographic" segments*: Thus, one segment might be considered "escapers" who look for adventure, and getting away from it all, while another might be considered "green" and actively seeking environmentally-sensitive products and services.

4) *By activity participation*: Thus, one segment might be "tent campers" while another might be "wildlife viewers". This method is easy, because the segments are easily identifiable. However, it should be noted that one visitor might engage in a number of activities. Each segment has different expectations of what they desire from an area.

5) *By frequency of participation*: Thus, one segment may be "frequent travellers" or "repeat visitors"; another "first-time visitors". Frequent travellers and repeat visitors usually have more informed expectations of the protected area, and may have more involvement and care more about it.

6) *By perceived product benefits*: Thus, one segment might expect to benefit from a challenging environment (e.g. through river floating or mountain climbing), while others might expect to learn about nature. Some might wish to socialise with friends or family, while others might simply expect to enjoy natural beauty. Segments can be identified by the product characteristics they prefer.

The value of segmentation is that it can predict behaviour, and thus help managers to plan for this behaviour. Segmentation by perceived product benefit can be used to develop an understanding of what tourists really seek in a visit to a protected area, and so establish an appropriate management response. In this way, visitors will gain greater satisfaction from the products and services offered.

Sophisticated research capabilities and procedures are normally required to understand the market in this way. Hall and McArthur (1998) point out that the behaviour of various market segments is best understood when *inferred* variables (rather than *objective* variables) are used. Inferred variables are obtained by directly questioning samples of a population (e.g. of visitors) about such things as motivations, expectations and attitudes. For protected area managers without sophisticated research capabilities, the best approach would be a combination of sample surveys and observing how services and facilities are used.

Different kinds of visitors tend to be attracted to various types of protected areas. For example, Lawton (2001) analysed this for each of the various IUCN categories of protected area (see Table 2.1). She groups tourism visitation into "ecotourism" and "other" types of visitation, and considers whether eco-visitors are 'soft' or 'hard'. Table 3.1 shows these types of visitors in relation to the IUCN categories of protected areas.

Table 3.1 Compatibility/suitability of forms of tourism with IUCN's Protected Area Management Categories (after Lawton, 2001)

IUCN protected area category (see Table 2.1)	Hard ecotourism (see para. 3.2.1)	Soft ecotourism (see para. 3.2.1)	Other forms of tourism
Ia	*no*	*no*	*no*
Ib	*yes*	*no*	*no*
II	*yes*	*yes*	*no*
III	*yes*	*yes*	*no*
IV	*yes*	*yes*	*no*
V	*no*	*yes*	*yes*
VI	*no*	*yes*	*no*

Source: after Lawton, 2001.

While not all visitors to protected area categories I–IV are in fact eco-tourists, in the absence of hard data and survey research this model of market segments can be helpful in planning to match tourist strategies to protected area types.

3.3 Potential benefits of tourism in protected areas

Tourism in protected areas produces benefits and costs. These effects interact often in complex ways. It is the responsibility of the protected area planner to maximise benefits while minimising costs. While this document does not provide a detailed analysis of all tourism impacts, the following sections identify the main costs and benefits.

Protected areas are established primarily to preserve some type of biophysical process or condition such as a wildlife population, habitat, natural landscape, or cultural heritage such as a community's cultural tradition (Table 2.2). Tourists visit these protected areas to understand and appreciate the values for which the area was established and to gain personal benefits.

Tourism planning and development aims to take advantage of the interest shown by tourists so as to: enhance economic opportunities, protect the natural and cultural heritage, and advance the quality of life of all concerned. These goals are expanded upon in Table 3.2 and briefly described below.

Table 3.2 Potential benefits of tourism in protected areas

	Benefits
Enhancing economic opportunity	▪ Increases jobs for local residents ▪ Increases income ▪ Stimulates new tourism enterprises, and stimulates and diversifies the local economy ▪ Encourages local manufacture of goods ▪ Obtains new markets and foreign exchange ▪ Improves living standards ▪ Generates local tax revenues ▪ Enables employees to learn new skills ▪ Increases funding for protected areas and local communities
Protecting natural and cultural heritage	▪ Protects ecological processes and watersheds ▪ Conserves biodiversity (including genes, species and ecosystems) ▪ Protects, conserves and values cultural and built heritage resources ▪ Creates economic value and protects resources which otherwise have no perceived value to residents, or represent a cost rather than a benefit ▪ Transmits conservation values, through education and interpretation ▪ Helps to communicate and interpret the values of natural and built heritage and of cultural inheritance to visitors and residents of visited areas, thus building a new generation of responsible consumers ▪ Supports research and development of good environmental practices and management systems to influence the operation of travel and tourism businesses, as well as visitor behaviour at destinations ▪ Improves local facilities, transportation and communications ▪ Helps develop self-financing mechanisms for protected area operations
Enhancing quality of life	▪ Promotes aesthetic, spiritual, and other values related to well-being ▪ Supports environmental education for visitors and locals ▪ Establishes attractive environments for destinations, for residents as much as visitors, which may support other compatible new activities, from fishing to service or product-based industries ▪ Improves intercultural understanding ▪ Encourages the development of culture, crafts and the arts ▪ Increases the education level of local people ▪ Encourages people to learn the languages and cultures of foreign tourists ▪ Encourages local people to value their local culture and environments

3.3.1 Enhancing economic opportunity

Tourism can increase jobs and income in a local area or region. It is often regarded as a source of foreign exchange, particularly since protected areas tend to attract international tourists. For example, nature tourism in Costa Rica was estimated to generate over US $600 million in foreign exchange in 1994 (Box 3.2). Visitors to Australia's Great Barrier Reef World Heritage Area spent AU $776 million (US $543 million) in 1991–1992 (Driml and Common, 1995). Governments often use tourism for economic development because it is relatively inexpensive to create a tourism job compared to one in manufacturing.

Box 3.2   Costa Rica's system of protected areas: an example of protected areas creating the foundation of a successful ecotourism industry

Costa Rica's national parks, wildlife refuges and biological reserves cover over 630,000ha, or more than 25% of the country. Much of the land was purchased and operated by government during the 1970s, but there was an economic crisis in the 1980s, and a reduction of international donations in the 1990s. Costa Rica chose to raise national park entrance fees. In addition, a two-tiered fee system was developed so foreigners paid more than residents.

Despite the increased charges, Costa Rica's parks remain a popular international tourist destination. The country had 1.03 million international arrivals in 1999, and – if the 1996 figures are a guide – 66% of those tourists visited a protected area. Annual tourism receipts in Costa Rica now total over US$1 billion, and it is the national park system which forms the foundation for its successful ecotourism industry.

Source: Honey cited in Brown, 2001.
Web site: http://nature.org/aboutus/travel/ecotourism/resources/

To gain such economic benefits, two conditions must be met: (1) there must be products and services for tourists to spend money on, and (2) it is necessary to minimise the amount that leaks out of the local area. "Leakage" can be a serious problem: for example, less than 6% of tourism income at Tortuguero National Park, Costa Rica, accrues to the local communities (Baez and Fernandez, 1992). So tourism should be as self-sufficient as possible, reducing dependence on out-of-region goods and services.

While some tourism developments in connection with protected areas will have a large initial cost, they may well generate significant revenues over the longer term. For example, in St. Lucia, most tourist arrivals currently visit the Sulphur Springs National Landmark. If the park were to be enhanced, estimates of costs and revenues show that not only would these costs be recovered, but also so would the costs of adding staff, programming, facilities and maintenance (Huber and Park, 1991). The estimated costs were expected to outweigh the estimated revenues for the first two years but, thereafter, benefits would exceed costs.

Box 3.3   Gorilla tourism, Parc National des Volcans, Rwanda: an example of economic benefits of tourism funding the protected area system

In Rwanda, gorilla tourism was so profitable that it was used to help fund conservation activities for a number of protected areas. From 1976 to 1980, income was lower than expenses, but this situation was then reversed and, by 1989, expenses were less than US$200,000, while fee income was $1million. In Rwanda's Parc National des Volcans, demand for visiting the mountain gorillas was so much higher than the visitation limit (24 tourists/day), that the government could increase fees to almost $200 per person for a one-hour visit. These fees were able to support other costs of conservation (e.g. guides and guards) as well as other services. This policy generated about $1 million annually until the civil war closed down gorilla tourism.

Source: Lindberg and Huber, 1993.

Tourism income from popular protected areas can be used to help finance others that cannot attract so many tourists, or where large numbers would be inappropriate. Box 3.3 illustrates such an example from Rwanda.

Conservation revenues may actually be higher than other land use revenues. For example, in the Devure Ranch in Zimbabwe, Pricewaterhouse Cooper estimated that cattle had the potential to generate Z $22/hectare/year, using a realistic stocking rate (which increased to Z $37 using a high stocking rate). By contrast, a small wildlife tourism operation (including viewing, hunting and culling) could generate Z$67/hectare/year (Lindberg, 1998). However, the Zimbabwe Government decided that land resettlement of local people was a more important objective. And in the last few years most wildlife tourism operations in that country have ceased to be viable, due to a loss of land for conservation and to a decline in the number of tourists.

Both the Rwanda and Zimbabwe examples illustrate that civil unrest impacts tourism, and the positive economic benefits of tourism, very strongly. Leisure travel is a luxury good, and people have a wide range of opportunities. Therefore, they will not travel to areas which they perceive as unsafe (see also section 3.1.9 above).

Protected area managers should aim to develop tourism development policies which support long-term economic development and encourage repeat visits. They should try to maximise local employment, social and cultural benefits through high visitor spending and low local leakage.

Guidelines for capturing economic benefits are:

- *Increase the number of visitors*: Increasing visitation is risky unless the financial benefits from the visitors exceed their costs. It may increase other impacts, some negatively.

- *Increase the length of stay*: Increased length of stay provides more opportunity to sell local products and services.

- *Attract richer market niches*: Different marketing tactics may bring in consumers with strong abilities to spend.

- *Increase purchases per visitor*: Offering more locally-made goods for sale, available directly and indirectly to the visitor, helps increase visitor expenditure and local incomes.

- *Provide lodging*: The costs of overnight accommodation are relatively large and are paid for locally. Local lodging also increases expenditures on meals, and local goods and services.

- *Provide guides or other services*: Since much tourist activity in protected areas is information intensive, there are usually good opportunities for guide services.

- *Host events*: Artwork, crafts and festivals based on local culture can increase local economic impact.

- *Purchase local food and drink*: When visitors, park staff and tourism employees consume locally grown food and drink, they provide important income to local farmers.

Some leakage of expenditure to sources outside the local area is unavoidable, simply because not all food, supplies and services are produced locally. However, tourism planners should try to minimise this leakage (WTO, 1999). Whatever the strategy employed, it is important that local communities are involved in planning for the economic impacts and how they should be measured.

3.3.2 Protecting the natural and cultural heritage

Tourism based on protected areas can be a key factor in supporting the conservation of the *natural* and *cultural heritage*. It can generate the funds through entrance and service fees, local taxes and in many other ways that can be used directly to help meet or offset the costs of conservation, maintaining cultural traditions and providing education. Indirectly, by demonstrating the economic value that protected area tourism can bring to a country or a region, it can build public and political support for conservation of natural heritage. Tourism enables some marine protected areas to prosper, for example in the Netherlands Antilles (Bonaire Marine Park), the Seychelles (Ste. Anne National Marine Park) and Kenya (Malindi/Watamu parks and reserves). Box 3.4 describes how tourism

---

Box 3.4   Madikwe Game Reserve, South Africa: an example of ecological restoration designed and paid for by tourism

Established in 1991, Madikwe reserve was once farmland, but now contains a restored African savannah ecosystem. Many derelict farm buildings and structures were removed, as well as hundreds of kilometres of old fencing, and many alien plants. Some preserved buildings now serve as Park offices and workshops, while new outposts have been built to house game scouts and other staff. Where possible, local business and labour was used for demolition and clearance, erecting fences and constructing roads, dams and lodges. Several game lodges have already been built; others will be developed in future.

Approximately 60,000ha of the reserve were enclosed in a 150km perimeter fence, electrified to prevent the escape of elephants and the larger predators. Operation Phoenix, begun in 1991, became the largest game translocation exercise ever undertaken. More than 10,000 animals of 28 species were released into the reserve, including elephant, rhino, buffalo, lion, cheetah, cape hunting dog, spotted hyena, giraffe, zebra and many species of antelope and other herbivores.

Madikwe is designed to benefit the three main stakeholders involved in the reserve. These are: the manager, the North West Parks Board of South Africa; the private tourism sector; and the local communities. All three work together in a mutually beneficial "partnership in conservation and tourism". The Parks Board is responsible for establishing the necessary infrastructure and the management to run Madikwe as a major protected area (IUCN Category IV). It also identifies suitable sites within the reserve to lease to the private sector for tourism-based developments and activities.

The private sector provides the capital to build game lodges, and markets and manages the lodges as well as the tourism and trophy hunting in the reserve. Operators pay concession fees to the Parks Board for permission to operate in the reserve. These fees are used to:

■ Pay back the development costs of the reserve;
■ Maintain the conservation infrastructure in the reserve;
■ Pay a dividend to the community for regional development; and
■ Develop similar conservation areas elsewhere in the North West Province through a Conservation Trust fund.

Thus private sector money, rather than State funds, is used to develop tourism. However, international development funding from the UK has been used to help local people acquire the entrepreneurial skills to exploit tourism opportunities. By 1999, with only 3 of 10 planned lodges constructed, the economic impact of the tourism was already larger than that of the farm operations that had been removed.

Source: Northwest Parks and Tourism Board, 2000.
Web site: http://www.parks-n.co.za/madikwe/index.html

Box 3.5 Montague Island Nature Reserve, Australia: understanding economic benefits

Montague Island Nature Reserve, off southeastern Australia, contains both natural ecosystems (penguins, seals, sea birds) and cultural features (European and aboriginal history) of national importance.

From 1990 to the present the management agency, the New South Wales National Parks and Wildlife Service, developed a system of use capacity limits, community consultation and monitoring of impacts. Measurement of the economic impact of the tourism showed the value of financial impact monitoring.

In 1998 the nature tours grossed AU $200,000 for the 4,300 participants that landed on the island. In 1999 a carefully done regional economic impact study determined that expenditures by visitors to the island contributed an estimated AU $1.4 million in gross regional output per year to the regional economy, which was linked to AU $965,000 in gross regional product, including household income of AU $468,000 paid to the equivalent of 19 people in the local economy. Knowledge of this impact helped the local community develop a better appreciation of the role of conservation and tourism in their area.

Web site: http://www.npws.nsw.gov.au/parks/south/sou018.html

---

funded an ambitious project in ecological restoration in South Africa. Box 3.5 describes how the economic benefits of tourism helped a local community in Australia to develop a better appreciation of the value of conservation. There are many thousands of other examples of such positive relationships between conservation of biodiversity and the natural environment, and protected areas-based tourism.

Well-managed tourism can also assist in protecting or restoring a community's or a region's *cultural heritage*. Protected areas have an important part to play in respect of the built heritage. Many protected areas contain significant historic, architectural and archaeological resources. This is especially the case with Category V protected areas in Europe, which are lived-in protected landscapes and often accommodate a wealth of attractive human settlements, as well as traditional features like stone walls and barns. Tourism can provide income to help in the upkeep or repair of such important buildings and landscape features. It may be collected directly, for example through entry or user fees or indirectly through local taxes.

The cultural heritage is also evident in local traditions. Tourists sometimes seek authentic experiences. It may therefore be possible to encourage the local community to maintain or re-establish important cultural festivals, traditions or events, and even to undertake the restoration of heritage buildings. There are many benefits from such activities. They will enrich the tourism experience within or near protected areas, thereby inducing tourists to stay longer and spend more. Exposure to cultural diversity can help modify tourist behaviour, change use patterns and create advocates for conservation among the tourist community. Moreover local communities may benefit when local traditions and values are maintained, and when they are encouraged to take greater pride in their communities or regions.

Chaa Creek Cottages, Belize

An increasing number of private nature reserves cater to ecotourism. © *Paul F. J. Eagles*

3.3.3 Enhancing quality of life in the host community

Tourism development should be designed to protect what is good about a host community and tackle those aspects that need to be improved. One way in which this can be done is to develop facilities and services for tourism which can also benefit the living conditions of local residents. Indeed protected areas can be the engines of sustainable rural development. IUCN advises that protected areas in Africa should be repositioned "in the context of community development and the local economy" (IUCN, 1999, page 51). It argues that protected areas, sustained by tourist income, not only create jobs and raise income but can also be used to support local communities' needs for:

- Improved communications: upgrading roads for tourism access gives neighbouring villages better access to the outside world. Telecommunications access to protected area offices can be vital to local communities in times of emergency;

- Education: some protected areas provide language, literacy and numeracy training to their staff, skills than can then be applied in the community as well;

- Training: the training that parks staff receive in such matters as vehicle maintenance or food hygiene will be of practical use in local communities;

- Health care: the medical services available to parks staff and visitors can be shared with local communities (IUCN, 1999).

Thus tourism to terrestrial and marine protected areas may be viewed as a tool to help communities to maintain, or improve, their living standards and quality of life. This may be measured in terms of:

- increased school graduation rates;

29

Box 3.6   Costa Rica: an example of environmental education shaping national values

Environmental education may assist a protected area system in shaping national valuation of natural heritage and conservation. In Costa Rica, for example, when the national park and wildlife reserve system started in the 1960s, there was a low public level of understanding of the need for natural heritage conservation. Thus it was first necessary to develop public understanding and appreciation of the country's exceptional biodiversity. This was accomplished in several ways:

- Encouraging park visitation by residents (valuing through experience);
- Channelled entry to education facilities in prominent national parks (e.g. via construction of an interpretive visitor centre at the entrance to Volcan Poas National Park);
- Interpretation on site (understanding acquired through displays, materials and interpreters);
- A national school environmental education programme (ensuring future generations understood the country's natural heritage); and
- Encouraging school visits (individual parks introduced active schools programmes).

A biological research industry emerged, as did a major ecotourism industry (Box 3.2), both in the private sector. Both led to increased employment for those with education. Over time, ecotourism development fostered local economic development, together with a strong national appreciation of the importance of the natural resources of the country. Through park visitation, environmental education and private ecotourism development, the national parks and the wildlife reserves are now seen as a fundamental feature of Costa Rican society.

Source: Eagles and Higgins, 1998.

- reduced infant mortality;
- elimination of water and air pollution;
- increased access to recreation sites, protected areas or subsistence resources; and
- better access to services, such as the park's programmes for interpretation and environmental education, which also benefit locals.

Protected areas can also be used to enhance the quality of life of a whole nation, by making them the foundation of a national policy to raise environmental understanding. Box 3.6 describes how this was done in Costa Rica.

3.4   Potential risks of tourism in protected areas

Negative effects can and do result from tourist visitation, but many of them can be competently managed and alleviated. Protected area stakeholders are in the position of gauging both the positive and negative effects of tourism, determining how acceptable the negative effects are, and suggesting how they can be managed. The costs of tourism are of three kinds: financial and economic, socio-cultural and environmental.

Box 3.7 Royal Chitwan National Park, Nepal: an example of a significant tourism industry, with insufficient local benefits

In 1994, the Royal Chitwan National Park in Nepal had over 60,000 tourists. Despite this, the economic impact on local peoples' household income was minimal, and limited to villages closest to the main park entrance.

A study found that "of the estimated 87,000 working age people living near the park, less than 1,100 were employed directly by the ecotourism industry". The report went on to say that "only 6% of the surveyed households earned income directly or indirectly from ecotourism". In fact the average annual salary of even these households from ecotourism was only $600. It is important to develop an understanding of the level of economic benefit that can occur and is appropriate. Tourism planners should not create unrealistic expectations of the degree of economic impact that may occur.

Source: Bosselman *et al.*, 1999, quoting WWF.

3.4.1 Financial and economic costs

Tourism brings increased demand for goods, services and facilities, such as lodging, restaurants, other attractions, and personal vacation properties. As visitor numbers increase, so do the demands for basic services such as policing, fire, safety and health care. Such increased demand brings increased costs and possibly higher tax burdens for the local community. In some cases, costs may rise so much that local residents can no longer afford to live there. This is particularly the case in destinations where local people have lower incomes than the visitors do. For example, wealthy foreign visitors to protected areas in developing countries may see economic opportunities and take control or buy out local businesses. Thus tourism can lead to increased foreign ownership and raised property values.

Increased visitation also means increased costs to the protected area management agency as it strives to add the additional personnel and facilities needed by the tourists. This cost of tourism must be weighed against the benefits. Therefore, the park agency must be able to apply the benefits earned from tourists against the costs.

As already noted, where the local economy and protected areas are heavily dependent on tourism, they may become vulnerable to external factors beyond their control, such as natural disasters, currency fluctuations, competitive capture of markets or political instability.

Some leakage of tourist expenditures will occur, whether it is out of the protected area, local community, region or the country. If local people do not benefit, they may look for other more profitable activities and land uses (Box 3.7). Hence the need to minimise leakage.

3.4.2 Social costs

Increased numbers of tourists may disturb community activities, and compete for recreation places and other services. Poorly planned tourism development can lead to increased congestion, littering, vandalism and crime. Governments may exacerbate these problems if they put short-term economic considerations before all else, for example by building inappropriate infrastructure or failing to establish the needs of local communities. When this happens, the local support for the protected area may be put at risk.

Sometimes tourism in protected areas calls only for seasonal employment, leaving residents underemployed during the slow or off-seasons. However, this may be to the local communities' liking. In the Klondike Gold Rush National Historic Park (Alaska, USA) the entire town of Skagway revolves around summer tourism. In the winter, many people leave, and then the community apparently enjoys its "quiet time", having earned sufficient income for the year during the busy season.

Where protected area agencies develop visitor management regulations that also affect local residents, there may be negative socio-cultural impacts (e.g. prohibitions on traditional uses such as fuelwood gathering or on spiritual uses which require entry to the protected area). Other negative impacts may occur where local traditions become commercialized, and lose their integrity or authenticity. An example would be dances, which had once had a vital social role but which are now put on only for the entertainment of visitors.

Negative impacts are most common when communities are not given choices, or have no control over their involvement with tourism. Outsiders often assign negative connotations to cultural change, while those undergoing the change may be positive about the new ideas or approaches. So it is important that those affected by cultural change be the ones that decide whether this change is acceptable. Appropriate planning is needed ahead of development, to avoid adverse impacts from the outset; but there are also management techniques that can be used to address problems should they arise.

The dangers are all the greater when there is a sharp contrast between the wealth of tourists and the poverty of the host community. Where this occurs, local communities are potentially vulnerable to exploitation and their voice may go unheard. Both the protected area manager and the tourist provider have a special responsibility in such circumstances to ensure that the community is listened to, and its views allowed to help shape the form of tourist development that takes place.

3.4.3 Environmental costs

Tourism, like many other forms of development, will always produce environmental impacts, even at low levels of intensity, and despite the best efforts of protected area managers. Such impacts occur both at the site level, and over larger areas. Because tourism in protected areas is drawn to environments which are inherently sensitive, it is vital that the impacts be assessed as accurately as possible beforehand to establish if they are acceptable. (However, in assessing these, it is important to consider what environmental impacts would have occurred if the park, and its tourism industry, were to be replaced by some other land use, such as agriculture, forestry, mining or urbanisation). Tables 3.3 and 3.4 set out two ways of listing the wide range of environmental risks.

Table 3.3 Negative impacts of human use on the environment

Trail creation (and deterioration)	Boats damaging banks
Camp-sites (and deterioration)	Habitat loss
Litter	Emissions and air pollution
Crowding	Firewood collection
Tracks and recreation vehicles	Visual and noise impacts
Pack stock impacts	Overfishing, undersized fishing
Human waste problems	Impacts on vegetation
Wildlife disturbance, habituation, or impact	Damage to sand dunes/reefs
User conflicts	Soil compaction or erosion
Water pollution (physical or biological)	Increased fire risk
Overdevelopment	Damage to archaeological sites
Weeds, fungi and exotic species	Trampling (human or horse)
Solid and human waste	Changed water courses
Cultural vandalism	Taking souvenirs (flora, fauna, etc)

Sources: Cole, Petersen and Lucas, 1987; McNeely and Thorsell, 1989; Buckley and Pannell, 1990; Dowling, 1993; Wight, 1996

Table 3.4 Environmental risks from tourism

Element	Examples of risk from tourism activities
Ecosystems	The construction of accommodation, visitor centres, infrastructure, and other services has a direct impact on the environment, from vegetation removal, animal disturbance elimination of habitats, impacts on drainage etc. Wildlife habitat may be significantly changed (travel routes, hunting areas, breeding areas, etc.) by all kinds of tourist development and use.
Soils	Soil compaction can occur in certain well-used areas. Soil removal and erosion also occurs, and may continue after the disturbance is gone.
Vegetation	Concentrated use around facilities has a negative effect on vegetation. Transportation may have direct negative impacts on the environment (e.g. vegetation removal, weed transmission, animal disturbance). Fire frequency may change due to tourists and park tourism management.
Water	Increased demands for fresh water. Disposal of sewage or litter in rivers, lakes or oceans. Release of oil and fuel from ships and smaller craft. Propeller-driven watercraft may affect certain aquatic plants and species.
Air	Motorised transportation may cause pollution from emissions (from plane, train, ship or automobile).
Wildlife	Hunting and fishing may change population dynamics. Hunters and fishers may demand the introduction of foreign species, and increased populations of target animals. Impacts occur on insects and small invertebrates, from effects of transportation, introduced species, etc. Disturbance by visitors can occur for all species, including those that are not attracting visitors. Disturbance can be of several kinds: noise, visual or harassing behaviour. The impact can last beyond the time of initial contact (e.g. before heart-rate returns to normal, or before birds alight, or mammals resume breeding or eating). Marine mammals may be hurt or killed by boat impacts or propeller cuts. Habituation to humans can cause changed wildlife behaviour, such as approaching people for food.

Table 3.5   Summary of types of costs incurred by protected areas

Costs	Description
Direct costs	Includes facilities construction, maintenance and administration of the site.
Environmental degradation	Degradation associated with use of the site; e.g. soil erosion, water pollution and disturbance of wildlife.
Congestion	An additional user imposes a cost on all other users by reducing solitude.
Cost of natural resources	Cost of the land and related resources.
Reduced welfare of locals	Negative impact on locals due to restricted access to protected area resources.
Resource opportunity cost	Resource values forgone because recreation or preservation is produced; the commercial value of the resource is lost to society.

Source: Brown 2001, quoting Binkley and Mendelsohn 1987; Ceballos-Lascurain, 1996; Walsh, 1966.

Table 3.5 summarises the types of costs associated with protected areas. There is moreover one more danger: that governments or management agencies will neglect those protected areas that have important conservation values, but limited appeal for tourists.

Ecotourism and sustainable tourism strategies are designed to manage park visitation to maximize positive benefits and minimise negative environmental impacts prior to their occurrence. This is best achieved through well-designed planning strategies. A key issue is to be sensitive to cumulative impacts, to practice *adaptive management* (viewing management actions as experiments), and to achieve consensus among stakeholders about how much impact is acceptable, and where, in the protected area. Later chapters of these Guidelines describe some of the tools available for this purpose.

3.5   Tourism in protected areas which are not publicly owned or managed

3.5.1   A trend towards diversity in protected areas

In IUCN's protected area category system (IUCN, 1994), areas may be publicly-owned, privately-owned, owned by the community or owned by a mixture of some or all of these possibilities. Management may be equally diverse. In some parts of the world, privately-owned conservation lands are becoming a significant force for both conservation and tourism, and are flourishing. Such areas include privately-owned parks, NGO reserves, private hunting reserves, and biological and research stations run by universities. Tourism at private nature reserves varies from large resorts with a reserve as an added attraction, to small ecolodges within large nature reserves. Private reserves are often found adjacent to or nearby major public parks. Also, particularly in Category V and VI protected areas, there are extensive tracts of privately-owned land which are farmed or otherwise managed for resource use, but which are important for their contribution to landscape protection and biodiversity conservation. Another rapidly growing area is that of indigenous, aboriginal and community-owned protected areas (Beltran, 2000).

Several forces are at work here, including: political empowerment of previously marginalised groups (e.g. indigenous peoples); devolution of power from central government; greater use of the private sector to deliver public services; and the desire of individuals, commercial operations and communities to benefit from the economic activity generated by tourism. Langholz (1999) noted that the growing trend towards private ownership of protected areas was explained by a greater public interest generally in biodiversity protection, governments' inability to safeguard all biodiversity, and the expansion in ecotourism. Also, some communities have developed communally managed reserves to generate income in ways that are compatible with their lifestyle. Tourism may be viewed as a way of financing conservation activities, as a means of making money, or as a more favourable alternative to some other form of land use.

Whatever the reasons, the reality is that, in many parts of both the developed and developing world, the initiative for setting up protected areas is no longer coming only or even mainly from central government. As a result, tourism in protected areas is no longer just about an activity affecting publicly-owned and publicly-managed land.

3.5.2 Private reserves, community-driven initiatives and tourism

The potential for generating economic activity through private reserves is indicated by a local example from Canada (Box 3.8).

Private reserves play an important role in Costa Rica, a country that has enjoyed political stability and has stable land ownership laws. An extensive system of both public and private reserves supports an ecotourism industry. There is a long tradition that links the scientific researchers and ecotourism. The ecological research highlighted the

---

Box 3.8   Haliburton Forest and Wildlife Reserve, Ontario, Canada

The Haliburton Forest and Wildlife Reserve is the largest private forest reserve in Canada, at 20,000ha. It is managed profitably for a range of activities, including fishing, camping, hunting, logging, mountain biking, snowmobiling, ecotourism, and adventure tourism, as well as tourist accommodation (in a converted logging camp) and other visitor facilities. A large, fenced, natural compound containing wild wolves is adjacent to the educational centre. There is a "walk in the clouds" boardwalk, throughout the treetops of the forest, which visitors pay up to CDN$70/ person to visit; this is so successful that at times reservations are required. The forest has become a major tourism attraction and, although remote, people travel long distances to experience the variety of outdoor experiences offered. This reserve is adjacent to the very popular Algonquin Provincial Park.

The Haliburton land was affordable when it was bought in the 1950s, because it had just been logged out, so the potential yield as a timber resource was distant in the future. However, it is now successfully managed for integrated uses, and is financially self-sufficient. Some 70% of revenues derive from ecotourism and adventure tourism activities. The remainder comes from forestry-related products and supplies. The owner is on an ecotourism committee of a local college. As a keen supporter of the concept of ecotourism, he has been able to lead the development of the forest, and develop new visitor experiences annually, such as a "star gazing" observatory, opened in 2001. His independent financial backing means that he can make decisions quickly and without depending on government policies.

Web site: http://www.haliburtonforest.com/

Box 3.9   Monteverde Cloud Forest Reserve, Costa Rica: an example of a self-sufficient private reserve

The Monteverde Cloud Forest Reserve protects cloud forest in the central mountains of Costa Rica. It has high biological diversity with 100 species of mammals, 400 species of birds, 120 species of amphibians and reptiles and 2,500 species of plants (among them 420 different kinds of orchids). It attracts around 50,000 visitors annually. Its 50,180ha are managed by a non-profit organization, the Tropical Science Centre. It charges entrance fees:

– US$23 for foreigners (this was US$2.75 in the 1980s)

– US$2 for residents

– US$1 for students

The income from tourism increased over time and by 1994 the reserve more than covered its operating costs. Thus, of the US $850,000 revenues, 90% went to operating costs, and 10% went to the Tropical Science Centre. In that year, this reserve generated more income from tourism than was generated by all Costa Rican national parks together.

Source: Church and Brandon, 1995.
Web site: http://www.cct.or.cr/monte_in.htm

---

importance of Costa Rica's tropical ecosystems, leading to increased demand for protection and ecotourism (Eagles and Higgins, 1998). Researchers established many of the private reserves, which are run more efficiently than those managed by government agencies, are able to respond quickly to the market, and are able to generate resources to support other types of conservation and development activities (Honey, 1999).

The average extent of private reserves in Costa Rica is small (101ha), and most owners are more concerned with quality of management than with size of the reserve. Profit is often a secondary consideration for reserve owners. Many of them value conservation and land stewardship more highly, and over 75% of owners placed bequest value very highly (Brown, 2001). However, a few private reserves are quite large, such as the impressive Monteverde Cloud Forest Reserve (Box 3.9).

Africa has had a long tradition of using private and community lands for tourism to supplement other activities. For example, until recently the CAMPFIRE communal areas management programme for indigenous resources in Zimbabwe generated 90% of its income from trophy hunting, with the remainder coming from photographic safaris, hides and ivory sales and other tourist-related activities. Similar community-based tourism is flourishing in Namibia (IUCN, 1999). In 1989, in 63 private reserves in Latin America and Africa, tourism accounted for 40% of operating income. By 1993, this had increased to 67% of the reserves' operating income. Approximately half of the respondents depended on tourism for 90% or more of their income, and just over one third were completely dependent on it (Langholtz and Brandon, 2001).

South Africa has thousands of private game reserves, each with its own mix of wildlife conservation and tourism. Many sell trophy hunting and harvest wildlife meat for sale. These reserves tend to provide high-cost visitor services, while leaving the more inexpensive operations to the national and provincial park services. In South Africa, as elsewhere, many private reserves are located near national parks. For example, much of

---

Box 3.10   The Royal Society for the Protection of Birds (RSPB) (UK): An NGO contributing significantly to protected area conservation

The RSPB owns and manages over 150 reserves in the UK covering approximately 110,000ha. The RSPB is one of the largest private landowners in the UK, with reserves scattered all over the country. Many of the UK's rarest birds now breed only on nature reserves and, for many others, they provide vital winter bases or stop-overs on long migration flights. They are very important sites for bird watching and nature tourism.

Most RSPB reserves are open to the public and many have facilities suitable for visitors with special needs. Some have hides that have been adapted to allow access for wheelchairs, and many have special paths and boardwalks installed.

The RSPB has well over 1,000,000 members. These members help finance the on-going acquisition of new areas, with at least one new reserve established each year.

Web site: http://www.rspb.org.uk

---

the west side of Kruger National Park is buttressed by adjacent private game reserves. The land in these reserves adds considerably to the area and conservation value of the entire ecosystem.

Many reserves are owned and managed by NGOs, mainly for biodiversity conservation, both in developing and developed countries. For example, The Program for Belize owns and manages the Rio Bravo Conservation and Management Area, covering 92,614ha, or approximately 4% of Belize's land area. Ecotourism is the largest single source of funds (45% in 1995) available to meet the costs of running the reserve.

The Nature Conservancy of the USA owns more than 1,300 reserves, making it one of the largest private systems of nature sanctuaries in the world. This private organisation recognised the importance of ecotourism to the long-term financial sustainability of protected areas and developed an international programme of planning, guide training, financial research, ecolodge development and business planning to assist private and public reserve managers. The Royal Society for the Protection of Birds (RSPB) in the UK is another large conservation NGO whose conservation achievements have largely been built on the back of visits to its reserves by the public (Box 3.10).

Like all protected areas, private reserves are vulnerable to political unrest, poaching, community opposition to loss of access to resources, squatters and sometimes antipathy towards tourism. Private reserves are also very susceptible to fluctuations in the ecotourism market (Langholtz and Brandon, 2001).

Success will depend upon a number of factors, including:

- extensive community involvement at the outset and subsequently;
- a non-forced negotiating position between parties;
- a legal framework to allow tourism revenues to be retained by private land managers;
- sufficient revenues from tourism for management, conservation and profits to support the enterprise and contribute to conservation;

- mutual understanding of differing goals between stakeholders;

- an understanding by the managers of the constraints over their operations;

- mechanisms to cover injury liability affecting tourists and residents;

- mechanisms which link public and commercial tourism; and

- commercial tourism being able to focus on heavily visited sites (after Buckley and Sommer, 2001).

The establishment of protected areas and providing for tourism often work best when they come from within the community, even if this is done with outside support from NGOs or government sources. Box 3.11 describes one such community-based project from Belize.

Box 3.11   The Community Baboon Sanctuary (CBS), Belize: community owned and managed lands for conservation and ecotourism

The CBS is located 53km outside Belize City. In 1985, 12 landowners cooperated to manage their lands for the benefit of the black howler monkey. However, since landowners' cooperation was critical, the sanctuary had to meet their needs as well as those of the wildlife. They were asked to follow voluntarily a land use plan, which would maintain a skeletal forest from which howlers and other wildlife could easily use the regenerating areas of cut forest. Landowners were asked to leave certain food trees, and forest strips uncut along riverbanks and other areas, thus providing aerial pathways, for the monkeys to use as travel routes in large cut areas. Such practices would also reduce riverbank erosion and shorten cultivation fallow time.

The first step in accomplishing this was circulating a petition among villagers calling for an investigation of the potential to set up a sanctuary. With WWF help, villagers drew up management plans and obtained landowner commitment. The sanctuary expanded to include over 120 landowners and 8 villages, covering 47km^2. Assistance is also provided by the Belize Audubon Society.

A manager has to meet landowners to make sure agricultural practices are consistent with the management plans that they agreed to follow, as well as guiding tourists, and organizing local tourist hosts. Tourists may rent rooms, or camp and take meals locally. Because tour group leaders often tried to avoid local guides, there is now a $2.50 charge per visitor, and local staff must accompany them. Visitors to the sanctuary and villages have increased significantly, from about 10 in 1985, to over 6,000 in 1990.

Source: Horwich *et al.*, 1992.
Web site: http://www.ecocomm.org/cbs.htm

3.6 Summary and guidelines

Based on the foregoing, the following **Guidelines** are suggested for increasing the benefits of tourism in all kinds of protected areas, whether owned or managed by public, private, voluntary or community bodies:

- Ensure that the measurement of park tourism activities, volumes and impacts is accurate, as complete as possible and that the data are effectively communicated;

- Match the services and products available in the park and locally to tourist travel motives;
- Make products and services available for tourists' expenditure (e.g. recreation services, accommodation, crafts, and foods);
- Aim for high service quality in all tourist services;
- Develop a constituency of satisfied and supportive park visitors, people who will argue for park objectives in the large political debates in society;
- Develop opportunities for park visitors to play a positive role in park management (through membership in Friends Groups, by providing donations to targetted programs, or providing personal assistance to staff);
- Ensure that all information and interpretation programmes create appropriate expectations;
- Minimise local leakage (retain local expenditures through maximum local self-sufficiency) by developing linkages with local industries;
- Provide local accommodation options;
- Provide recreation activity options;
- Encourage consumption of locally-grown foods;
- Ensure local participation and control (e.g. local guide services);
- Ensure revenue-sharing or direct payment programmes;
- Understand the role of the protected area in regional and national tourism activities;
- Understand the fiscal and economic roles of park tourism;
- Host special events;
- Provide opportunities for local people to celebrate their cultural traditions;
- Where needed, assist in the education of local people in the skills necessary for tourism;
- Evaluate all tourism services provided by the private sector to ensure service quality and adherence to park policy;
- Ensure that the park has staff trained in tourism planning and management;
- Continuously evaluate all tourism programmes to ensure that goals are met;
- Ensure that tourism programmes are based upon competent financial management;
- Price appropriately; and
- Earmark the income from fees appropriately.

Guidance for minimising the adverse economic, environmental and social impacts is contained in the following chapters 4 to7.

4. Planning for protected area tourism

4.1 Protected area plans, policy and planning

The following key planning terms are used in these Guidelines:

- *Policy* is a written course of action adopted and pursued by a stakeholder, such as a park management agency;

- *Planning* is the process by which policy is placed into a structure that enables implementation;

- A *plan* is a document that articulates the policies, park goals, decision processes and the actions needed to implement the policies;

- A *management plan* is a tool to indicate how a park is to be protected, used, developed and managed;

- The *planning process* consists of the steps to be gone through in preparing a plan, which usually involves much public participation and debate at all stages.

Each park and protected area needs a plan that describes how tourism and associated development will be managed. The plan represents the desired future state or condition of the protected area and the most efficient and equitable path to that future. Such a plan details the specific goals and objectives mandated for the area in its founding legislation, decree or government policy, describes the objectives for tourism development, and specifies the management actions, budgeting, financing and park zoning needed to achieve those goals. In a sense, park plans for managing tourism attempt to maximize the benefits of tourism while minimising its costs. Tourism policies are an important component of the overall document, sometimes called a *management plan*.

In the distant past, protected area management planning tended to be *ad hoc*: often individual developments took place without an overall policy structure or goal. As the limitations of this approach became apparent, one large plan, typically called a *master plan*, was developed, following the approach used in city master planning. There was a reaction in the 1980s towards a more streamlined approach, with a strategic statement of goals, policies and actions, sometimes based on a "visioning exercise". In many quarters these documents became known as *management plans*. In the 1990s, in a search for still greater simplicity, the concept of management plans was in some cases slimmed down to mere policy statements. Despite these developments in practice, the importance of management planning has grown over time and, increasingly, many protected area agencies are required by law or policy directives to produce and follow management plans of some kind.

It is important in designing a planning process to adopt a procedure that is understandable, defensible, where decisions can be traced and where the value judgements inherent in protected area planning are made explicit. Most of all, it is essential that all stakeholders are appropriately involved in the process. Making management decisions

Figure 4.1   Protected Area Management Planning System

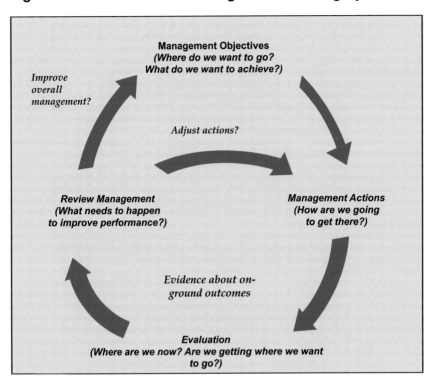

about tourism in protected areas is not easy; it involves not only protected area managers but also affected citizens, including the local public, visitors, private operators and scientists. To ensure that each group can contribute its different type of knowledge to decision making, it is essential to establish a *public involvement programme*, which may be modest or comprehensive, depending upon the needs.

Many park agencies have developed a set of guidelines and best management practices for use in writing management plans. For example, the Australia and New Zealand Environmental Conservation Council (ANZECC) has produced many Best Practice reports related to protected area management, all available on the Internet. The model in Figure 4.1 identifies the key stages of objectives, actions, evaluation and management review (Tasmania Parks and Wildlife Service, 2000). Other publications in IUCN's WCPA Best Practice Protected Area Guidelines series also address a number of topics which are relevant to management planning, notably in respect of:

- marine protected areas (Kelleher, 1999),
- financing protected areas (IUCN, 2000),
- management effectiveness (Hockings *et al.,* 2000), and
- transboundary protected areas (Sandwith *et al.,* 2001).

IUCN plans to publish general guidance on the form and content of management plans in this series in 2003.

Tourism and protected areas will be considered in several plans and policy statements at government levels senior to the protected area itself. Examples include:

- *National* or *regional sectoral plans* which address broad topics and affect protected areas within them. Examples are a Regional Development Plan, a Natural

42

Resource Management Plan, a National Plan for Tourist Development or a Transportation Strategy;

▪ A national level *protected area tourism policy,* for which some agencies have government approval. Appendix C contains the policy of the USNPS.

4.2 Tourism in the Park Management Plan

The park management plan is the vehicle for determining and listing all park policies. It is comprehensive in character. Park plans contain a variety of subjects, one of which is how tourism should be managed, impacts mitigated, and opportunities enhanced. Developing a park tourism plan requires that it be integrated with other plans for the protected area, such as a wildlife management plan, fire management plan and vegetation management plan. While such plans are often strong in how the natural resources are managed in the park, they are often weak in describing the objectives for tourism and how those objectives will be achieved. Therefore, the issue of tourism in protected areas is most importantly addressed in the policies relating to *tourism and recreation* within the management plan. But it may also be covered in greater detail in a *protected area tourism plan* developed from those policies.

Whether a separate protected area tourism plan is required, and the breadth and level of detail in it, will depend upon the complexity of issues to be considered. This plan may detail specific tourism management practices to be deployed, facility location, policies to guide tourism operations, level of fees charged to tourism operatives etc.

Black Bear in camp-site in Killarney Provincial Park, Ontario, Canada

Management of the interface between dangerous wildlife and park visitors is a unique challenge.
©*Paul F. J. Eagles*

The topic may be further developed through still more *specialised plans* or *strategies* intended to guide tourism and recreation within a protected area. Examples are a Visitor Use Plan, the Visitor Activity Management Process (VAMP), the Tourism Optimisation Management Model (TOMM), the Limits of Acceptable Change (LAC) or a Visitor Impact Management Plan (VIM) – see also Section 6.3.1 below.

Given the potential complexity of plan making, it is important that policies and plans should be integrated with those at different levels, that their relationship should be made clear, and that all management actions in different plans should be co-ordinated.

Listed below are several **Guidelines** that can be used to guide the development of the park tourism policy and plan:

- The natural and cultural environment within the protected area should form the basis for all other uses and values affecting the park and its management. These fundamental assets must not be put at risk;

- Protected area tourism depends on maintaining a high quality environment and cultural conditions within the area. This is essential to sustaining the economic and quality of life benefits brought by tourism;

- The protected area management organisation exists to protect the values for which the area was originally established through, among other things: active management of tourism and tourists; sharing of responsibility for management with tourism operatives, local communities and visitors; and providing potential economic opportunities for tourism;

- Protected area visitors expect to find facilities, programmes, and recreational and learning opportunities within the park, but not all demands can be met, as some of these expectations may be inconsistent with park goals and objectives;

- Visitors actively seek the best service quality they can afford for the money they have available. They do not necessarily seek the cheapest opportunities available;

- Visitors desire diversity in the recreational opportunities afforded, but not all parks can or should set out to provide for every demand;

- Planning should occur within, and acknowledge, the regional context of a particular protected area. This means that the types of tourism opportunities afforded in other protected areas should be inventoried as part of the planning process; and that the planning of tourism within a protected area should take account of tourism demands and provision in nearby areas; and

- Managing expectations is jointly the responsibility of park managers and other tourism operators.

4.3 Developing goals and objectives

Goals are defined here as the broadly stated social purposes for which a protected area is established. *Objectives* are more explicit statements of what is to be accomplished.

The goals for a protected area provide the overall policy framework for managing tourism in that area. Fundamental goals are often articulated in legislation, government policy directives, and in legal agreements with local stakeholders or through other mandates. Sometimes these are vague (e.g. to "protect the resource") or contain conflicting elements (e.g. the U.S. National Park system is designed to provide for the enjoyment of park resources while leaving them unimpaired for future generations).

Table 4.1 Guidelines for successful protected area planning objectives

Characteristic	Guidelines	Examples
Output-oriented	Objectives deal with the results or accomplishments of an activity. They describe what is to be accomplished, but not how. The "how" is part of the local protected area manager's creativity.	"Provide 3,000 visitors annually with a world class wildlife viewing opportunity" "Maintain an average annual population of 500 lions" "Increase the average ecological knowledge of visitors by 50% within 5 years"
Time-bound	Goals and objectives should maintain or move toward a desirable future condition. A time frame for an objective should be specified. Time-bound objectives provide the direction needed to develop the appropriate management actions, and require accountability.	"Within five years, provide 3,000 visitors annually with a world-class wildlife viewing opportunity" "Over the next 3 years, labour income from park tourism should increase 4% per year"
Specific	Objectives should provide all parties with a clear vision of what is to be accomplished. Once stakeholders agree to the objective, everyone is clear as to the meaning, and everyone becomes accountable for their role in achieving the objective.	"Over the next 3 years, labour income from park tourism should increase 4% per year" (The time frame is fixed, the increase is explicit and the term "labour income" has a shared meaning).
Measurable	Measurable objectives provide a clear basis for evaluating progress. Measurable objectives allow managers to determine where efforts need to be placed in the future. They indicate what elements in the protected area need to be monitored, where, and with what frequency.	"Over the next 3 years, labour income from park tourism should increase 4% per year" (Indicates that local labour income needs to be measured at least once per year over the first three years of the protected area plan)
Attainable	Objectives must be realistic over the time frame of the park plan. Objectives must be achievable with the available funding and staffing resources. Objectives represent a compromise between an idealistic vision (e.g. without impairment of park resources) and the reality of the impacts of tourism. Attainable objectives provide a motivation for action. Realistic objectives provide managers, visitors and operators with a sense of foreseeable accomplishment. By focusing on desired, rather than existing, conditions, objectives point towards an improvement in conditions. Attainable objectives may require trade-offs between a perfect world and a realistic one.	"Increase the average ecological knowledge of visitors by 50% within five years"

Source: In part from Schoemaker, 1984.

While such broadly written goals provide a sense of social purpose, they are not necessarily specific enough to guide the management of tourism. Since the development of protected areas tourism has other important social purposes (e.g. to develop local economic opportunity or enhance the quality of life), it is necessary to elaborate specific goals and objectives for these and other purposes. In order to measure progress towards the achievement of objectives, *indicators* need to be developed for monitoring (see also section 11.1.1).

Defining goals and objectives is the first step in the planning process, and the most difficult component of park planning for tourism. They must reflect the fundamental purpose of the protected area. The goals stated in the management plan should reflect the importance attached to attributes of the protected area by various interest groups, and interpret the legislation or decree establishing the park. The more groups of people and interests that are involved in goal refinement, the more difficult it will be to achieve agreement on them. However, it is worth overcoming this obstacle as the rest of the planning process can then be accomplished with greater ease.

The wording of objectives is very important. They should be specific, measurable statements that provide guidance in making decisions about appropriate levels, types and amount of tourism and tourism developments. More specifically, objectives should have five characteristics: (1) output-oriented; (2) time-bound; (3) specific; (4) measurable; and (5) attainable (Schoemaker, 1984). Table 4.1 sets out **Guidelines** for the development of appropriate protected area objectives.

4.4 Characteristics of successful protected area planning processes

A successful planning process has several characteristics. When embarking on the preparation of a new or updated plan for a protected area, managers should consider how the need for these characteristics will be addressed. Table 4.2 highlights the most important of these, with **Guidelines** for their implementation, and comments of explanation.

Table 4.2 Guidelines for successful planning

Criteria	Planning guidelines	Comments
Clarity in plan production	n State how the protected area is to be managed. n State how surprises are to be dealt with. n State how funding and personnel will be raised and allocated. n State how monitoring will occur. n State a specific time frame. n Provide for periodic review.	n Protected area personnel may change, so the document "outlives" any one person. n Provides continuity between changes in government.
Implementation oriented	n Make provisions for implementation during the planning process. n Indicate roles and responsibilities. n Work with politicians, interest groups and local communities to ensure implementation.	n Plans are written to change or work toward future conditions. This only happens if they are implemented. Without implementation, plans are useless.

Criteria	Planning guidelines	Comments
Socially acceptable	n Invite input from a large range of interests. n Use consensus-building processes. n Use technical planning assistance. n Social acceptability increases potential for implementation.	n Those affected by plans must find them acceptable, as must those with "veto" powers. n Consensus is not necessarily unanimity.
Mutual learning oriented	n Obtain expectations about anticipated experiences/ programmes/facilities from visitors. n Determine how park plans and business plans affect each other, jointly define the tourism product, and develop marketing plans cooperatively. n Managers should outline legal mission of the park, implications of different management strategies, and mitigation approaches. n Scientists should determine cause-effect relationships, and social-environmental consequences of actions. n Determine importance of benefits and values from citizens. n Techniques that empower stakeholders to become more aware of the issues increase their ability to generate innovative approaches.	n Enabling different publics and stakeholders to come together provides opportunities for mutual learning and appreciation. n Many-way dialogue helps active mutual involvement. n Avoid underestimating the competence of citizens. n Providing a range of venues for this learning is helpful, not only formal venues. n Do not forget associated agency staff and volunteers.
Responsibility and shared ownership	n Use many involvement techniques at all stages of the planning process (e.g. workshops, field trips, open houses, focus groups, advisory committees, etc.). n Create responsibilities for stakeholder groups. n Encourage stakeholder participation in issue identification, evaluation of alternatives and implementation. n Share information (e.g. about briefings or meetings) rather than provide information (e.g. displays, draft plans) – this creates more legitimate stakeholder involvement.	n Implementation of the plan is much enhanced if all stakeholders take responsibility and ownership of the plan. n The publics "own" the plan, not the agency. n Some workshops can be run over several days to build strong sense of ownership.
Representative of wide interests	n Recognise that protected area tourism affects, and is affected by, many political and social interests at national and community level. n Embody a wide range of values and interests through public participation. n Conduct a stakeholder analysis to identify the types of values affected by plan.	n Active engagement of stakeholders secures support. n Even those fundamentally opposed to park's objectives can benefit from seeing their interests honestly handled.
Relationship building oriented	n Use planning process to strengthen relationships, secure community commitment and build support for funding and personnel. n Demonstrate to local communities how they might benefit from tourism in the protected area. n Seek information, rather than provide information: this builds greater levels of trust.	n Agencies need to overcome distrust or other problems, by openness. n Open communication is necessary with the community and within the agency.

4.5 Involving stakeholders

4.5.1 Who are the stakeholders?

Protected area-based tourism has many stakeholders. Each group has its own particular values and objectives – its own "culture" indeed. This complex mosaic of stakeholder interests makes constant demands upon park management. The groups who have a direct interest in, and are affected in different ways by, park and tourism management policies, include:

Signing of the Federal-Provincial Agreement creating Bruce National Park, Ontario, Canada

Park planning typically involves high levels of public consultation and political involvement. ©*Paul F. J. Eagles*

- Park planners and managers
- Park volunteers
- Park visitors
- Park employees
- Local community
- Native or indigenous community
- Landowners (in and around the area)
- Residents (in and around the area)
- Resource extraction interests
- Government ministries
- Allied and sometimes competing government agencies
- Profit-making private sector
- Non-governmental organizations
- Environmental groups
- Economic development organizations
- Concessionaires, licensees and permit holders
- Hospitality industry
- Tour operators
- Destination marketing organizations
- Educational institutions
- Research bodies
- Media

Among all these interests, four groups are particularly important in the management of tourism in protected areas: (1) society in general, including local communities, (2) park managers, (3) tourism operators, and (4) visitors and users. Each group views park tourism from its own unique perspective (Figure 4.3).

4.5.2 Involve the range of stakeholders

Protected area planning encompasses two different, but related, domains: (1) a technical component, and (2) a public participation element for the stakeholders described in the section above. A key to success is the integration of these two inputs into a single, coherent planning process. Figure 4.2 illustrates this relationship and places public involvement on a par with the technical planning processes.

Successful planning generally involves all groups in such a way that each can contribute constructively to the various components of the process, and thus feel "ownership" of the plan. The entire decision-making process must be designed for stakeholder involvement throughout, not just added on to the process, after the fact.

Consensus-building is needed for acceptance, so that public resources can be allocated to implement the plan or measures taken to manage and sometimes restrict public use of the protected area. Therefore, developing a stakeholder involvement programme is an important element of success.

Each participation programme should be designed to meet the specific needs of the situation, rather than imposing a pre-determined methodology that may have worked well in other conditions. It is important too to avoid tokenism: managers should not tell the stakeholders they want their involvement, and then only budget two weeks for it. This will lose credibility for the whole project. Managers should also explain decision-making and the planning process in simple, everyday language.

Suggested **Guidelines** for the process are set out in Figure 4.3.

Figure 4.2 Effective planning

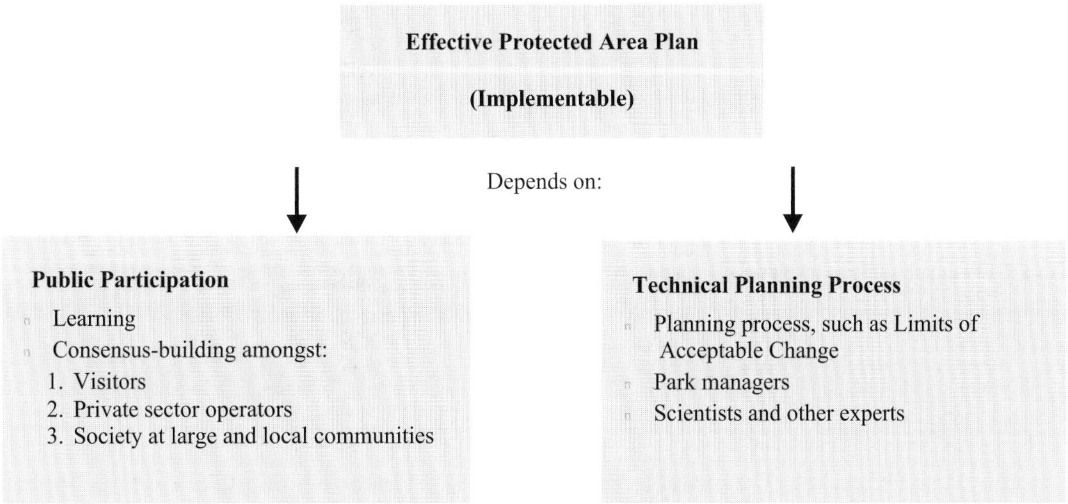

Effective Protected Area Plan

(Implementable)

Depends on:

Public Participation

- Learning
- Consensus-building amongst:
  1. Visitors
  2. Private sector operators
  3. Society at large and local communities

Technical Planning Process

- Planning process, such as Limits of Acceptable Change
- Park managers
- Scientists and other experts

Figure 4.3   Guidelines for a stakeholder involvement programme

Phase 1 **Early involvement**	◦ Consult informally to determine the major issues raised. ◦ Estimate level of public interest, and the most likely stakeholders. ◦ Identify key individuals.

Phase 2 **Initial planning**	◦ Chart agency's decision-making process. ◦ Identify stakeholders and publics. ◦ Determine information exchange needs. ◦ Clarify public involvement objectives.

Phase 3 **Development of a** **public involvement** **programme**	◦ Choose detailed methods of stakeholder involvement. ◦ Establish internal agency communications. ◦ Commit resources. ◦ Schedule and assign work.

Phase 4 **Implement the programme**	◦ Carry out the programme. ◦ Monitor the public involvement programme. ◦ Evaluate the results of involvement.

Phase 5 **Post decision public** **involvement**	◦ Develop post decision requirements (at the least notify public of decision, and how their comments were used). ◦ Implement as required.

Box 4.1   The Tanzania Community Conservation (CC) Project: an example of community outreach

Tanzania National Parks (TANAPA) developed the community conservation project to involve local communities better in park management. Community meetings are used as a way to understand and begin to address the needs of local people. Each protected area has a community liaison officer, whose job it is to develop community knowledge and trust. He/she also represents the communities' interests in management planning.

Since tourism income to TANAPA exceeds expenditures, there are funds available for community outreach projects. The park liaison officer works with the local community, identifies community needs and then directs funds towards the needs. The projects funded vary, but examples include local school education projects and repair of community facilities. For example, funds were provided for the repair of the roof of the council building in a community near Ruaha National Park. From then on every town council meeting was held under the roof provided by funds raised by tourism in the nearby national park.

Box 4.1 illustrates how these general ideas for stakeholder involvement in protected area planning have been adapted to the needs of a national protected area programme. Boxes 4.2, 4.3 and 4.4 describe case studies in community involvement in three protected areas.

4.5.2 Stakeholder motivations

The long-term viability of a protected area, and of its agency, depends upon the support of government and of the people. Park tourism is a critical component of the development of that support. All planners and managers, both in the public and the private sector, should understand stakeholders' attitudes towards the area. Each category of stakeholder has its own motivations and perspectives on the benefits of tourism in protected areas, whether physiological, psychological, social, economic or environmental. Stakeholders' perspectives and motivations are summarised under grouped headings in Table 4.3.

Box 4.2 Wakatobi Marine National Park, Indonesia: an example of an NGO involving the local community in a marine national park

Wakatobi Marine National Park (MNP), declared in 1996, is the second largest MNP in Indonesia. It contains 1.39 million hectares of marine, coastal and tropical forest environments in the Wallacea region between Borneo and New Guinea, and includes Sulawesi, a site of very important biodiversity.

Operation Wallacea is a UK-based NGO. It began biological surveys of the Wallacea region in 1995, and upon recognising its ecological importance lobbied for the creation of a national park. This lobbying, working with a counterpart in Jakarta, the Wallacea Development Institute, stimulated the Indonesian government to create the national marine park in 1996.

Operation Wallacea operates a dive and marine research centre in the national park, and each year runs a series of scientific wildlife survey and conservation expeditions, using substantial numbers of scientific volunteers. Each volunteer pays for the experience. In 2000, 300 volunteers stayed an average of 5 weeks in the area, between June and October. Each volunteer is responsible for a research project dealing with some aspect of marine biology, ecotourism research, forest ecology, wildlife management or community conservation. In 1999 students and professors from 22 British and Irish universities were involved. In addition, volunteer naturalists, divers and photographers completed a range of research and community development projects. The park has 55 rangers involved in the protection of the park and in the implementation of a management plan. The park rangers have dramatically reduced the level of destructive and illegal fishing techniques.

The project is designed so that the visitors have a positive economic impact on local communities. Approximately 60 local families gain all or a significant proportion of their income through employment, contract work or provision of supplies. Overall, 50% of all monies paid by the volunteers are spent in the local communities. Five local people are supported for each volunteer visitor. The project constructed an environmental education centre to provide reef biology courses to over 1,000 children each year. Funding is provided for community work, in order to provide sustainable economic opportunities for the local people.

Operation Wallacea is one of the largest examples of a coordinated, volunteer-based, park research project in the world. Park managers report that scientific research findings and the presence of scientists help enormously in achieving the park's management objectives. Operation Wallacea successfully manages to bring the benefits of tourism to the grassroots. This empowers local people by providing a new and lucrative source of income. It enables local communities to see the value of protecting natural resources, such as rain forests and coral reefs, rather than depend upon their exploitation.

Sources: Operation Wallacea, 2000; Wakatobi Dive Resort, 2000.

Web sites: http://www.opwall.com/ and
http://www.wakatobi.com

Box 4.3 Kakum National Park and Conservation Area, Ghana: an example of a successful community-based approach to tourism in a protected area

Kakum National Park was designated in 1991. The area provides habitat for globally endangered Forest Elephants, Bongo, Yellow-backed Duiker and Diana Monkey, an estimated 550 butterfly species, 250 species of birds, and 100 mammal, reptile and amphibian species. This area is part of the Guinean Forest Region of West Africa, a globally important area of biodiversity.

In order to provide better viewing of the wildlife, an aerial walkway was constructed, the first of its type in Africa. The walkway is 333m in length and is suspended approximately 27m off the ground by eight huge emergent trees. The canopy walkway offers students, tourists and researchers access to the rainforest canopy.

Financial support and guidance came from Conservation International and the U.S. Agency for International Development. The Kakum Conservation Area project was planned and implemented in the belief that ecotourism can be both an effective conservation tool and a successful community development model. It uses a community-based approach to tourism development, which is part of a successful conservation strategy. Tangible benefits to local people include:

- Purchase of agricultural products for the restaurant
- Purchase of furnishings, crafts and services from local artisans
- Provision of guide training to local teachers
- Creation of full-time, direct and indirect employment

Local people were helped to assist and manage their own ecotourism businesses, which create jobs that directly depend on a healthy environment, and motivate people to protect their surroundings. Visitation increased from 700 in 1990 to 80,000 in 1999.

The success of the Kakum project is due to four critical aspects:

1. It was a well-conceived local government initiative;

2. US AID provided long-term and significant financial support;

3. There was consistent and high-quality technical direction provided by Conservation International; and

4. Ghana had a stable political environment and an expanding economy over the period of project development.

The project exemplifies the best of environmentally sustainable tourism. It is an excellent example of local community development, carefully structured to create an ecotourism economic alternative to resource exploitation.

Web site: http://www.conservation.org/xp/CIWEB/regions/africa/west_africa/westafrica.xml

Box 4.4   Soufrière Marine Management Area, St. Lucia: an example of tourism management in a sensitive marine environment

Soufrière Marine Management Area was established in 1994 near the island of St. Lucia in the Caribbean Sea after a lengthy negotiation process between the government, the local fishing community, dive operators and other shore-based interests. Park tourism income replaced some of the local reliance on fishing, which had caused reef damage. The fishermen gave up access to near-shore fishing areas, in return for other employment opportunities, provision of small business loans and other economic alternatives. The marine reserve now provides excellent fisheries, spawning and replenishment functions for a much larger area.

The marine management area is funded by various government agencies, the sale of goods, user fees and an active "Friends Group" of volunteers. The park is managed by the Soufrière Foundation and Department of Fisheries, under the guidance of a Technical Advisory Committee consisting of key management authorities and user groups. The park attracts around 3,600 yachts, 5,000 boats a year, with 21,000 snorkellers and 12,000 divers.

The park area is divided into zones, each with an activity profile. Some potentially polluting activities are accepted in certain zones. The park managers established a visitor management programme, with specific emphasis on controlling the numbers and activities of the divers attracted to the marine resources. Yacht anchoring is restricted to a few selected areas. In these yacht zones approximately 60 mooring systems have been installed for anchoring. Marine biologists have confirmed that some reefs are already recovering from previous damage.

The park has an active education and interpretation programme. Lectures, brochures, videos and the internet are used to disseminate information on the park and its use. Private dive operators are required to give specific training and guidance to divers.

The Soufrière Marine Management Area also has monitoring programmes designed to measure the change of the ecosystem in response to human activities and environmental enforcement. Routine measurements attempt to track environmental, biological and socio-economic variables at key locations in the area over the long term. Research projects are designed to improve the understanding of the structure and function of the marine ecosystem of the Soufrière coast; they range from studies of coral fish migration to profiles of the Soufrière community.

Soufrière Marine Management Area (St. Lucia) is a good example of careful community development, sensitive tourism development, good planning and multi-stakeholder management. The management frameworks allow visitor use without negative impact on the marine resource. As a result of all the efforts, an important marine resource in the Caribbean Sea is protected and well managed.

Source: SMMA, 2000.

Web site: http://www.smma.org.lc/

Table 4.3   Stakeholders' views of tourism in protected areas

Groups	Motivations
Society and local communities	▫ Redistribute income and wealth ▫ Provide opportunities for local businesses to benefit from local resources ▫ Increase opportunities for employment ▫ Contribute to improved quality of life ▫ Gain foreign currency ▫ Assist community development ▫ Promote the conservation of natural and cultural heritage ▫ Sustain and commemorate cultural identity ▫ Provide education opportunities to members of society ▫ Promote health benefits ▫ Expand global understanding, awareness and appreciation ▫ Create employment and income ▫ Promote conservation and heritage appreciation
Specific to local communities	▫ Securing additional income ▫ As a source of employment ▫ Enhance respect for local traditions, cultural values, local environment ▫ Access to better services ▫ Enhancement of self esteem
Protected area managers/experts	▫ Promote conservation ▫ Develop heritage appreciation ▫ Generate revenue (to make a profit or reduce operating costs) ▫ Create employment and income ▫ Learn from others ▫ Build alliances with the local community ▫ Develop long-term sustainable economic activity ▫ Manage resource extraction ▫ Foster research ▫ Create a positive experience ▫ Generate repeat visits
Tourism operators	▫ Operate profitably ▫ Respond to market demand ▫ Identify target markets ▫ Develop target markets ▫ Exploit market advantage ▫ Develop products for target markets ▫ Provide markets with services ▫ Support visitors and assist them to understand the resources
Tourists	▫ Enhance personal experiences, which include: ➢ cognitive objectives (for example, learning about nature and wildlife) ➢ affective concepts (for example, gaining peace of mind) ➢ psychomotor desires (for example, getting exercise) ▫ feel personal accomplishment ▫ gain health benefits ▫ participate in a social experience ▫ spend quality time with peers ▫ meet people with similar interests ▫ achieve group team building ▫ achieve family bonding ▫ explore family history ▫ provide the opportunity for courtship ▫ reaffirm cultural values ▫ promote conservation and preservation

An effective and comprehensive management plan for a park must incorporate an understanding and appreciation of the perceptions of these groups. Failure to recognise and address all of the driving forces of tourism will result in short-sighted management that considers only a small proportion of potential users. When that occurs, there is the potential for troublesome political problems. It is critical that public participation be a central component of all management plan development.

The process used to identify the values, choose amongst alternatives, and to make decisions must be open, participatory, equitable and visible. Those stakeholders whose views are not given priority must be assured that their opinions were nonetheless considered fully.

4.5.3 A range of stakeholder involvement processes are available

Many public involvement techniques exist, and Table 4.4 shows these as a continuum. During the course of stakeholder involvement, it may be desirable to use a variety of techniques.

Table 4.4   A continuum of stakeholder involvement approaches and selected techniques

Approach	Description	Selected techniques	Message to the public
Public information/ education	"Knowledge about a decision"	Advertising Newspaper inserts Posters	*You want them to know and understand about it*
Information feedback	"Being heard before the decision"	Briefs Focus groups	*You want them to understand and support your programme*
Consultation	"Being heard and involved in discussions"	Community meetings or gatherings Conferences Workshops/Problem-solving meetings	*You want to understand them and value their views and input*
Extended involvement	"Having an influence on the decision"	Advisory groups Task forces	*You seriously expect to implement most of their advice*
Joint planning	"Agreeing to the decision"	Consultation Mediation Negotiation	*You are fully committed to using the results in all but the most exceptional circumstances*

Key: From top to bottom = Increasing degree of stakeholder involvement

Source: Wight, 2002b.

As a general rule, the higher the degree of involvement:

- The more staff time and energy is required;
- The more money it costs to support the process;
- The more detailed and sophisticated resource information is requested by participants;
- The greater is the expectation of stakeholders that their contributions will be valued and used; and
- The greater the visible commitment that must be made to use the results, keep stakeholders informed, and explain any deviations from recommendations or decisions.

Since the views of the various stakeholders are often in conflict, it is critical that stakeholders should know which protected area management objectives are paramount, and why. This is discussed further in the following section.

4.6 Managing conflict

4.6.1 Understanding conflict in protected areas

Conflicts occur whenever two or more groups compete for similar resources and one finds that another group interferes with its pursuit of a particular goal – such as recreation, indigenous hunting or collecting. Within recreation management, conflict may be thought of as *goal interference*. Some conflict is inevitable in protected areas, so the major question confronting managers is how to manage and resolve this.

Four main kinds of conflicts that may occur are discussed below:

Conflicts between visitors and managers: Managers have a paramount responsibility for the protection of protected area values, so their view may conflict with what park tourists are seeking. For example, managers may want to minimise human interference with wildlife habits, and thus restrict where and how visitors view and photograph animals. Visitors may want to get as close as possible to animals in order to take a good photograph. These two groups thus experience goal interference with each other. Managers may help to reduce the conflict by explanations (e.g. why it is important for visitors to remain distant from wildlife).

Conflicts between recreationists in the same activity: Conflicts can occur within one recreational activity. They may arise when an area is crowded or when a group is engaged in behaviour considered to be inappropriate, unacceptable or obnoxious by others. Inter-recreation conflict can occur due to different skill/experience levels amongst the recreationists. For example, amateurs with naïve approaches can upset experienced nature-photographers. Zoning, education and information, dispersal of use or enforcement of regulations may reduce such conflicts.

Conflicts between recreationists engaged in different activities: Conflicts can occur between different recreation activities (e.g. between people engaged in motorised and non-motorised recreation, and between people engaged in *active recreation*, such as bicycling or four-wheel driving, and those engaged in *passive recreation*, such as wildlife viewing, photography or nature study). Zoning, either spatially or temporally, is one of the best ways of reducing these conflicts.

Conflicts between recreation and non-recreation activities: Strong conflicts can occur between recreation and non-recreation activities (e.g. in those protected areas where land is used for farming, timber harvesting or mining for example). Wildlife viewers and timber harvesters often hold conflicting views about protected area use. Careful zoning, management of visitors and of the non-recreational activity, and information about why the activity is permitted, may help reduce the extent of the conflict. In protected areas where such uses as traditional forms of agriculture are considered part of the landscape heritage and support wildlife (mainly Category V areas) such information will need to emphasise the conservation benefits that some resource use can bring. In many parks the non-recreation activity is banned, thereby removing the on-site conflict, and moving it into the larger political arena.

Table 4.5 Assessment of community involvement techniques

Techniques	Objectives				Assessment			
	Information giving	Information receiving	Information sharing	Participatory decision-making	Level of contact with community	Ability to handle specific interests	Level of two-way communication	Ability to resolve conflict
Information sheets and brochures	•				✓✓	✓	✓	✓
Displays and computer simulations	•				✓	✓	✓	✓
Media campaigns	•				✓✓✓	✓	✓	✓
Draft documents (plans and policies)	•				✓	✓	✓	✓
Review of plans and publications		•			✓	✓	✓	✓
Political environmental assessment		•			✓	✓✓	✓	✓✓
Information hotlines	•	•			✓✓	✓✓	✓✓	✓
Discussion papers	•	•			✓	✓	✓	✓✓
Individual stakeholder interviews	•	•			✓	✓✓✓	✓✓✓	✓✓
Telephone polling and surveys	•	•						✓
Guided tours	•	•	•		✓✓	✓✓	✓	✓✓
Public meetings	•	•	•		✓✓	✓	✓✓	✓
Stakeholder meetings	•	•	•	•	✓	✓✓	✓✓✓	✓✓✓
Advisory committees	•	•	•	•	✓	✓✓✓	✓✓✓	✓✓✓
Focus groups	•	•	•	•	✓✓	✓✓✓	✓✓✓	✓
Workshops	•	•	•	•	✓✓✓	✓✓✓	✓✓✓	✓✓✓

Key: • Most appropriate for achievement of objectives: ✓ limited performance; ✓✓ reasonable performance; ✓✓✓ good performance
Source: Hall and MacArthur (1998) adapted from various sources.

4.6.2 Public involvement techniques to reduce conflict during planning

Since recreation conflict is due to goal interference, there are two basic approaches to the resolution of conflict. One is to develop an understanding of the goals, and then establish a management regime that allows for goal fulfilment without interfering with the goals of another. The other is to try to change the goals. To resolve differences, there has to be acknowledgement and some integration of a range of values. A range of approaches is possible: all the way from forcing one group or interest to capitulate, or at least compromise, on a strongly held position, to a more constructive collaborative approach.

Table 4.5 assesses a range of community involvement techniques. As some conflict is unavoidable, the main focus in its resolution should be management rather than prevention. Also, not all conflicts can be successfully resolved. Resolving conflicts requires that managers use a variety of tools and involve those impacted by the conflict in the management process. Usually, resolution involves better and more communications. In some cases, formalised conflict resolution, processes such as negotiation, and arbitration, will help resolve matters. In others, more informal co-operative and collaborative processes may be successful.

The outcome of a dispute is likely to involve one of three approaches:

Prohibition of certain activities: Prohibition is a controversial, but sometimes necessary approach. However, once potential visitors know the rules, they can choose whether or not to visit.

Separation of activities in time or in space: Temporal and special zoning are common planning outcomes. Zoning is relatively easy to understand, communicate and implement.

Box 4.5   Marine Protected Areas, Republic of Maldives: An example of successful prohibition of activities for protection

In 1992, a survey by the Government of the Maldives found that over US$2 million was spent per year by divers who came to watch sharks. It was estimated that reef sharks are about 100 times more able to generate revenue if they are the basis of dive operations, than if they are the basis of a shark fishery. Thus there was a sound economic case for protecting reef sharks, at least within the tourism zones (25 selected sites).

In these areas, prohibited activities included: anchoring (except in an emergency), coral and sand mining, rubbish dumping, removal of any living and non-living resources, and fishing of any kind. Objectives were to protect important dive sites, conserve biodiversity and sustainable development of tourism.

Tourist divers were used to keep track of people breaking the law deliberately or through ignorance. They report their findings. This has created awareness among locals of the importance of many values. As a result, there has been no illegal mining or garbage dumping. However, there is still a need to restrain some visitor practices, such as casual boat anchoring.

The lessons from this project are that marine life can be preserved and protected through regulations, but increasing public awareness is an essential part of this strategy.

Source: WTO, 2001.

Provision of information and education: Information can be used to influence a visitor's goals and his or her activities. However, those with strongly held views are often not amenable to education programmes.

Once decisions on how to address a conflict have been taken, action should follow and must be made to stick. For example, if zoning is instituted, an activity is banned or a permit system developed, the park managers should ensure implementation. Since some people may not accept the decisions, there is, unavoidably, a need for enforcement. It may even be necessary to use legal and policing powers to enforce the agreed-upon measures. Box 4.5 describes a successful outcome of enforcement action of this kind.

4.7 Plan development and implementation

Once a plan or a policy has been agreed upon, it must be implemented. A first step is its communication to all stakeholders. Typically, a published document is distributed to all those involved in the plan or policy's development and implementation. Recently, many protected area agencies have placed their policies and plans onto Internet sites, for easy and rapid distribution.

Chapters 5, 6 and 7 flow from Chapter 4, and provide details of plan development and implementation. Chapter 5 deals with the sensitive and sustainable design of park infrastructure and services. Chapter 6 addresses challenges in park tourism planning, and sets out various management frameworks which have been developed by park agencies to assist with the task. Chapter 7 reviews the tools that can be used to manage park visitation and tourism. The choice of these tools and their application within the protected area management plan is at the heart of tourism planning in protected areas.

Implementation involves the carrying out of the plan, and involves the deployment of financial and human resources. Chapter 8 deals with the economic aspects of protected area tourism. Chapter 9 describes financial aspects of park management, and Chapter 10 those of human resource management. Implementation must of course be kept under constant review, and Chapter 11 therefore covers the questions of monitoring and evaluation.

5. Sensitive development of infrastructure and services

All protected areas, other than those in IUCN Category Ia, require some level of visitor service infrastructure. This may be no more than an information sign in a nature reserve, or as prominent a feature as a village or small town of importance to tourism in a protected landscape. All infrastructure must be located with care because it can be so intrusive. Tourism-related structures must also be very carefully designed and operated. They should reflect protected area values and clearly accord with park policy.

Protected area managers need to reflect on the fact that they manage a cultural and a natural area, and a site that often assumes a very different state from that which once prevailed. Some protected areas accommodate "pockets of urbanisation" within a larger environmental and cultural matrix. Infrastructure and services serve the people now using the area, and these are often much different from that which occurred previously. These services fulfil needs such as sanitation, food provision, lodging, information, transport and safety. The key is the provision of the services that best fulfil visitor needs, while minimising negative impacts.

Tendele, Royal Natal National Park, Kwa-Zulu Natal, South Africa

Culturally and environmentally sensitive structures enhance the park visitor's experience.
©*Paul F. J. Eagles*

While some protected areas are rarely visited, others accommodate large numbers, far exceeding the size of the local population. For example, in Kakadu National Park, Australia, there are now thousands of people around the visitor centre on many days during the peak visitor season, whereas 30 years ago, before the proclamation of the first part of the park, only a handful of people visited the area annually. In the case of several UK national parks (Category V areas), visitor numbers occur in the range 10 to 20 millions annually.

It is clear that visitor services both stimulate park use by people and also direct these uses. Wherever possible, therefore, park infrastructure and visitor services should help to enhance visitor understanding of key park themes and values. Good design makes visitors more comfortable and responsive to the special place that they are visiting. Visitors who feel they are well looked after will value the park more and are likely to assist in its protection. An increasing emphasis on a customer focus has developed in recent decades. Park visitors' needs are now more carefully investigated through planning and research, and monitored through comments cards and satisfaction surveys. Indeed, a mark of a well-managed protected area is that the planning of the infrastructure and services for visitors is based on an understanding of the needs of existing and potential users.

Good design is important because well-designed enterprises are the most successful. They function better, and attract more visitors. Moreover, good design need not be expensive. Often success depends on simple solutions and easy maintenance.

5.1 Culturally sensitive design and operation

Culturally sensitive design and operation are essential in the provision of visitor services. This calls for patience, tolerance and a sense of fairness on the part of the protected area manager but most of all it requires a sensitivity to heritage issues and values. *Heritage* is a broad concept, encompassing not only wildlife and landscapes, but also historic sites, architectural features, collections, past and continuing cultural practices, including ceremonies, rituals, events, even language, traditional knowledge and living experiences. Moreover, different nations, peoples and individuals have varied notions of heritage: for some, it is buildings and structures; for others a way of life and a living culture. Some communities view the historic heritage as dating from, say 150 years or more; for others, less than 50 years will suffice.

Because heritage is so culturally specific, great care should be taken to understand heritage values before designation of protected areas. While tourism may provide a special impetus towards the conservation of such areas, both by raising profile and providing funds, managers of protected areas should always be sensitive to the special needs of cultural sites of all types. Cultural resources designated as heritage under legislation will require special attention, but since the cultural impact of tourism can extend well beyond designated heritage sites, there is always a need for careful cultural impact understanding and management. A key issue for managers is who is involved in making the decisions that affect cultural heritage, and what is the process for decision-making.

The International Council on Monuments and Sites (ICOMOS) develops approaches to the conservation and use of cultural heritage. For example, the organisation has developed guidance, or charters, for handling a broad range of situations, including:

- Historic gardens and landscapes
- Historic towns
- Archaeological heritage
- Underwater cultural heritage
- Monuments
- Cultural tourism

ICOMOS developed a Charter on culture and tourism in 1999, the key management elements of which are presented in Table 5.1.

Table 5.1 Guidance from the 1999 ICOMOS Charter

Element	Guiding directions
Authenticity	Retention of authenticity is important. Interpretation programmes should: • Enhance the appreciation and understanding of that cultural heritage; • Present the significance of the culture in a relevant and accessible manner; • Use appropriate, stimulating and contemporary forms of education, technology and personal explanations; and, • Encourage high levels of public awareness and support of heritage.
Employment	Tourism should: • bring benefits to host communities and provide an important motivation and means to maintain their heritage and cultural practices; • Promote equitable distribution of benefits of tourism, through education, training and creation of employment opportunities; and • Encourage training and employment of local guides and interpreters. Managers should: • Carefully address the potential impact of visitors on the characteristics, integrity and biodiversity of the place, local access and the social/economic/cultural well-being of the host community; and • Select circulation routes to minimise impacts on integrity of place.
Respect	• Respect sanctity of spiritual elements, values and lifestyles of the host. • Respect rights and interests of the community, property owners and indigenous peoples, who may have traditional rights over their own land, or wish to restrict certain activities, practices or access. • Encourage and help all parties to understand and resolve conflicting issues. • Conservation should provide well-managed opportunities for visitors and members of the host community to experience and understand that community's heritage and culture, first hand.
Culture	• Encourage visitors to experience the wider cultural/natural heritage of the region. • Involvement of all parties, including local and/or indigenous community representatives is necessary to achieve a sustainable tourism industry.
Economic returns	• Allocate a significant proportion of revenues to protection, conservation and presentation of places, and tell visitors about this allocation. • Ensure that distribution and sale of crafts and products benefit the host community.
Visitor satisfaction	• Ensure that the visitor experience is worthwhile, satisfying and enjoyable. • Present high quality information to optimise visitors' understanding of heritage and need for protection. • Provide appropriate facilities for comfort, safety and well-being of the visitor. • Ensure tourism promotion creates realistic expectations. • Minimise fluctuations in visitor arrivals and even the flow as much as possible.

Element	Guiding directions
Consultation and evaluation	▫ Continuing research and consultation are important to understanding and appreciating the heritage significance of the place. ▫ Involve host communities in planning for conservation and tourism, and establishing goals, strategies, policies and protocols. ▫ Evaluate the ongoing impacts of tourism on the place or community.

Source: ICOMOS, 1999.
Web site: http://icomos.org/tourism/charter.html

5.1.1 Protection and use of the built heritage

There are basically four approaches to protecting and using the built heritage:

1. *Preservation:* the stabilisation and protection of existing structures and artefacts;

2. *Restoration:* the repair of the structures and artefacts where replacements of missing parts should integrate harmoniously with the whole;

3. *Re-creation:* the creation of a new structure or artifact that faithfully replaces one that is lost, destroyed or too fragile to use; and

4. *Adaptation:* the restoration of part of the structure, but with change in another part, to make it more useful, for example for tourism.

The tourism use of the built heritage raises difficult technical issues, such as accommodating human movement, disseminating visitor information, safety and security for buildings and people, food provision, and services like electricity, sanitation and water distribution. Employees' needs must also be considered. Tourism demands can be handled within a restored and adapted building, though imaginative solutions are often required. The preservation and restoration of built heritage must be very carefully planned and executed: the aim should be to provide for tourists in the best possible way, using good interpretation, while ensuring high quality heritage preservation.

Guidelines for any new building (for tourism use, for example) in the context of the historic built heritage include:

▪ Work with the character of existing buildings;

▪ Be sympathetic to the local vernacular style and materials (though this is not incompatible with contemporary architecture);

▪ Pay careful attention to the setting; and

▪ Involve the stakeholders in finding the architectural solution.

5.1.2 Interpretation and education for cultural heritage

Cultural heritage only really comes alive for the visitor through well-designed and implemented interpretation and education programmes. Interpretation is required to communicate the significance of an area to visitors, and to members of the host community, and the need for its conservation. Interpretation should aim to develop awareness of, and respect for cultural and heritage values, the present-day community and indigenous custodians of the heritage, and the landscapes and cultures within which that heritage has evolved. It should help develop support for the stewardship of the site.

A professionally-planned heritage interpretation programme involves: the careful determination of interpretation themes; the choice of media to present the themes; the presentation of the material; and the evaluation of the presentation. In selecting themes, managers should note that individual aspects of the heritage within a protected area would have differing levels of significance, from local to international. Interpretation programmes should present that significance in a manner relevant to the visitor but also to the host community. The visitor should always be informed of the cultural values of a particular resource.

Cultural heritage interpretation differs somewhat from natural environment interpretation because of the fragile and irreplaceable aspects of many cultural artefacts and because much heritage is still "owned" by a living culture. Moreover, cultural presentation often involves careful analysis of the cultural conflicts involved in the presented themes. For example, a war site commemorated in a national historic site has different interpretations for the different cultures involved in the conflict. Each of these must be presented honestly and openly. Getting the message right can be challenging: failure to do so can lead to politically-charged situations.

5.2 Environmentally sensitive design and operation

5.2.1 Standards and guidelines

Tourist facilities and programmes within protected areas should act as standard-setters in environmentally sensitive design and operations. Good design and sympathetic operations can increase local and visitors' awareness of key park values, and demonstrate to all visitors the protected area management's commitment to environmental protection. This can be done by:

- Minimising the negative environmental impact of visitor support services;

- Creating an atmosphere in which visitors feel they are in a special place; and

- Setting an example of environmentally sensitive design and operation practices, to educate and demonstrate the value and practicality of sustainable, innovative and effective solutions.

The need for, and level of detail of, each aspect of planning and design will vary according to individual circumstances. The Tourism Council of Australia (1998) and the National Park Service of the USA (1993) have both published excellent guides to environmental design in parks and tourism. Table 5.2 provides **Guidelines** for environmentally and culturally sensitive design and operation. Boxes 5.1 and 5.2 are two examples of some of these values put into practice.

Table 5.2   Guidelines for environmentally and culturally sensitive facilities

Aspect	Guidelines
Environmental impact assessments	Consider whether or not a statutory or informal environmental assessment is required, including ecological, social, cultural and economic evaluation. Develop a mitigation plan, where required.
Landscaping and site design	Develop a context plan – examining the entire surrounding area and community, including valued views and resources. Develop a management plan for the site, including the relationship with the surrounding/ adjacent protected area, addressing zoning and access. Develop a site plan, focusing on detailed design. This should minimise site disturbance, physical intrusion and intervention. Tree management considers tree retention, relocation or replacement. Plant vegetation to supply a more natural environment that provides habitat for birds, mammals and other wildlife. Use indigenous species for landscaping. Consider cultural aspects of site. Ensure linkages are considered (for land use, human circulation, nearby trails, other facilities, outpost camps, etc.).
Built facilities	Height and mass should be in scale with existing vegetation and topography. Design guidelines should recognise the history of place, cultural characteristics and indigenous or vernacular design features, colours, etc. Facilities should be constructed for energy efficiency, using renewable energy wherever possible.
Resource conservation and consumption	Design and operate services so as to minimise use and production of water, energy, waste, sewage, effluent, noise, light and any other emissions. Encourage the use of renewable sources of energy. Consider a permaculture approach (which mimics the interconnectedness and diversity of flora and fauna in natural systems) to turn waste into resources and problems into opportunities.
Materials	Materials should be indigenous, appropriate to the area, and involve low maintenance. Materials used in construction should be "sourced" to ensure that they come from sustainable production systems, or should be recycled where appropriate. Ensure that all materials brought onto the site for construction are used – apply a "no waste" condition to contractors.
New and low impact technologies	Use new technologies in construction and operations where appropriate, practical, cost effective, and where there are no perverse effects elsewhere (e.g. "smart" room controls and sensors, low heat transfer glazing assemblies, free cooling/heating, energy from solar/ wind/micro-hydro, power controls for energy savings, re-use of produced heat, etc.). Use new technologies, which are more effective in stand-alone equipment and vehicles, as well as in facilities.
Services	Develop and implement service standards to meet the needs of all stakeholders – visitors, agencies, private sector, staff.
Quality control	If guidelines and conditions of operation of the protected area agency are clear, reporting or decisions should be simple and clear. Baseline information should be maintained (ideally from pre-construction) so as to assess what, if any, impacts may occur as a result of construction and operations. These may be very simple observations, or quite complex. Set conditions of operation and timelines such that the developer/concessionaire can afford to invest in quality and visitor satisfaction, as well as obtain a reasonable return on the investment. Initiate regular meetings with managers and facility operators to help resolve problems or issues.

Aspect	Guidelines
Green practices	Develop green purchase policies. Use biodegradable cleaning products. Use alternatives to watering, such as mulching, alternate mowing and composting. Develop an integrated pest management plan. Use bulk or re-usable storage containers. Keep all systems and equipment well maintained, since all systems degrade in efficiency over time. Encourage staff vehicle pooling for staff transport to site. Ensure marketing materials are environmentally sensitive, and use electronic communications.
Programming	Reward staff for creativity and monitoring. Involve visitors in developing ongoing improvements. Manage human use – a human use strategy (see above) assists this. Consider partnerships with others (e.g. other public agencies) to assist in programming. Develop high staff to client ratios. Build monitoring into programme activities.
Relationship with the local community	Consult with the local community before development or significant changes in activities. Donate surplus or left over goods to local charities or causes (e.g. soaps, bed linens, amenities, foods). Maximise employment opportunities with the local community. Buy goods and services locally, and encourage "green" products and services, where none are available. Assist local organisations, provide discounted services, or donate a percentage of fees or profits to a worthy local cause. Encourage visitors to spend more time locally. Offer work experience or training options locally.

Box 5.1 Sabi Sabi Private Game Reserve, South Africa: an example of environmentally sensitive sewage management at a private reserve

Sabi Sabi is an 800ha private game reserve, adjacent to Kruger National Park, which was used for cattle grazing prior to its purchase in 1974. It has had a lion and white rhino reintroduction programme, and is now used for big game viewing. It supports 130 employees, over 100 locals, together with their families. Its main contribution to conservation is to protect the area from clearance for settlement, agriculture or cattle grazing, through low-volume, high-value tourism. Its contribution to community development is through employment, training and purchase of local products and services.

There are three operating lodges. An artificial wetland is a key part of the sewage treatment system. Sewage is collected by gravity feed to a 3-chambered 10,000-litre holding and separation tank. Sludges are pumped out and trucked away, as needed. Liquids are pumped to settling ponds, and electrified fences protect adjacent vegetation. Water drains gradually through plant roots to a small swamp area. The ponds and swamp support a range of waterbirds, including the saddle-billed stork, which feeds on frogs.

Source: Buckley and Sommer, 2001.
Web site: http://www.sabisabi.com/

67

5.2.2 Design of public and private sector facilities

There is a continuing debate on the appropriate mix of operating approaches to visitor facilities. The most common options are: park agency, concessionaire, Friend's Groups, NGOs and local communities. However, in situations where land is mainly under private ownership, services like accommodation and catering will be provided by the private sector without direct control from the protected area agency (though it may be able to determine the location and form of that service through controls operated under a land use planning system). Each option has its advantages and disadvantages. The key factors in making the decision are: government policy on private involvement; fiscal considerations; the administrative structure of the protected area agency; and its capability to manage. Whatever option is chosen, the facilities need to be designed and managed as sensitively and efficiently as possible, following the guidance in Table 5.2. In the following sections, key aspects of the design of camp-sites, roofed accommodation, interpretation facilities and transport facilities are each considered.

Camp-sites

The provision of comfortable accommodation in camp-sites, and in roofed accommodation (see below) in the North American national parks was probably crucial in building the strong constituency that the parks movement enjoys today.

Many countries provide camping facilities within protected areas, ranging from basic camp-sites in remote areas, to large constructed camp-sites with extensive infrastructure. Parks Canada's (1992) Camping Manual illustrates one agency's approach to camp-sites. It describes the role of camping in national parks, the development of a service strategy, and the design, construction, maintenance and operation of camp- sites.

Facilities associated with camping in wilderness and backcountry situations should be as simple as possible, appropriate to the level of use, and appropriate to the degree of allowable impact. Well-designed facilities for backcountry camp-sites can minimise human impact on remote sensitive environments: for example, simple pit toilets are much preferable to widespread distribution of human waste. "Front country" camp-sites often include showers, laundry facilities, children's play facilities and interpretation facilities. All should follow principles of environmentally sensitive design (Table 5.2).

Box 5.2   River Cove Group camp-site, Kananaskis Country Provincial Park, Alberta, Canada: Use of solar power at an unserviced camp-site

The River Cove camp-site serves provincial, national and international visitors. Most of the camp-sites in the area have toilets and shelters, but have no power supply for lighting. In 1988 photovoltaic (PV) powered fluorescent lighting systems were installed to extend camp-site use after dark. One was at a public shelter, and one at a public toilet. The systems are triggered by motion sensors, and are turned off by a delay switch.

Installation of a PV system is more cost effective than connecting with a utility grid. Although initial capital cost is high, there is virtually no maintenance cost once the system is installed. It is simple, reliable, and requires minimal maintenance. Visitors have shown a lot of interest in the system, and ask questions about it, thus creating an opportunity to give out "green" messages.

Waste disposal is an important issue for all camp-sites. Solid garbage waste requires landfill disposal either inside or outside the protected area, so plans to reduce waste generation are highly desirable. Self-composting toilets can significantly reduce sewage disposal problems. Many protected areas near cities and towns especially can take advantage of collection and recycling programmes for metal, paper and glass. Others can generate their own solutions. For example, Algonquin Provincial Park in Ontario, Canada introduced a ban on cans and bottles for all backcountry hiking and canoeing areas. The private sector responded by providing a full range of food and supplies in packages that are light, easy to burn or carry back out. The result was the virtual elimination of the garbage problem in the interior of the park.

Roofed accommodation

Many visitors require overnight accommodation. If the protected area is small, they are probably best accommodated in nearby towns, villages or home stays; the same of course will apply in the case of protected areas, usually Category V, that contain such settlements within their boundaries. In such cases, there will be a particular need for good transport, preferably public transport, to provide access to and within the protected areas, and especially to such focal points as information centres and take-off points for walking trails and toilets.

There is a vigorous debate about the merits of allowing built accommodation within Category I to IV protected areas (in principle, their presence in Categories V and VI protected areas is not controversial). In the early days of national parks, it was almost axiomatic that protected area-based tourism and built accommodation went together. Today, too, many of the larger parks and game reserves in Africa, for example, construct accommodation in the parks to serve their visitors. In many other countries, however, there is opposition to accommodation in these kind of protected areas; instead it is felt that such development should take place in nearby communities.

There are some good arguments for locating built accommodation (ranging from resort-style buildings to lodges or cabins) within Category I to IV protected areas, particularly where the areas are large:

- The protected area managers have stronger control over the accommodation complex and the ways visitors use the protected area;
- The visitors spend most or all their time within the protected area, which should increase their appreciation of it, and there is less need to use transport;
- Well-designed accommodation and service facilities can attract visitors to under-utilised areas; and
- Through fees and other financial arrangements, the protected area benefits from the money spent on accommodation and meals.

Against that, it can be argued that:

- Tourist accommodation is *per se* out of character with an essentially natural area, being often visually intrusive and potentially polluting;
- Tourist development requires a range of services, usually brought in by road, which create a secondary impact on the protected area;
- Tourist accommodation has an in-built potential to grow and, once established, is difficult to restrain; and

▨ By providing the centre of tourist activity outside the protected areas near established settlements, it is easier to bring benefits to local people (especially to women, who need to be near their children) and will minimise their need to travel to work.

Decisions on the location of accommodation in relation to protected areas involve many other issues, especially financial ones. Construction costs are always higher in remote areas. Where visitation is highly seasonal, it is difficult to attract capital for such a venture, whether from government or the private sector. Often, too, only limited term leases are allowed inside the protected area, which makes the project less attractive to the private sector and venture capital. Nonetheless, there have been a number of new accommodation centres built in important Category I to IV protected areas in recent years, for example the relocation of cabins in Sequoia National Park, California, and several new lodges constructed in Tarangire and Serengeti National Parks in Tanzania. But wherever such roofed accommodation is constructed, it should be done in the most culturally and environmentally sensitive way.

Information, orientation and interpretive facilities

Signage, and other information and interpretation can be used to influence visitor behaviour and thus assist protected area management, for example by safeguarding fragile environments. Though the movement of visitors in vehicles or on foot is likely to cause far more impact than the signs, they can be overbearing and intrusive; and many protected area management agencies conduct periodic audits to guard against the overuse of signs. Some park agencies have signage policies, to ensure standardised approaches throughout the park, indeed throughout the protected area system. A few protected areas have developed special arrangements with local transport authorities, so that road and transit signs to, and within, the protected areas contain directional information.

Visitor centres represent major investments in protected areas, and provide a broad range of information, interpretation, safety and recreation services. Since they are focal points for traffic, they should:

▨ be appropriately located, normally near the park entrance in the case of Category I–IV protected area; and

▨ adhere to the basic guidelines of construction and operation illustrated in Table 5.2.

Although visitor centres are not essential, they are used to fulfil important management tasks, especially in protected areas that attract large numbers of visitors. Many such protected areas have two or more visitor centres, often sited near the main entrances to the park.

In the past, visitor centres were rarely targeted to any particular market segment, and no arrangements were made to obtain feedback from visitors. Many centres have become quite dated, and need upgrading to remain stimulating to visitors and to fulfil their role. Because they are expensive to build and operate, they are often the most costly single item of investment in the protected area. The danger is that they can become a "white elephant", whether due to poor location, out-of-date design, inappropriate messages or lack of maintenance.

The best of today's new visitor centres are located in positions which attract the most visitors and fulfil many functions. Though they need to be discreetly designed, carefully sited and sympathetically landscaped, they must nonetheless work. In other words, they should draw visitors into the building, persuade them to look at the displays and lead them out, better informed, into the real protected area itself. Thus, to be successful, visitor centres must build in a strong interpretive component, help visitors to understand the significance of the area, and thus assist the protected area manager as well. Many centres also contain stores and restaurants, providing useful services to the visitors and important sources of income to the park. Providing the fundamental mission of the protected areas is not lost sight of, the provision of services of this kind can be beneficial to all concerned.

5.3 Transportation and infrastructure

Transportation infrastructure within protected areas provides visitors with access to opportunities for understanding, appreciation and enjoyment. In many parks such transport will also be important as a service to local people. However, this usually means motorised transport, which can have major negative impacts. Noise, pollution and dust can disrupt wildlife, damage vegetation and affect water quality. Visitors, too, may be affected, although this is a matter of perspective: those who are hiking in a remote chasm will probably be much more annoyed by the noise of a helicopter than the sightseers within the aircraft.

Transportation infrastructure (roads, tracks, airstrips, boat landings, etc.) often has very significant impacts on protected areas, even when its primary purpose is to allow better access by managers (e.g. airstrips to assist in surveillance or fire trails). Trails for the use of management alone are often one of the most difficult parts of protected area infrastructure to manage. Infrastructure of this kind can be expensive to put in and to maintain. It may also fragment ecosystems and seriously affect wildlife movements. Therefore, its design, routing and management must be carefully planned, especially since there is often pressure to open it to public use.

Many protected areas inherited some infrastructure (e.g. tracks or airstrips made by miners or loggers), which tends to be retained, or only slightly modified. While this may be the easiest option, it is rarely the best in the long term. Provided there are no urgent matters, e.g. those involving visitor safety, it is worth considering whether such roads should be taken out entirely.

Older infrastructure can be unsafe, especially as tourist traffic increases, and this can lead to accidents. For example, in 1997 an old "pre-park" road, designed to be used for only a few years, collapsed due to a leaking water pipe, leading to the death of 18 people in Kosciusko National Park, New South Wales, Australia. While older transport infrastructure may be unable to handle increasing numbers of visitors, this can be the stimulus to innovative solutions. In Kosciusko, again, the chronic overcrowding of roads into the Perisher Valley ski area was resolved by constructing a train tunnel through the mountain. Skiers and other visitors now leave their cars just inside the park boundary and travel to the ski area by train.

In many protected areas, the road system is essentially a part of the public road network and in many protected areas of all kinds, the roads are owned and managed by the local transportation or highways authority. Some protected areas indeed are traversed by national highways. This can create access, cost and communication problems, since people moving through the protected area mix with the park's recreational traffic. Such situations require careful negotiation and plan development, so that the protected area's objectives, and its environment, are not compromised.

5.4 Evaluating development proposals

Protected area managers are frequently faced with proposals for developments of various kinds related to recreational development, while those in Category V areas may be asked to determine all kinds of development projects. Developers seeking permits or licences to build or in other ways affect the environment are normally asked questions about physical aspects of the proposed development so as to help the protected area agency to determine the impact of the proposal. Working with partners, the former UK Countryside Commission (now Countryside Agency) has developed a checklist of questions that can be asked regarding tourist-related development in national parks. They are modified here and developed as **Guidelines**, in the form of a checklist for the use of managers and developers:

Checklist of questions for proposed facilities and services in the protected area

- Is the scale of development right for the protected area, both physically and in terms of visitor numbers, and timing of their visit?
- Are there alternative uses of the site, which should be considered?
- How will the character of the site be conserved?
- What economic value will the development bring to the protected area and to the local community?
- How important will the proposed development be to supporting the protected area's goals and objectives, and will it support any other (traditional) activities?
- What, if any, will be the effect on traffic?
- What is the level of demand for the proposed facility or service, and the value to the visitor?
- Do similar facilities exist now in the general location, and how well used are they?
- What are the proposals for the subsequent management and maintenance of the site?

Answers to these questions will assist in evaluating the need for the proposal itself, as well as establishing any modifications that are required to it.

Box 5.3 is an outstanding example of many of the applications, in a developing country, of the good practices advocated in this chapter.

Box 5.3 Chumbe Island Coral Park, Tanzania: Private ecotourism with environmentally and culturally sensitive design

Chumbe Island is the first private marine park in Tanzania. It is located in the Indian Ocean, and centred on a 24ha uninhabited island, surrounded by a very significant coral rag forest and coral reef of exceptional biodiversity and beauty, in an otherwise heavily over-fished and over-exploited area.

In 1992, the Chumbe Island Coral Park Ltd (CHICOP) was created for the purpose of creating and managing the park. This operation aims to create a model of sustainable management, where ecotourism supports conservation and education. The reserve includes a reef sanctuary and a forest sanctuary.

Funding came from several sources. About two thirds of the US$1 million cost was provided by a private individual who initiated the project. The remainder came from many government and private donors. The idea of developing an ecotourism site that could contribute to conservation and community development was attractive to many people. As a result more than 30 volunteers, from several countries, provided professional support to the project.

The management of the site by CHICOP is assisted by an Advisory Committee with representatives of neighbouring fishing villages, the Institute of Marine Sciences (IMS) of the University of Dar es Salaam and Government officials of the Departments of the Environment, Fisheries and Forestry respectively. The Committee meets one or more times per year.

The tourism facilities include seven bungalows that accommodate up to 14 guests at any one time. In addition, day trips are offered to 12 more visitors. The environmentally sensitive design is revealed in the eco-bungalows, which all employ eco-architecture, in the following ways:

- *Rainwater catchment*: There is no fresh water on the island, so rainwater is collected from the roof in the rainy season, passed through a natural filter, and stored in underground cisterns.

- *Solar water heating*: Rainwater is pumped up from cisterns through a solar-powered heating system into hot and cold-water containers for the shower.

- *Greywater recycling*: Water from showers is recycled through plant beds so that no polluted water seeps into the Reef Sanctuary. Beds are planted with species with high water and nutrient requirements, appropriate for the shower water rich in nitrates and phosphates.

- *Natural ventilation*: All the buildings have natural ventilation.

- *Composting toilets*: Toilets economise on water. They also prevent sewage seeping through the porous ground into the Reef Sanctuary. The human waste quickly decomposes to natural fertiliser when mixed with compost (aerobic-composting) in the compost chamber.

- *Photovoltaic power*: Lights are powered by photovoltaic panels on the roof, which provide enough energy for average use.

Cont.

73

Box 5.3 Chumbe Island Coral Park, Tanzania: Private ecotourism with environmentally and culturally sensitive design (cont.)

The Chumbe Island development reveals considerable long-term vision in the selection of objectives and in planning. Besides the design features, there are a number of socio-economic benefits. Five former fishermen from adjacent villages trained as park rangers for the island participate actively in monitoring the Reef and Forest. They have had guide training for visitors, including snorkellers. Marine and intertidal nature trails have been developed and equipped with "floating underwater information modules" and laminated information cards. These trails and materials are available to both tourists and local people. CHICOP cooperates with NGOs, and re-invests profits in conservation, land management and free schoolchildren's day visits for environmental education.

Web site: http://www.chumbeisland.co

6. Managing the challenges of tourism in protected areas

6.1 Management of risk and safety

All outdoor recreation involves some level of risk. Dealing with such risk is an important component of park tourism management. Visitor risk management is the systematic identification, analysis and control of the broad range of visitor risks, which threaten an agency or its ability to achieve its objectives.

6.1.1 Risk management

A *risk*, in the broadest sense, involves exposure to an unintentional event or situation that can cause a loss. The loss for a protected area management might be as simple as the pain of a twisted ankle or as complex as a liability claim ending in a lawsuit. Risk is often expressed in terms of an equation: *Risk = Frequency of Incident x Severity of Consequences*. Risk has some element of chance to it, but "risk management" involves foresight and control. *Foresight* is essential in risk management because, by being proactive, it is possible to reduce the level of risk. The concept of *control* means action: only through thoughtful action can an organisation reduce the probability of a risk and limit its negative consequences.

Effective visitor risk management practices are important in managing protected areas. Many forms of visitor activity and recreation have inherent risk associated with them: indeed this may be an integral component of the recreation. However, the potential for large personal injury claims and payouts, the aggressive pursuit of such claims in the courts, and the greater recourse to the courts which now occurs in many countries, means that it is important to identify hazards in a systematic way.

6.1.2 Shared responsibility

Protected area managers need to understand their existing and potential visitors, and what they want and do. Visitor management is a client-oriented approach to planning and service delivery that considers the visitors' needs, expectations and satisfaction. Visitor management techniques are useful in understanding the factors that lead to incidents (e.g. lack of experience, or the willingness of visitors to take risks).

The prevention of public safety incidents, and when necessary the delivery of public safety, and of Search and Rescue services, should be a shared responsibility between protected area managers, tourism operators and other stakeholders, visitors and users. Box 6.1 illustrates one example of this shared responsibility, as utilised by Parks Canada.

Box 6.1   Shared safety responsibilities (agencies, operators, visitors)

Park managers

- Identify and address priority risk issues related to the environment, infrastructure, communications, visitor characteristics and programme management
- Plan visitor risk management and public safety for their area of responsibility
- Organise targeted prevention education, and information programmes that encourage self reliance
- Communicate site-specific hazards to tourism operators, stakeholders, visitors and other users
- Establish and maintain appropriate levels of search and rescue services
- Establish co-operative agreements, training and communications with other government departments, NGOs, tourism operators, concessionaires and service providers

Tourism operators

- Identify and where appropriate address priority risk issues unique to their business operations
- Plan visitor risk management and public safety for their business operation
- Carry out targeted prevention education, and information programs for their clientele
- Communicate site-specific hazards to their clientele and to park managers
- Establish appropriate levels of search and rescue services, including training of staff as first responders
- Establish co-operative agreements, training and communications with park managers, government departments, NGOs and service providers

Visitor/tourists

- Recognise the risk inherent in their activities and ensure that they have the knowledge, skills and physical fitness to participate
- Get trained, be properly equipped, and, if necessary, be prepared to deal with an emergency situation until professional help arrives
- Seek and heed advice from park managers and tourism operators concerning risks and how to prepare for them

Visitors/tourists should observe and adhere to regulations, information brochures, fencing barriers and signs. Both park managers and tourism operators must place a high priority on the prevention of incidents to ensure the provision of opportunities for high quality visitor experiences and to limit their exposure to liability.

Source: Parks Canada, 2002.

6.1.3 Emergencies and emergency planning

An *emergency* is considered here as an abnormal situation that requires prompt action beyond normal procedures to prevent or limit injury to persons or damage to physical property or the environment. Emergency planning, which may overlap with public safety questions (such as risk assessment and prevention, and search and rescue services) is concerned with developing proactive and reactive responses to high frequency-low impact/consequence events (e.g. overdue party, broken limb). It also deals with the broader area of emergency programming for lower frequency-higher impact/consequence events (e.g. floods, tornadoes, hurricanes, fires, landslides and avalanches). It is primarily reactive. Through the risk evaluations described above, these types of events can be identified, and emergency plans developed.

6.1.4 Visitor risk management programme

Essentially, evaluating risk requires:

- Assessing – asking what can go wrong?
- Controlling – asking what can be done about it?
- Financing – asking how it can be paid for?

The approach advocated here is to develop a visitor risk management programme, which involves a broad-based understanding of risks, and deploys the staff time and funds in a cost-effective way so as to minimise possible incidents.

The components of a Visitor Risk Management Programme include:

- Staff training;
- Inspection and identification of risk areas;
- Networking with legal advisors, insurers and other agencies;
- Reporting incidents.

The main elements of such a programme include:

- a policy statement setting out the goals, objectives, strategies and performance indicators (to help monitor how well objectives are achieved);
- a structured process to (1) identify risks, (2) assess them, (3) manage them, and (4) monitor what happens and review policy (ANZECC, 2001). This is set out as **Guidelines** in Figure 6.1. An alternative approach is Parks Canada's (2002) Visitor Risk Management Process, which is a little more complex, with seven steps.

Figure 6.1 Guidelines for the Risk Management Process

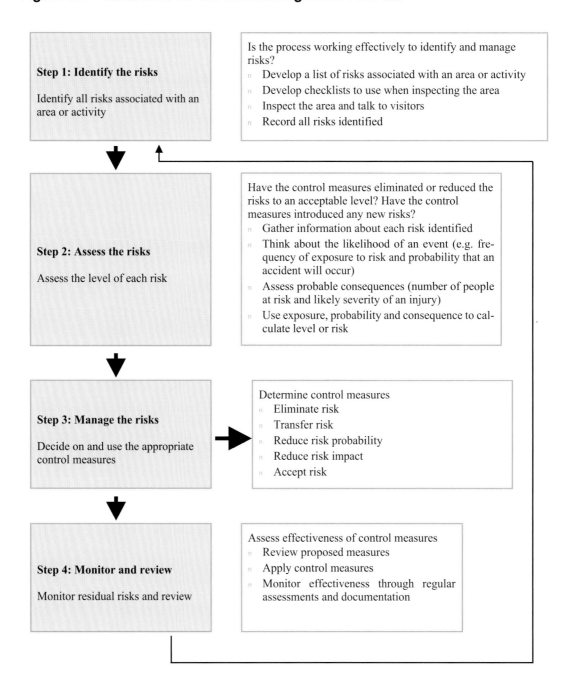

Step 1: Identify the risks

Identify all risks associated with an area or activity

Is the process working effectively to identify and manage risks?
- Develop a list of risks associated with an area or activity
- Develop checklists to use when inspecting the area
- Inspect the area and talk to visitors
- Record all risks identified

Step 2: Assess the risks

Assess the level of each risk

Have the control measures eliminated or reduced the risks to an acceptable level? Have the control measures introduced any new risks?
- Gather information about each risk identified
- Think about the likelihood of an event (e.g. frequency of exposure to risk and probability that an accident will occur)
- Assess probable consequences (number of people at risk and likely severity of an injury)
- Use exposure, probability and consequence to calculate level or risk

Step 3: Manage the risks

Decide on and use the appropriate control measures

Determine control measures
- Eliminate risk
- Transfer risk
- Reduce risk probability
- Reduce risk impact
- Accept risk

Step 4: Monitor and review

Monitor residual risks and review

Assess effectiveness of control measures
- Review proposed measures
- Apply control measures
- Monitor effectiveness through regular assessments and documentation

Source: adapted from ANZECC, 2001.

6.2 Principles of visitor management in protected areas

Park tourism depends on the quality of the natural and cultural resources of the protected area. The impacts of visitation on these resources must be carefully managed, directed and mitigated wherever possible. Even small levels of recreational use can lead to negative impacts, and all recreational use causes some impact. Some of the consequences of protected area tourism, for example the generation of income, may be desirable, and indeed the reasons behind park establishment. Therefore a certain level of impact may be acceptable. The principal question confronting park tourism planning is to determine what *degree* of impact is acceptable. Such decisions, while informed by science, represent value judgements about the relative worth of the trade-offs involved. How much damage to the natural environment is worth the positive economic and quality of life gains from park tourism? What impacts on natural and cultural resources would occur if park tourism did not exist and the resources were utilised for some other purpose?

To help answer such questions, Table 6.1 sets forth some key principles for visitor management.

Table 6.1 Principles of visitor management

Principle	Description
1. Appropriate management depends on objectives	<ul><li>Objectives provide definitive statements of the outcomes of protected area management.</li><li>They identify the appropriateness of management actions and indicate acceptable resource and social conditions.</li><li>They allow evaluation of success of management actions.</li><li>The specific objectives are likely to be more contentious than general value statements.</li><li>The process of establishing objectives is essentially political; therefore, public participation is essential.</li></ul>
2. Diversity in resource and social conditions in protected areas is inevitable and may be desirable	<ul><li>Impacts, use levels, and expectations of appropriate conditions tend to vary (e.g. impact of a camp-site in periphery vs. centre of the protected area).</li><li>Environmental variables influence visitor use and level of impact (e.g. topography, vegetation, access).</li><li>Managers can identify this diversity, then make decisions on its desirability, thereby separating technical decisions from judgmental ones.</li><li>Using zoning explicitly to manage for diverse recreation opportunities is more likely to preserve important values.</li></ul>
3. Management is directed at influencing human-induced change	<ul><li>Protected areas often protect natural processes as well as features, so management is generally oriented to managing human-induced change since it causes most disturbances.</li><li>Human-induced change may lead to conditions considered to be undesirable.</li><li>Some changes are desirable and may be the reason for the creation of the park. For example, many parks are created to provide recreation opportunities and local economic development.</li><li>Management actions determine what actions are most effective in influencing amount, type and location of changes.</li></ul>
4. Impacts on resource and social conditions are inevitable consequences of human use	<ul><li>Even small amounts of recreational use can lead to disproportionately large biophysical or social impacts, so any level or use leads to some impact.</li><li>Many impacts are purposefully designed, for example providing a certain level of environmental education for park visitors.</li><li>Managers must ask: "How much impact is acceptable or desirable?"</li><li>The process to determine the acceptability of impact is central to all visitor planning and management.</li><li>Managers must utilise appropriate actions to create and manage this acceptable level of impact.</li></ul>

Principle	Description
5. Impacts may be temporally or spatially dis-continuous	◻ Impacts from visitor use or management activities may occur out of the protected area, or not be visible until later (e.g. prohibitions of use may displace that use to other areas; or poor water treatment may result in water pollution downstream). ◻ Planners need substantial knowledge of relationships between use and impacts to predict relationships at a variety of scales and over time.
6. Many variables influence the use/impact relationship	◻ Many variables other than level of use affect the use/impact relationship in protected areas (e.g. behaviour of visitors, travel method, group size, season, and biophysical conditions). ◻ Education and information programmes, as well as regulations aimed at restricting visitor behaviour, may be necessary in addition to limits of use.
7. Many management problems are not dependent on numbers of users	◻ Management issues relating to the density of human use often have relatively simple technological solutions (e.g. parking, toilet facilities, water supply). But the relationship to use is not always linear. For example, the facilities designed for a few users may have very large impacts, but facilities designed for many more users have proportionally less additional impact. ◻ Similarly, social conditions (e.g. visitor satisfaction) are not always density-dependent.
8. Limiting use is only one of many manage-ment options	◻ A use-limit policy is only one of a number of potential management actions available, and is one of the most intrusive actions that protected area managers can employ. ◻ There are many issues involved in employing limits to use, such as choosing appropriate allocation or rationing techniques. ◻ Limiting use can have major political problems because of the necessary decision of who does not get access, and how access is allocated.
9. The decision-making process should separate technical decisions from value judgments	◻ Many protected area management decisions are technical (e.g. location of trail, design of visitor centre). But others reflect value judgments (e.g. decisions to limit use, and how, types of facilities, tourism opportunities provided). ◻ Decision processes should separate questions of "existing conditions" from "preferred conditions."

6.3 Protected area management frameworks

During the 1970s, carrying capacity was advanced as a technique for managing tourism in sensitive environments. This encouraged managers to try to solve visitor use problems merely by setting limits to numbers based upon a pre-determined level, derived from ecological, social and other analyses. However, this approach has serious limitations. It is basically a restrictive concept, founded on limits and constraints. As a result it can be seen as working against protected area objectives designed to encourage appropriate visitor enjoyment and valuation of the resource. When the limitations of this approach became evident, a number of more sophisticated frameworks were developed to provide a structure for the management of protected area visitation and tourism.

6.3.1 A choice of frameworks for management

Some frameworks which have been used in various parts of the world include:

1) Limits of Acceptable Change (LAC)

2) Visitor Impact Management (VIM)

3) Visitor Experience and Resource Protection (VERP)

4) Visitor Activity Management Process (VAMP)

5) The Recreation Opportunity Spectrum (ROS)

6) Tourism Optimization Model (TOMM).

There is literature about each approach and their pros and cons have been documented in Appendix D and Table 6.2, which compare and contrast these frameworks.

A number of challenges arise when approaches like these are adopted:

▓ They all require staffing, funding and time to implement;

▓ There are often gaps in scientific knowledge about visitor impacts, so judgments have to be made subjectively, or with limited information; and

▓ The management action called for is not always taken, even when limits are far exceeded, because of the lack of staff resources or because management is unwilling to face up to hard choices.

While these Guidelines introduce the reader to the existence of these frameworks and their main features, managers intending to apply them should consult the relevant documents and contact planners with experience in their application. However, a rather fuller overview of the LAC technique is provided below. It is featured because of its widespread use and acceptance, and because there is abundant literature and experience available to assist novice users in its application.

6.3.2 The Limits of Acceptable Change Planning Process (LAC)

It is essential to develop goals for tourism in protected areas. All subsequent actions, such as building facilities, developing recreation programmes and assigning levels of tourism service, flow from these goals.

The LAC offers a way to do this that does not focus so much on the relationships between levels of use and impact, but on determining the desirable environmental and social conditions for the visitor activity, and the management actions required to achieve these conditions. It uses a process that is systematic, explicit, defensible and rational, and involves public participation.

Guidelines for the application of the LAC framework are presented in Table 6.3. An example of the practical application of LAC is given in Box 6.2 below.

Table 6.2 Assessment of visitor management models (see also Appendix D)

Characteristic	Limits of Acceptable Change (LAC)	Visitor Impact Management (VIM)	Visitor Experience and Resource Protection (VERP)	Visitor Activity Management Process (VAMP)	Recreation Opportunity Spectrum (ROS)	Tourism Optimization Management Model (TOMM)
Main areas of application	Protected areas, especially IUCN Category Ib	Sites within protected areas	Primarily National Parks in the USA	Primarily Canadian National Parks, but applicable elsewhere	Any protected or multiple use area with nature-based tourism present	Australian system, but applicable in situations of communities with nature-based tourism
Able to assess and/or minimise visitor impacts	+	+	+	+	+	+
Considers multiple underlying causes of impacts	+	+	+	+	+	+
Facilitates selection of a variety of management actions	+	+	+	+	+	+
Produces defensible decisions	+	+	+	+	+	+
Separates technical information from value judgements	+	+	+	+	+	+
Encourages public involvement and shared learning	+	+	+	+	+	+
Incorporates local resource uses and resource management issues	+	+	+	+	+	+
Planning investment needed	- -	-	- -	- - -	- -	- -
Overall effectiveness based on experience	- - -	-	-	-	- - -	- -

Key: + = Positive attributes; - = Negative attributes (with scale from - to - - -)
Sources: Based on and adapted from Hall and McArthur, 1998; Farrell and Marion, 2002

Table 6.3 Limits of Acceptable Change: Process and guidelines

Steps	Guidelines	Comment on Purpose
1. Identify special values, issues, and concerns attributed to the area	Citizens and managers: n Identify special features or qualities that require attention n Identify existing management problems and concerns n Identify public issues: economic, social, environmental n Identify role the area plays in a regional and national context and political/institutional constraints	Encourages a better understanding of the natural resource base, a general concept of how the resource could be managed, and a focus on principal management issues.
2. Identify and describe recreation opportunity classes or zones	*Opportunity classes* describe subdivisions or zones of the natural resource where different social, resource, or managerial conditions will be maintained n Identify opportunity classes for the natural resources n Describe different conditions to be maintained (Bob Marshall Wilderness Complex case study, Box 6.2 below illustrates the opportunity classes used there)	Developing classes (or zones) provides a way of defining a range of diverse conditions within the protected area.
3. Select indicators of resource and social conditions	*Indicators* are specific elements of the resource or social setting selected to be indicative of the conditions deemed appropriate and acceptable in each opportunity class n Select a few indicators as indicative measures of overall health n Use economic, social, environmental, political indicators n Ensure indicators are easy to measure, relate to conditions in opportunity classes, and reflect changes in recreational use	Indicators are essential to LAC because their condition as a group reflects the overall condition of the opportunity class and guides the inventory.
4. Inventory existing resource and social conditions	n Use chosen indicators to guide the inventory of resource and social conditions n Use inventory data to provide a better understanding of area constraints and opportunities n Map inventories to establish status (location and condition) of indicators By placing the inventory as step 4, rather than the first step as is often done, planners avoid unnecessary data collection and ensure that the data collected is useful	Inventory data are mapped so both the condition and location of the indicators are known. Helps managers establish realistic standards, and used later to evaluate the consequences of alternatives.
5. Specify standards for resource and social conditions in each opportunity class	n Identify the range of conditions for each indicator considered desirable or acceptable for each opportunity class n Define conditions in measurable terms, to represent the maximum permissible conditions allowed (limits) n Ensure conditions are attainable and realistic	Provides the basis for establishing a distinctive and diverse range of protected area settings, serving to define the "limits of acceptable change."

83

Steps	Guidelines	Comment on Purpose
6. Identify alternative opportunity class allocations	This stage identifies alternative allocations of opportunities n Identify different types/location/timing of alternatives, using steps 1 and 4 to explore how well the different opportunity classes meet the various interests and values	Provides alternative ways of managing the area to best meet the needs, interests, and concerns.
7. Identify management actions for each alternative	n Analyse broad costs and benefits of each alternative n Identify the kinds of management actions needed to achieve the desired conditions (direct or indirect)	This step involves an analysis of the costs and benefits of each alternative.
8. Evaluation and selection of a preferred alternative	n Review costs vs. benefits of alternatives with managers, stakeholders and public n Examine the responsiveness of each alternative to the issues n Explicitly state the factors considered, and their weight in decision-making n Select a preferred alternative	Builds consensus and selects the best alternative.
9. Implement actions and monitor conditions	n Develop implementation plan with actions, costs, timetable, and responsibilities n Develop a monitoring programme, focusing on the indicators developed in step 3 n Compare indicator conditions with standards to evaluate the success of actions If conditions do not correspond with standards the intensity of the management effort might need to be increased or new actions implemented	Ensures timely implementation and adjustment of management strategies. Monitoring ensures that effectiveness of implementation is known. If monitoring shows problems, actions can be taken.

Box 6.2   Bob Marshall Wilderness Complex, Montana, USA: an example of wilderness management using Limits of Acceptable Change

The Bob Marshall Wilderness Area is a Category Ib type protected area (a wilderness area), where, by law, no permanent human habitation is allowed. When LAC is applied to Category II, III or V areas, for example, a far wider range of activities, facilities and use types would be permissible.

The Bob Marshall Wilderness Complex is located in north central Montana, and managed by the US Forest Service (USFS) under provisions of the 1964 Wilderness Act. It comprises 600,000 hectares of un-roaded temperate forest, and attracts 25,000 visitors, primarily from June through November. June to September is dominated by backpacking and horse- supported backcountry trips. In the autumn, most use is for big game hunting.

In 1982, the USFS embarked on a planning effort based on the LAC process. It involved continuous public participation through a taskforce consisting of a range of stakeholders: the public, scientists and managers. The process took five years. LAC focused effort on addressing how much change in wilderness, biophysical and social conditions is acceptable. By designing a public participation process that incorporated the full range of values involved in the Wilderness area, participants developed a set of management actions that were effective in reducing and controlling human-induced impacts, and achieved the social and political acceptability necessary for implementation.

The plan has three broad characteristics:

(1)   It establishes four opportunity classes (zones) designed to protect the pristine character of the wilderness, yet realistically permits some trade-offs between recreation use and human-induced impacts.

(2)   It identifies indicator variables – things to monitor to ensure conditions remain acceptable and to use to establish the effectiveness of actions implemented to control or mitigate impacts. For each indicator, quantifiable standards exist, indicating what limit of change from the natural baseline is acceptable in each zone.

(3)   It indicates for each zone the management actions in order of their social acceptability. This gives the manager a choice of tool, and determines what management action will be most acceptable in controlling impacts. This procedure thus encourages the least intrusive management action first.

Zones thus form the framework for managing human-induced impacts. Each zone is described by the biophysical, social and managerial setting conditions that are acceptable. The opportunity classes represent amounts of impact permitted on a continuum with Opportunity Class I being most pristine, while Opportunity Class 4 is least pristine (see table below).

LAC Opportunity Classes in Bob Marshall Wilderness

Zone	Setting	Description
Class 1	Biophysical	Unmodified natural environment. Environmental impacts minimal
	Social	Isolation and solitude, no evidence of human activities. Few encounters with users. High opportunities for cross-country travel, with maximum outdoor skills
	Managerial	Strong emphasis on enhancing natural ecosystems. Little direct management of visitors. Communication of rules outside the area (e.g. trailheads or boundary gates)
Class 2	Biophysical	Unmodified natural environment. Environmental impacts of use are low
	Social	High isolation. Few user encounters. Good opportunities for independence and self-reliance
	Managerial	Emphasizes enhancing natural ecosystems. Minimum on-site management contact.
		Communication of rules outside the area (e.g. trailheads or boundary gates)

Zone	Setting		Description
Class 3	Biophysical		Unmodified natural environment. Some natural processes affected by users. Moderate environmental impacts, mostly along travel routes and sites.
	Social		Moderate isolation, and low to moderate encounters with users. Moderate opportunities for independence and self-reliance
	Managerial		Emphasises enhancing natural ecosystems. Routine visitor contact on-site. Communication of rules outside the area (e.g. trailheads or boundary gates)
Class 4	Biophysical		Predominantly unmodified natural environment. Conditions may be affected by impact of users, especially on travel routes, river corridors, shores, and entry points
	Social		Moderate to low opportunities for isolation. Encounters likely. High opportunity for interaction with environment, but with low to moderate challenge or risk

7. Tools for visitor management

7.1 A toolbox of strategies and tactics

This chapter concentrates on the management of park visitation that already exists, and is occurring at levels that justify intervention of some sort. Note though that, while well-established protected areas in developed countries often receive large numbers of visitors, newly established ones can struggle to attract them. This is especially so in some developing countries, where protected areas often depend on tourism income, and the number of visitors may be too low to provide even a small portion of the necessary income to run the park. Therefore strategies to manage the problems of large numbers of visitors in some protected areas often need to be complemented by other strategies designed to attract them to other areas.

Managers have at their disposal a wide array of strategies to manage the impacts of park tourism. Their choice will be determined by any restrictions that legislation or agency policy places upon them, by the efficiency and appropriateness of the management strategy, and the resource implications. The main features of these strategies to control, influence and mitigate visitor impacts are described below.

Highway in Fiordland National Park, New Zealand

Roads and other transport facilities are critical determinates of the locations and levels of park tourism use. ©*Paul F. J. Eagles*

Broadly speaking there are four strategic approaches which can be used to reduce the negative impacts of visitors on protected areas:

1. *Managing the supply* of tourism or visitor opportunities, e.g. by increasing the space available or the time available to accommodate more use;

2. *Managing the demand* for visitation, e.g. through restrictions of length of stay, the total numbers, or type of use;

3. *Managing the resource* capabilities to handle use, e.g. through hardening the site or specific locations, or developing facilities; and

4. *Managing the impact* of use, e.g. reducing the negative impact of use by modifying the type of use, or dispersing or concentrating use.

Table 7.1 sets out a list of possible strategies and options for managing visitor numbers and coping with high levels of use. These and other approaches are expanded upon in the rest of this chapter.

Table 7.1 Strategies and tactics for managing high levels of use

Strategy	Management tactics and techniques
1. Reduce use of the entire protected area	1. Limit number of visitors in the entire protected area 2. Limit length of stay 3. Encourage use of other areas 4. Require certain skills and/or equipment 5. Charge a flat visitor fee 6. Make access more difficult in all wilderness
2. Reduce use of problem areas	1 Inform about problem areas and alternative areas 2. Discourage or prohibit use of problem area 3. Limit number of visitors in problem areas 4. Encourage/require a stay limit in problem areas 5. Make access harder/easier to areas 6. Eliminate facilities/attractions in problem areas, improve facilities/attractions in alternative areas 7. Encourage off-trail travel 8. Establish different skill/equipment requirements 9. Charge differential visitor fees
3. Modify the location of use within problem areas	1. Discourage/prohibit camping/use of horses 2. Encourage/permit camping/horses in certain areas 3. Locate facilities on durable sites 4. Concentrate use through facility design or info 5. Discourage/prohibit off-trail travel 6. Segregate different types of visitors
4. Modify the timing of use	1. Encourage use outside of peak use periods 2. Discourage/ban use when impact potential high 3. Fees in periods of high use/high impact potential
5. Modify type of use and visitor behaviour	1. Discourage/ban damaging practices/equipment 2. Encourage/require behaviour, skills, equipment 3. Teach a wilderness ethic 4. Encourage/require a party size and/or limit on number of horses 5. Discourage/prohibit horses 6. Discourage/prohibit pets 7. Discourage/prohibit overnight use

Strategy	Management tactics and techniques
6. Modify visitor expectations	1. Inform visitors about appropriate wilderness/PA uses 2. Inform about potential conditions in wilderness/PA
7. Increase the resistance of the resource	1. Shield the site from impact 2. Strengthen the site
8. Maintain/ rehabilitate resource	1. Remove problems 2. Maintain/rehabilitate impacted locations

Source: Manning, 1979; Cole *et al.*, 1987.

The following section discusses some of the key tools for visitor management used by protected area managers.

7.1.1 Seasonal or temporal limit on use level

Definition: *Use limits* are direct restrictions on the number of people that may enter a recreation area.

Examples:

- when all camp-sites are occupied, other people are not permitted access;
- to limit the number of day users, managers can restrict the size of car parks; and
- where public transport is a major means of access, it is possible to set a limit on bus numbers, size of boats or frequency of trains.

Frequency of use: Use limits are commonly applied in wilderness hiking, canoeing situations and access to historic buildings and sites. They are becoming more common in front country situations.

Benefits: Use limits maintain use at a predetermined level, potentially controlling biophysical and social consequences of fast growing, or excessive use levels.

Costs: Use limits tend to generate controversy, particularly in how they are implemented, so the process used to determine the use limit is critical. Restriction of access to an area has financial costs. The costs of enforcement can be high, especially in the early stages.

7.1.2 Group size limit

Definition: *Group size* limits the maximum number of people in one group of tourists or recreationists travelling together.

Examples:

- a limit is set to the number of people that can camp together on a back-country camp-site; and
- a limit is set to the size of party that is permitted to snorkel on a coral reef.

Frequency of use: Group size limits are commonly used in many back-country, dispersed recreation and remote zones of protected areas.

Benefits: Larger group sizes tend to have greater social and biophysical impacts; group size limits reduces these impacts. Over time, users become familiar with the limits and adapt their expectations of the site accordingly.

Costs: The approach restricts access to any area for larger groups, which has cost implications. Tourism operators may not welcome the imposition of limits. The administrative costs of enforcement and the educational costs can be high.

7.1.3 Pre-assignment of recreation site

Definition: *Pre-assignment* (through pre-registration or pre-booking) involves the allocation of individual sites to specific individuals or groups before entry into a recreation area, much like a reserved seat on a passenger aircraft.

Examples:

■ pre-booking a camp-site; and

■ pre-booking entry to an historic site.

Frequency of use: This approach is becoming more common at car camping sites, back-country camp-sites, river access sites, historic sites and trekking trails. When demand is high, pre-registration for use is desirable for both the users and the managers. The big issue is the method used for pre-registration. Agencies use telephone, mail and increasingly, the Internet. Six months is a common maximum length of time between the first time allowed for pre-registration and use.

Benefits: This approach optimises use of sites with known area and limited capacity, and minimises inter-party competition. The technique spreads the number of visitors over time but yet assures them access. Knowing the level of demand well in advance, the manager is able to assign appropriate staff levels, supplies and equipment. Pre-registration is highly appreciated by most park visitors.

Costs: There can be a substantial management cost for the pre-registration procedures. Fees are often used to recover these costs. This approach requires all potential visitors to know the rules and procedures for pre- registration, and so can be problematic for foreign tourists. It assumes all visitors will comply and has limited flexibility for accidental violations.

Fox Glacier, Westland National Park, New Zealand

Dynamic physical phenomena, such as an active glacier front, attract people into dangerous situations. *©Paul F. J. Eagles*

90

7.1.4 Area closures

Definition: *Area closures* include prohibiting all, or some types of, tourist use of particular areas.

Examples:

- prohibiting camping in a designated part of the park;
- allowing camping only at specific sites;
- closing an area to all recreational use;
- requiring a permit before entry to the area; and
- prohibiting camping within certain distances of surface water.

Frequency of use: Area closures are common at historic sites and museums and other high use locations, such as near visitor centres at high-altitude locations. They are used in protected areas at environmentally sensitive sites, near wildlife concentrations, or in the habitat of endangered species. Usually visitors are provided with reasons for the closure, but this can be counterproductive if the features are attractive and encourage use.

Benefits: If closures are obeyed, all direct human influences and negative impacts at the site are removed.

Costs: This approach restricts visitor freedom. It requires explanation and enforcement.

7.1.5 Restrictions on the use of fire

Definition: *Fire restrictions* aim to reduce the visible and biological effects of using fire.

Examples:

- fire may be prohibited entirely;
- fire may be permitted only in designated sites;
- fire of a certain type may be forbidden (e.g. green wood or locally collected firewood); and
- in high altitude situations, fire may be allowed only with stoves fuelled by gas.

Frequency of use: Fire restrictions are frequently used in front country, less frequently in back-country. Occasionally, fire prohibitions are implemented in periods of high fire danger.

Benefits: This approach significantly reduces the potential of wildfires, reduces fuelwood use, and reduces ecological impacts due to wood gathering. The sale of campfire wood can be a lucrative source of income for parks.

Costs: The costs of fire prohibition include enforcement and loss of the experience value associated with campfires. Some parks have the legal authority to collect costs from those tourists who cause wildfires. If wood collection is prohibited, but fires are permitted, some alternative supplies of wood must be made available.

7.1.6 Restrictions by group characteristics

Definition: The *characteristics* of *groups* are used to prohibit entry.

Examples:

- groups with certain equipment, e.g. guns, vehicles; and
- groups planning to undertake certain activities, such as orienteering or hunting.

Frequency of use: Nearly all national park and other recreation areas employ restrictions on some visitor group types. Most frequent are prohibitions on the use of motorised or mechanised conveyances, such as powered boats, all-terrain vehicles and bicycles. Some backcountry areas prohibit users on horse.

Benefits: Significant reductions in biophysical impacts and visitor conflicts; increased visitor safety and satisfaction for those who gain access.

Costs: Reduction in some visitor freedom and accessibility occurs. Information must be provided on the restrictions, and enforcement is required.

7.1.7 Length of stay limits

Definition: *Length of stay limits* set the amount of time an individual or group may stay in a recreation area.

Examples:

- no-one may stay overnight; and
- no-one may stay longer than three nights at any one place.

Frequency of use: Length of stay limits are frequent in areas with more demand than supply. Along linear features, such as trails and rivers, users are required to move camp-sites every night, in order to keep the flow of people moving through the area.

Benefits: Increased accessibility to the area for more visitors.

Costs: This approach reduces the opportunity for visitors to enjoy longer visits to the area. There are enforcement and administrative costs.

7.1.8 Technology requirements

Definition: *Technology requirements* make it mandatory that tourists carry specialised equipment for environmental or safety reasons.

Examples:

- visitors must be prepared for cooking with gas stoves only (i.e. no wood burning);
- visitors must be prepared for personal waste disposal (e.g. portable toilets); and
- visitors must have appropriate safety equipment.

Frequency of use: It is becoming common on specialised sites, such as white water rivers and other wilderness settings, to demand certain levels of equipment and supplies. For example, since some wilderness parks ban bottles and cans, this effectively requires that all supplies must be carried in burnable containers, thereby reducing the amount of garbage. Some protected areas require all hikers to carry remote sensing devices to enable easier rescue, if lost.

Benefits: This approach can reduce biophysical impacts, and increase safety levels.

Costs: There is an administration and enforcement requirement. Education concerning proper use of technology is needed. The equipment may be expensive.

7.1.9 Trip scheduling

Definition: *Trip scheduling* involves establishing the location and timing of individual group use of a recreation area.

Examples:

- timing of raft launches on rivers;
- group naturalist tours of wildlife concentrations; and
- designated times for viewing historic sites, interpretive films and displays.

Frequency of use: Trip scheduling is common in front-country situations involving historic resources and visitor centres. It is used occasionally on white water rivers, especially in conjunction with camp-site assignments. It is appropriate for sensitive wildlife species that are easily disturbed by visitors at certain times.

Benefits: Trip scheduling can reduce congestion; provide opportunities for solitude; facilitate interpretation; and reduce competition for limited space. This approach can make management much easier, since it results in a fairly constant and predictable stream of visitors.

Costs: Visitors lose the freedom to see what they want when they want. There are costs to administer schedules and permits. Personnel costs for tours may be high.

7.1.10 Barriers

Definition: A *barrier* is a deliberately established obstacle to visitor movement.

Examples:

- a fence to keep people out of the breeding grounds of rare species;
- a ditch to keep people from walking into a sensitive wetland; and
- a low barrier to keep vehicles off the grass.

Frequency of use: This technique is common in front country, uncommon in back-country. Not all barriers need to be obvious. There are many park facility designs that allow for the construction of effective, but unobtrusive barriers.

Benefits: There is a reduction of visitor impacts, reduction of vandalism, and efficient movement of people through a site.

Warning Sign, Hawaii Volcanoes National Park, USA

High levels of physical danger to park visitors require active risk management, including abundant information. © *Paul F. J. Eagles*

Costs: The costs include reduction of visitor freedom to walk/drive wherever they want, construction and maintenance costs and enforcement. Poorly designed barriers can be an unwelcome visual intrusion.

Royal Albatross Centre, New Zealand

A visitor centre is a very effective component of the visitor interpretation programme in many parks.
©*Paul F. J. Eagles*

7.1.11   Site hardening

Definition: *Site hardening* involves constructing facilities and locating trails and roads to reduce the impacts of visitors on sensitive soils and vegetation, and to help meet the visitors' needs for usable access.

Examples:

- hard surfacing materials used to reduce erosion on trails; and
- hard topping of roads.

Frequency of use: This approach is widely used where the natural surface is unable to cope with the pressures of feet and wheels. It is seldom used in back-country situations.

Benefits: Hard surfacing is effective in reducing erosion; and may reduce maintenance costs.

Costs: The approach is relatively expensive. It can be unsightly and out of character, and can cause damage to vegetation if the wrong materials are used. Especially in areas defined as natural zones in the management plan, paved roads and other hard surface features will be incongruous.

7.1.12   Park information (see also section 7.5 below)

Definition: *Park information* involves the provision of data, facts and advice to visitors concerning the park, its biology and geology, locations of visitor facilities, rules and regulations, and appropriate behaviour.

Examples:

- leaflets, books, maps etc.;
- website, local radio;
- signs, information points;
- visitor centres;
- Internet web sites; and
- face-to-face provision of advice.

Frequency of use: The communication of park information is commonly used. Nearly all protected areas contain some level of information about some aspect of the area. Those parks with insufficient funds often depend upon private sector tourism operators to provide most of the information.

Benefits: The benefits include data, facts and advice which help inform the visitor of what is happening where in the park. It may result in more visitors adopting appropriate behaviours that will reduce impacts and provide the visitors with a more satisfying visit.

Costs: Some forms of information provision are costly. There are personnel, printing and display costs. Information is not universally effective. Brochures, signs and other messages must be placed where visitors will take notice of them. They must be presented in the appropriate language for the visitors, at an appropriate level of educational attainment. The use of the Internet is a very cost-effective way of distributing information very broadly for a low cost. When parks do not provide their own information, they run the risk of others providing inaccurate or misleading information.

Visitor Interpretation in Great Barrier Reef Marine Park, Australia

Visitor learning and satisfaction are highly influenced by effective interpretation programmes.
©*Paul F. J. Eagles*

7.1.13 Interpretation (see also section 7.5 below)

Definition: *Interpretation* involves providing information to visitors in such a way that they will be stimulated to learn more and gain more appreciation. Thus interpretation is more than the presentation of data and facts (see Information), but includes weaving them together so that visitors come to understand, and appreciate the values for which the park was established.

Examples:

- nature trails and trail-side signs;
- field guides, trail leaflets, maps;
- guided walks or tours; and
- interactive displays, interpretation centres.

Frequency of use: In wealthier countries, many protected areas provide some type of interpretive materials. In developing countries, protected area managers rarely have the resources for more than modest interpretive provisions. In many places, the private tourism sector also provides interpretation through specialised programmes and guides.

Benefits: The primary benefit from effective interpretive programmes is a visitor population which gains understanding and appreciation of the protected area. This in turn can help reduce visitor impacts and provide greater public support for the park.

Costs: The costs of interpretation vary depending on the interpretive methods used. Brochures are relatively inexpensive, whereas major interpretive centres are expensive to construct and operate, though they may be very popular. Visitors to protected areas often pay for their interpretation, through the purchase of programmes or materials. Guiding services are a major source of employment in many protected areas.

7.1.14 Differential pricing (see also section 7.4 below)

Definition: *Differential pricing* involves establishing two or more prices for the same recreation opportunity.

Examples:

- higher fees during peak holiday periods;
- differential fees according to location or outlook of accommodation;
- discounts for children and pensioners; and
- differential charges for park entry, so that foreign tourists pay more than residents do.

Frequency of use: Most park systems use some form of differential pricing, which combines an element of social justice (e.g. differential charging rates for less privileged groups), market response (e.g. raising prices when demand rises), and management tactics (e.g. to help redirect visitor pressures).

Benefits: Differential pricing can redistribute use levels, achieve a social purpose and maximise income in periods of peak demand.

Costs: Differential pricing policies are more complicated to administer, may cause confusion amongst employees and guests, and resentment when the reasons for use are not clearly communicated.

7.1.15 Visitor and/or operator qualifications

Definition: *Visitor and/or operator qualifications* means limiting entry only to those possessing required qualifications.

Examples:

- scuba divers must be qualified to use a marine protected area;
- ecotour leaders must have a certificate of competence; and
- users of the protected area must be accompanied by a qualified local guide.

Frequency of use: Specialised qualifications are common for high-risk activities, such as scuba diving or mountain climbing. They are common too, for commercial businesses that provide guide services to visitors. Some African game parks allow their visitors to view game only from a specialised vehicle with qualified guides, while tours on foot are often permitted only with an armed guard.

Benefits: This approach is attractive to the protected area manager. Only those with the necessary training, equipment and group co-ordination are allowed. It increases local employment in training and guiding. When visitors are more competent, they pose less threat to protected area values and make fewer demands on the time of staff. When operators, such as guides, are licensed, managers have additional control over tourism operations. Qualified operators provide better services to visitors. Major benefits are higher levels of safety, and lower search and rescue costs.

Costs: Arrangements of this kind are challenging to set up and require external systems of qualification, certification and verification. The development of the proper requirements may involve difficult negotiations with the user groups. The enforcement costs can be high.

7.1.16 Tourism marketing

Definition: *Marketing* is the practice of connecting people's demands with a supply of goods and services.

Examples:

- web site information for tourists;
- briefing of tour operators; and
- agreements on protected area promotion by the national tourist agency.

Frequency of use: It is important for protected areas to develop a market of customers that are interested in the environments and services that they can offer. Yet protected area managers seldom use professional marketing to develop the appropriate tourism market. This is changing, as protected area managers develop an understanding of marketing, and staff trained in tourism enter park agencies. The best approach is *target marketing*, (i.e. going after the sector of the population that is most suitable for the resources, the services and the products available). Protected area managers can also consider *de-marketing*, that is trying to convince potential park visitors to go elsewhere by reducing promotional activities or promoting alternatives. Some parks in a system encourage visitors to visit other parks in the same system.

Benefits: Higher incomes result when the visitors are interested in, and agree with park management policies. Lower conflict occurs when the visitor suits the environments and services available within the protected area.

Costs: While protected area management should aim to understand their visitors' characteristics, wants and needs, research and advertising can be expensive.

7.2 Zoning in protected areas

Protected area managers face a strategic choice between *concentrating* or *dispersing* recreational use. Often, a dispersal strategy is chosen to deal with negative impacts in a small area or several areas, and this will work effectively in biophysical settings that are relatively resilient to use. But such a strategy is less effective in more sensitive settings, where damaging impacts may just be spread more widely by this approach. A concentration strategy focuses recreational use on small areas with high levels of management, thereby confining the impacts, although their occurrence will be more intense. Since a concentration strategy places development in small areas, it may effectively discourage visitors from gaining access to other parts of the protected area.

Zoning is the principal method used to deploy visitors, and hence it is critical in achieving the appropriate combination of concentration and dispersal. It is designed to allocate geographical areas for specific levels and intensities of human activities and of conservation. Typically, it involves a range of spatial zones with varying levels of intensity of human activity (and therefore development). At one end are developed areas, such as service centres or, in the case of protected landscapes, villages or towns with a strong emphasis on tourist provision; at the other end are remote and even wilderness areas with effectively no development at all.

Zoning can also be temporal, that is an area set aside for different uses at different times, within the course of the day, over the week or seasonally.

Zoning requires two steps:

1. A *descriptive* step, which identifies important values and recreational opportunities. It requires an inventory of resource characteristics and types of existing recreational opportunities.

2. An *allocation (prescriptive)* step, in which decisions are made about what opportunities and values should be provided where in the protected area. It involves managers working with operators, visitors and other stakeholders to determine what should be protected, what facilities will be provided, what programmes should be set up, and where and when.

There are several benefits of zoning:

1. The process of zoning helps managers, operators, visitors and local communities to understand what park values are located where;

2. Zoning oriented to establishing standards of acceptable human impact helps to control the spread of undesirable impacts; and

3. Zoning provides a better understanding of the distribution and nature of different recreation and tourism opportunities within and around the protected area.

Zoning should apply to all activities occurring within a protected area: conservation, other land uses, and of course recreation and tourism. The zones, with the policies applied to them, should appear in the protected area management plan and thus guide the way in which the area is managed.

For tourism, zoning involves decisions about what type of recreational opportunity will be provided, and where. For example, should some provision be highly developed in character? Should provision be made elsewhere for more basic conditions, requiring survival skills, for example? Typically, zoning of this type is based on the degree of impact which a type of recreation causes. This, of course, requires a sound information base related to the function and sensitivity of ecosystem structure, as well as the opportunities and impacts of existing and potential visitor experiences.

Useful frameworks when considering zoning include the Recreation Opportunity Spectrum (ROS – section 6.3.1 above) (developed in the USA) and the Tourism Opportunity Spectrum (TOS) (developed in Australia). Both the ROS and TOS operate at the large-scale, involving whole landscapes extending well beyond protected areas in categories I to IV. Though these areas may be beyond the protected area managers' mandates, every effort should be made to co-ordinate recreation and tourism planning across this wider scale so that there is a sub-regional context for provision within a protected area.

Many park agencies have standardised zoning frameworks that are applied to all protected areas across their system. The national parks zoning system in Canada is an integrated approach by which land and water areas are classified according to ecosystem and cultural resource protection requirements (Table 7.2). Each zone is considered for its suitability and capability to accommodate visitors for a range of opportunities. The result is a framework for the area-specific application of policy directions, such as those for resource management, appropriate activities and research. Thus, zoning provides direction for the activities of managers and visitors alike. Box 7.1 is a practical example of the application of zoning theory to a particular protected area.

Lava Flow, Hawaii Volcanoes National Park, USA

The continuous flow of lava in Hawaii National Park attracts large numbers of visitors to a very dangerous situation. Management must deal with high levels of risk. ©*Paul F. J. Eagles*

Table 7.2 Parks Canada zoning system summary

Zone class	Zone purpose	Boundary criteria	Management framework	
			Resources	Public opportunity
I Special preservation	Specific areas or features, which deserve special preservation because they contain or support unique, rare or endangered features or the best examples of features.	The natural extent and buffer requirements of designated features.	Strict resource preservation	Usually no internal access. Only strictly controlled and non-motorised access.
II Wilderness	Extensive areas which are good representations of each of the natural history themes of the park and which will be maintained in a wilderness state.	The natural extent and buffer requirements of natural history themes and environments in areas of 2,000ha and greater.	Oriented to preservation of natural environment setting.	Internal access by non-motorised means. Dispersed activities providing experiences consistent with resource preservation. Primitive camping areas. Primitive, roofed accommodation including emergency shelters.
III Natural environment	Areas that are maintained as natural environments and which can sustain a minimum of low-density outdoor activities with a minimum of related facilities.	The extent of natural environments providing outdoor opportunities and required buffer areas.	Oriented to preservation of natural environment setting.	Internal access by non-motorised and limited motorised means, including in the north, authorised air charter access to rivers/lakes, usually dispersed activities, and with more concentrated activities associated with limited motorised access. Rustic, small-scale, permanent, fixed-roof accommodation for visitor use and operational use. Camping facilities are to be the semi-primitive level.
IV Recreation	Limited areas that can accommodate a broad range of education, outdoor recreation opportunities and related facilities in ways that respect the natural landscape and that are safe and convenient.	The extent of outdoor opportunities and facilities and their area of immediate impact.	Oriented to minimising impact of activities and facilities on the natural landscape.	Outdoor opportunities in natural landscapes or supported by facility development and landscape alteration. Camping facilities will be of the basic serviced category. Small and decentralised accommodation facilities.
V Park services	Towns and visitor centres in certain existing national parks, which contain a concentration of visitor services and support facilities as well as park administration functions.	The extent of services and facilities and their immediate area of impact.	Oriented to emphasising the national park setting and values in the location, design and operation of visitor support services and park administration functions.	Internal access by non-motorised and motorised means. Centralised visitor support services and park administration activities. Facility based opportunities. Major camping areas adjacent to, or within, a town or visitor centre to the basic serviced category. Town or visitor centre.

Box 7.1 Saguenay–St. Lawrence National Marine Park, Québec, Canada:
An example of a marine park using a standardised zoning system

In April 1990, the governments of Canada and Québec signed a federal-provincial agreement providing for the establishment of the marine park at the confluence of the Saguenay River and St. Lawrence Estuary. The agreement stipulates that both levels of government retain their respective jurisdictions over the area and will work towards its protection. The management plan confirms the stated objectives of both governments to involve the public in the management of this area through a co-ordinating committee. Complementary legislation was prepared at the federal and provincial levels for park establishment and management.

The Saguenay Fjord and St. Lawrence Estuary National Marine Conservation Areas of Canada consist of a series of islands scattered along an 80km stretch of the St. Lawrence River. Each island is managed as a distinct environment with facilities ranging from docks, trails, camping facilities, a boat launch, interpretive displays and day-use areas. This park manages four of the five zoning classes described in Table 7.2.

There are nine Special Preservation areas intended to protect sites that represent both the natural and cultural heritage resources of the Thousand Islands region. Wilderness (Class 2) is not an appropriate zone for St. Lawrence Islands because the park only encompasses 869ha and a wilderness zone requires a land mass of 2,000ha or more. It is, in fact, Canada's smallest National Park.

There are many areas that have been zoned as Natural Environment (Class 3), to provide a variety of opportunities for visitors to experience the Park's natural values through low-density outdoor activities, and appropriate facilities and services. These facilities include picnic shelters, primitive camp-sites, trails, interpretive panels, toilets, and docks.

There are also Recreation (Class 4) areas, for outdoor recreation and related facilities. A full range of visitor uses is permitted in this zone.

The least protective zone for a park is Zone 5 – park service areas. These areas provide a place for visitors' services, support facilities and the administrative functions required to manage and operate the park.

7.3 Transportation management

The complex challenges of transportation within protected areas were addressed in Section 5.3. Some solutions to these problems can be achieved through zoning. For example, the zoning policies within the management plan should also address transportation matters, such as:

- regulations governing numbers, types and speed of road vehicles;
- the use of public transport to reach and travel within the protected area;
- corridors indicating where off-road vehicles, boats and aircraft may move; and
- the times at which movements can take place.

All this requires proper legislative regulation and policing.

Box 7.2   Traffic/visitor management techniques used in protected areas

Road closure: for part of the year no vehicles allowed.

Full public transit: in special sites, all visitors must use public transport. This may include the park employees and the employees of businesses in the park.

Partial public transit: where some visitors (certain segments, or those to certain park destinations) may be required to use public transport.

Optional public transit: where visitors are encouraged to use shuttles or transit systems, but not compelled. There may be incentives (e.g. free guided walks for public transport users).

Special use fees: fees for public transport are sometimes incorporated into the park entry charge, or identified as a special charge.

Specialised transit: may be used for unique environments, such as an historic railway, an aerial car or a passenger boat.

Restricted type of transport: may be used. For examples some lakes have prohibition on all powered boats.

Educational information: about potential impact of human transport on the park, via signs, exhibits, and recommended behaviour.

Integrated systems: of all public transport systems and tours (e.g. guided walks linked to bus times).

Partnerships: collaborating with other transport agencies outside protected areas, communities and governments.

Road hierarchies: hierarchies of the road network (with appropriate signing) to encourage the use of the most appropriate roads by the different types of road user (e.g. priority traffic, vacation traffic), or at different speeds.

Technology: computer screens showing public transport network (and waiting times) at key locations.

Many tools are available for managing traffic etc. Box 7.2 shows a range of them which have been used in a number of protected areas.

7.4   Pricing for visitor management

As briefly noted in section 7.1.14, charging visitor fees can fulfil several management objectives. Examples include: earning income, decreasing use, increasing use, moving use to an alternative area or time, creating an attitude of respect, or (in the case of differential fees) achieving some desirable social purpose, such as favouring local residents or encouraging less privileged sectors of society to use protected areas.

High fees can be used to lower visitation and reduce congestion and/or ecological damage at sensitive sites. Fees can be used to distribute visitors away from heavily-used places or peak times. For example, in Tasmania, national park entry fees are higher on holidays (AU$12 vs. AU$5 per person; and AU$30 vs. AU$9 per vehicle). Similarly, in the US, the White River National Forest charges a US$5 fee per person on weekends for cross-country skiing and snowmobiling, but only a US$2 fee during the week (Lindberg, 2001). People are much more likely to value something they pay for. Some parks have found that they had to increase the fees for their interpretive programmes before people were persuaded to attend: it appeared that visitors were not convinced that suitable programme quality was present until commensurate fees were in place.

Experience indicates that modest fees generally do not have a significant effect on park visitation. Nevertheless, the impact on visitors of raising charges should be monitored and changes introduced if necessary – in other words, take an adaptive management approach.

There is evidence that people will be put off (and go elsewhere) if the entrance fee to a protected area is a large proportion of the total trip cost, such as would often be the case with local visitors who have few travel costs to meet, or when the fee is quite large. However, where the cost of visiting the destination is only a small proportion of the total trip cost, fees may have very little influence. This is a particularly important consideration for protected area managers in developing countries which receive large numbers of long haul visitors from wealthier parts of the world.

Increases in fees, or the introduction of new fees, are best done with the clear intent of improving services for visitors. Park visitors are much more willing to agree to pay when they can see that the fee revenue is used to provide a product or service.

Insufficient warning of fee changes is a common concern of the tourism industry, since operators need to be able to incorporate this cost of doing business into their tour package prices, which are established at least a year or two ahead of delivery. Lindberg

Glass bottom boat, Great Barrier Reef Marine Park, Australia

Provision of effective and safe means of visitor transport combined with interpretation is important in visitor management. ©*Paul F. J. Eagles*

(2001) reports that the Great Barrier Reef Marine Park Authority decided to increase the environmental maintenance charge for tourists on commercial tours. The industry strongly opposed this, and the Government backed down. While the size of the planned increase was part of the problem (from AU$1.00 to AU$6.00), the timing was also a problem. It did not allow operators to incorporate this increase into tours that were sold more than a year in advance. A common industry recommendation is for at least 18 months prior warning of price increases.

The staff employed to collect fees can also inform, regulate and count visitors, and can contribute to educational and other functions. This is always important, but particularly so if fees are being used as a management device, when every opportunity for public contact should be taken to inform visitors of the purpose behind the fee or levy.

7.5 Regulation of visitor use

In general, there is also a choice between a strategy of *direct regulation, directive measures* and *indirect measures.*

Direct regulation of visitor behaviour relies on the force of law. It therefore requires that the legal powers be in place to adopt the regulations, and to enforce them with appropriate penalties. Regulations enforcement may rely on a firm, policing approach, or managers may decide that violation of a regulation is an opportunity to educate visitors. Either way, enforcement of the rules is important: if it is absent, protected area management will lack credibility and be undermined.

Trail Erosion, Hohe Tauern National Park, Austria

What level of trail erosion is acceptable? What procedure is in place to determine the Limits of Acceptable Change?
©*Paul F. J. Eagles*

Directive measures include design features that gently guide, but do not force, visitors in desired directions. Nature trails are often directive: their layout, trail surface preparation, and signage guides visitors towards desirable features, while at the same time subtly guiding people away from other features. Many of the approaches described in the previous section fall under this heading.

Indirect measures aim to make the visitor aware, but leave the decision to him or her on where to go and what to do. A strategy based on indirect measures will use information, interpretation and various learning opportunities (see next section) so that the visitors will adopt and employ the desired behaviour. The effectiveness of indirect measures depends on co-operative tourism operators, the general level of education and other characteristics among the visitors, and choosing the appropriate communication medium for particular messages.

In practice, of course, a combination of direct regulations, directive measures and

104

indirect measures is usually used: many managers employ indirect or directive measures first, and with the majority of visitors, and fall back on regulation where these fail.

Table 7.3 sets out a range of problem situations requiring management action, and the degree to which they are likely to be responsive to a strategy based on the indirect measures of information and education alone.

Table 7.3   Using information and education to assist in solving management problems

Type of problem	Example	Potential effectiveness of information and education	
Illegal actions	Collecting fish, birds or other wildlife Use of wilderness zone by motorised vehicles	Low	
Unavoidable actions	Human body waste Loss of ground cover vegetation in camp-site	Low	
Careless actions	Littering Noise or other nuisance activities	Moderate	Increased effectiveness of education
Unskilled actions	Touching coral when diving Selecting inappropriate camping spot	High	
Uninformed actions	Boating too close to marine mammals Collecting dead wood for firewood	Very high	

Source: Modified from Manning and Lime, 2000.

Protected agency managers are not able to solve all the problems which may affect the protected area, particularly when they originate from outside it. The degree of control they can exercise is at three levels, as shown graphically in Figure 7.1:

1. The agency has *direct control* over its own operations, and can thereby minimise any negative impacts (e.g. by adhering to certain minimum standards for visitor centre or trail construction);

2. The agency can have an *indirect impact* on the activities of others (e.g. it may require or prohibit private sector tourism operators from undertaking certain activities); and

3. The agency can *influence* others – individuals, agencies, communities, operators, etc.

In respect of level 3, where the agency exercises influence but no form of control, it should employ collaborative approaches based on partnerships with other interests which can help it achieve its aims.

Figure 7.1   Protected area managers' spheres of influence on tourism activities

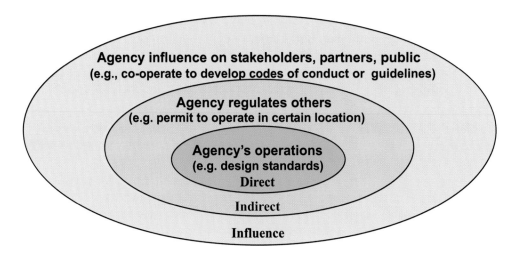

Source: Wight, 2002b.

Voluntary arrangements made between the protected area agency and partners are now widely used. They may arise out of the initiative of the protected area manager, or of a particular group which has an interest in the protected area. The scope for using such voluntary arrangements is very wide, but success depends on a good understanding of the other stakeholders' perspectives. Therefore protected area managers and their staff should develop the communication and negotiation skills needed to build good relationships, and to persuade other stakeholders to co-operate for the benefit of the protected area as well as doing so in their own interests.

Codes of practice, charters and certification schemes can underpin such voluntary arrangements. In relation to tourism and protected areas, these can be of several kinds:

▪ *Systems of standard setting and certification* applied to the tourist facility and/or provider. The Green Globe 21 scheme (see Box 3.1) is one such system; another is described in Box 7.3.

▪ *Charters, which set general principles for tourism in protected areas.* An example of a regional system of this kind in Europe, the European Charter for Sustainable Tourism in Protected Areas, is described in Appendix E, though in its development it is moving towards the next type of scheme.

▪ *Systems of standard setting and certification applied to protected areas*, ensuring that both the site itself and recreation within it are properly managed. Another example of a regional system in Europe is shown in Box 7.4 below.

▪ *Advisory codes for visitors,* which indicate appropriate behaviour in protected areas.

Box 7.3   Pacific Rim National Park Reserve, Canada; Voluntary Guidelines for Marine Tourism Operators

The Pacific Rim National Park Reserve, located on the west coast of Vancouver Island, British Columbia, is in three parts, and includes sand beaches, an island archipelago, old-growth coastal temperate rainforest, and significant archaeological sites. Its territory extends offshore to include a marine component of approximately 155km². However, management had little control over marine tourism operators within the area despite its legal status as a park reserve. Staff could only provide ecotourism and other commercial operators with recommendations and guidelines.

The manager's major objectives were to develop guidelines for the tourism industry, specifically commercial operators, which would assist in managing the natural resources of the area, particularly its wildlife. Management challenges included:

- Operators who were constantly pushing the park reserve for more access, greater numbers, or uses considered inappropriate for the park by agency staff;
- Some operators who were unwilling to adapt to change, or accept that the creation of the park was intended to increase protection;
- Insufficient park management resources (dollars, staff, time);
- Visitor pressures increasing as the off-season gained in popularity; and
- Difficulties in getting all players together on a regular basis (cost, distance, time commitment).

The manager decided to take a collaborative approach to developing cooperation, so as to influence the activities of tourism stakeholders, and solve or prevent potential problems. Staff worked with marine operators to develop an extensive package of voluntary guidelines. They were particularly concerned because the area is recognised as being vulnerable, unique and ecologically sensitive. The aim of the proposed guidelines is to provide strong protection to essential habitats, and to minimise disturbance to whales foraging in high and low tide conditions. Guidelines were developed for:

- Shoreline wildlife viewing;
- Seabird viewing;
- Seal and sea lion viewing;
- Killer whale/Orca viewing;
- Gray and Humpback whale viewing; and
- Grice Bay (a particularly sensitive location).

The Pacific Rim Guidelines not only covered wildlife viewing in general, but also detailed aspects of relevance to marine wildlife viewing such as: Getting into Position; Viewing; Leaving the Area; Distance Viewing; and Waiting. The voluntary initiative resulted in a set of documents related to key sensitive species in the region, and to a sensitive habitat.

By no means have all the problems been solved. For example, issues which remain to be resolved include: location of group camping areas and the identification of outfitting services to maintain the wilderness character and visitor experience. However, the collaboration has:

- Generated cooperation between agency and operators, and between operators themselves;
- Developed a willingness among visitors to adhere to the viewing guidelines and codes of conduct on a voluntary basis;
- Initiated regular information exchanges between operators and protected area staff; and
- Developed respect between agency staff and operators.

Box 7.4   PAN Parks, Europe

The PAN (Protected Areas Network) Parks Initiative began in 1997 with encouragement from WWF. The idea of this initiative was "to introduce a marriage between nature conservation and tourism on a European scale" (Hogan, 2000). The initiative aims to put the economic value generated through tourism into the protection of Europe's nature. 17 PAN Parks had been recognised by 2001. These are protected areas in Europe that met certain agreed standards, principles and criteria. Visitors to them know that conservation will be undertaken to the highest standards. Aware of the dangers of overwhelming protected areas with tourism, PAN Parks partners endorsed a decision that the minimum size of a PAN Park will be 25,000 ha, of which 10,000 ha will be a core zone, "off limits to visitors and free of management intervention".

Web site: http:// www.panparks.org

7.6   Information and interpretation

Potential and existing park visitors often require information. This varies from simple information on park location, times of operation and fees, to much more complex interpretation of cultural history and local ecology. Interpretation and education go beyond simply informing, towards developing an understanding and appreciation. There are three fundamental objectives of interpretation – to promote management goals, to promote understanding of the agency, and to improve understanding of the protected area (see Table 7.4). To be used as a visitor management tool, interpretation has to affect visitors' behaviour, and in order to do this, motivate through an appeal to human needs and emotions.

Table 7.4 Interpretation objectives

Goal	Comments
Management goals	• Provide information to visitors on management policies. • Direct behaviour towards acceptable practices. • Encourage behaviour that minimises negative environmental impact and maximises positive impacts.
Promote understanding of agency	• Assist with creating positive public relations for the agency. • Develop positive public attitude towards protected area agency, staff members, policies and management. • Assist park management in carrying out new policy initiatives.
Understanding of park	• Develop awareness, appreciation and understanding of park cultural and natural environments. • Develop heightened visitor satisfaction with recreation experience.

Source: Sharp, 1976.

Since the concept of a protected area first developed in its modern form, many authors, poets and painters have provided their interpretations of the meaning of parks and their environments. The provision of such interpretation by protected area agencies themselves began in the early years of the last century, with the initiation of education programmes for visitors. Over time, these grew in number and sophistication. By now, many protected area managers have become very professional in the supply of educational material to visitors, and many visitors, at least those in developed countries, have developed high expectations in this respect.

Protected area agencies should develop an information and interpretation policy. The goals set by the policy should aim to meet the needs of both the visitor and the manager. Many protected areas will require an interpretive plan to implement the policy. Table 7.5 provides a brief summary of the main interpretation techniques that should be considered in preparing the plan.

Table 7.5 Interpretation techniques

Technique	Comments
Personal services	Provide information directly to visitors by park staff or private individuals. Information duty at park gate, trail head and visitor centre. Special programmes such as guided walks, campfire programmes and theatre dramas. Personal services are highly effective, can adapt to a wide range of circumstances, but are very expensive per visitor contact.
Non-personal services	Provide information to visitors using technology. Wide range of technology available, including publications, signs, films, Internet sites and radio broadcasts. Non-personal services are less effective than personal services, are less adaptable to questions and changing circumstances. Non-personal services can make information widely available at a relatively low expense per visitor contact.
Supporting activities and facilities	Common facilities include: visitor centres, outdoor amphitheatres, nature trails, information boards, signs. Common activities include: highly trained interpretive specialists, media specialists, specialised audio and visual equipment, programme effectiveness evaluation. Many interpretive programmes involved park staff, private tour guides and volunteers. All the various types of services must be coordinated within an overall interpretive plan.

Source: adapted from Sharp, 1976.

Visitors require some basic information before they arrive, for example about the existence of the protected area, how to get there, what it will cost, the natural and cultural resources of the park, and its facilities and programmes. It is critical that suitable expectations are set in advance, so that upon arrival the visitor is aware of what can and cannot be experienced. Protected area managers have a responsibility to help create appropriate expectations.

Once people get to the park their needs change, becoming more detailed and complex. They will want to know more about the resources and facilities available, what activities are permitted or forbidden, and about safety and security. As their understanding of the area grows, visitors show more curiosity about its natural environment and history, about the culture of people living in or near the protected area, and about the visitor's role. This is the demand to which interpretation should respond. The result of well planned interpretation should be a more fulfilling visitor experience for thousands of people.

But, as already noted, interpretation also has a strong role in the management of visitors and of their impact on resources. It can be used to modify human behaviour so that it is appropriate to the area; in so doing, the environment and cultural heritage resources are better protected and supported.

Early interpretation services were usually provided to the visitors at little additional cost, and without levying a user fee. As the public appetite for information and education grew, many agencies found it too expensive to provide the full range of information and interpretation services themselves, let alone to provide these free of charge. All such services cost money, but few agencies can meet the full cost. While some protected areas have just cut back on interpretation provision, alternative approaches are possible, several of which are listed in Table 7.6.

Table 7.6 Information and interpretation management approaches

Approach	Comment
Free information provision	Basic information provision by park staff, local communities, tour operators and non-governmental organisations at no direct cost to the consumer.
	Used for travel directions, safety, programme availability, and information on cultural and environmental services.
Park user pay principle	Provided to those who pay directly for the services.
	Used for value-added programmes, such as specialised personal services, books, art, film, drama, and databases.
	Widely accepted by visitors when the cost is clearly tied to the service.
Non-profit, friends groups	Many parks encourage the development of community groups to provide interpretive services.
	Costs are covered by volunteer donations and payment by users.
	Provides park visitors with the ability to contribute to the park, with time, money and influence.
Profit-making tourism sector	Tour companies provide a specialised guide paid for by a user fee.
	Critically important in protected areas that are structurally unable to operate cost recovery operations.
	Many companies provide information to attract consumers, with the costs recouped by a later sale of a product or a service.

With the development of information technology and the use of multi-media techniques, some interpretation has become very sophisticated. While this can be an effective way of transmitting information to visitors, many of whom have access to similar technology in their work place and at home, there are dangers:

- it is often expensive to install, even if the cost of some IT equipment is falling, and therefore rarely appropriate in developing countries;

- its protection may need additional security (e.g. from fire, flood or theft);

- it will make on-going demands for energy that may be at variance with green energy policies; and

- upkeep of such equipment requires skilled maintenance (nothing is more depressing than some sophisticated display that does not work).

But perhaps the most important concern is that the medium can get in the way of the message. Nature is something often best appreciated in the natural environment itself. While the use of cutting-edge information technology to put across environmental or cultural messages within an information centre may be superficially impressive, it can be a barrier between visitors and nature rather than a bridge to it. Outstanding tourist experiences, watching geese gather at dusk, for example, can never be replicated by technology.

Nonetheless, providing there is a realistic awareness of the limits of technology as an aid to interpretation, it can help resolve certain visitor management problems, as shown in Box 7.5.

Box 7.5 ArchaeoLink Prehistory Park, Scotland, UK. An example of technology assisting with visitor management problems

ArchaeoLink is a 40-acre (18ha) prehistory park in Scotland. It is a tourist attraction and educational venue for a range of visitors. It has an "underground" interpretive centre in a huge earth mound, as well as an outdoor component, with Pictish farmstead, a Roman Marching Camp, and hill fort. Indoor elements include interactive computer educational tools.

The computer software "ArchaeoQuest" was tailor-made for the site, and has two elements, Browse, and Quest. The Browse feature allows visitors to look at all the sites in the region. Icons on the map represent various types and periods of archaeological site (e.g. stone circles, hill forts, the Picts or Symbol stones). Further information is available via images, detailed dossiers, a video display or a map. This allows visitors to determine which types of sites are most interesting.

Quest is intended to assist the tourist in visiting the sites of interest to them. It allows the visitor to enter personal details, and to respond to visitor interests as well as to advise on site conditions. The categories of visitor question include:

- Party size – 1; 2; 3–4; 5–12; 13–20; over 20
- Level of fitness – low, average, high
- Mode of transportation – foot, bike, car, coach, public transportation
- Time available – up to 1 hour, <3 hours, <6 hours, 1 day, more than a day
- Level of archaeological knowledge – low, average, high
- Eventual destination today – a series of regional options is presented for selection on the map
- Topics of interest – a menu of choices is presented. Choices are the same as in Browse

Once visitors answer these questions, the on-screen map shows an individualised proposed route. Part of the analysis includes site constraints (e.g. if there is inadequate parking for certain sizes of parties, sites which would match in every other way are eliminated from the route selection). This allows the programme to manage visitor parties and vehicles by matching these to resource constraints. This software has potential to be further modified to manage visitors to destinations at many scales. It is of educational, entertainment and information value, gives improved visitor satisfaction, and helps manage resources.

Source: Wight, 2002a.
Web site: http://www.archaeolink.co.uk/home.htm

8. The economics of tourism in protected areas

8.1 The economic value of tourism

Tourism based on protected areas is a large and growing part of the economy of many countries. For example, protected area tourism in the USA and Canada in 1996 had an economic impact of between US$236 billion and US$370 billion (Eagles *et al.*, 2000). But in general, economic evaluation data of this kind are scarce, and often unreliable when available. As a result, societies and governments tend to undervalue the benefits derived, and therefore do not provide the funds needed to maximise the flow of benefits.

The absence of systematic large-scale gathering of economic data from parks means that key parts of the economy are overlooked. The absence of adequate statistics causes an information blind spot; these natural places are valued, on a financial basis, at a zero price. This leads to excessive destruction of natural areas, implying that present economic performance in many countries will be reduced, and future economic performance will be severely curtailed (IUCN 1998).

At the same time, there is near-universal under-investment in nature protection (Wells, 1997). Most protected area systems in the world are under-funded; many are starved of funds, even when they are the central focus of a major tourism industry. Therefore, a major purpose behind this section of the Guidelines is to encourage the widespread application of economic valuation in relation to protected area tourism in order to help demonstrate the true economic value of such places.

The total economic value of a protected area is the sum of the *use values* and the *non-use values*. Use value may be direct or indirect. Direct values are considered to be market values. Indirect values are non-market values. Non-use value may also be broken into different categories: *option*, *existence* or *bequest* value (Figure 8.1). There is some debate about whether option value is a use or non-use value, because it is a non-use value in the present, and a use value in the future. All non-use values are also non-market values.

Park tourism is most often considered a direct use value of a protected area, and will be treated as such in these Guidelines. However, park visitation influences the other values. After people visit a park, they are more aware of its existence and therefore may be more willing to donate money, to argue for its existence, and to request that it be protected for future generations. In effect, they are expressing their recognition of both use and non-use values.

Figure 8.1   Total economic value of a protected area

	Use value		Non-use value
Economic value of parks =	1. ***Direct***: Recreation, education, research, wildlife harvesting. Associated with direct use of the area. (market values) 2. ***Indirect***: Ecological functions of an area, watershed protection, wildlife habitat, climate influence, carbon sequestration. Associated with indirect uses of the protected area. (non-market values)	+	1. ***Option value***: Insurance to retain option of potential future site use. Protected areas act as a resource bank. 2. ***Existence value***: Benefit of knowing a PA exists. Often measured by willingness to donate money or time. 3. ***Bequest value***: Provides benefit of knowing the areas will be around for future generation. (all non-market values)

Source: Adapted from Wells, 1997 and IUCN, 1998.

8.2   Measuring the economic impacts of tourism

Many approaches can be used to measure the economic impact of park tourism. It is beyond the scope of these Guidelines to describe the details and advantages of each method: only a brief introduction is given.

Economic impact assessment measures the value of all financial transactions made by groups (e.g. tourists or governments) related to the protected area, and their impacts on a local, regional or national economy. Impacts can be measured in such terms as Gross Domestic Product (GDP), labour income or the number of jobs created by the park.

An *economic impact* occurs with any financial transaction in an economy, for example a protected area agency buys supplies or a tourist purchases services. This impact exists, regardless of the origin of the funds or the home location of the tourist injecting the funds. All economic impacts are measurable in the marketplace.

Economic benefits are the gains that a protected area brings to the local, regional or national economy. An economic benefit occurs when there is an increase in wealth to the area under study. The increase will be affected by the region defined in the analysis: one area's cost can be another area's benefit. Benefits are more than financial: they also consist of the non-market values, but they are generally reported in unit figures of the currency. During the creation of protected areas, economic benefits should be weighed against the opportunity costs of other land use options, and this information should be used in any benefit-cost analysis to determine land allocation decisions.

When a central government protected area agency spends government money in a park, there is an economic benefit to the local community: the funds come from outside the region, and thus represent an increase in its wealth. However, from a national perspective, no increase in wealth has occurred, just a redistribution of resources within the country. So there is economic benefit at the local level, but no economic benefit at the national level. This also applies in cases where protected area agencies are partly or wholly funded by local taxes, since those moneys are raised and spent in the region. However, where funds come from international sources, such as via development assistance programmes or from the Global Environment Facility, they do represent a real benefit to the local economy.

Similarly, a *foreign* visitor represents a potential outside source of injected capital and increased wealth, to both the country and the local area: so a foreigner's expenditure represents both a benefit and an impact. However, any expenditure by a *local* resident in the community represents a redistribution of capital – an impact, but not a benefit.

Non-market benefits are measured in protected areas by two techniques – the Travel Cost Method (TCM), and the Contingent Valuation Method (CVM).

TCM is based on the value of a protected area to the society as measured by the amount of money that people pay to travel to it. The method assumes that users will react to hypothetical increases in entry fees in the same manner that they would to increased travel costs. TCM recognises that the total cost each individual pays for his or her trip depends on the cost of travel to the site; this in turn affects an individual's frequency of visitation. These two factors make it possible to draw a demand curve at the site. TCM is only used for the measurement of consumer surplus – a direct use value, and cannot be used for measuring option, existence or bequest values.

CVM is based on the assumption that consumers can accurately assign a value to recreation experiences and that these values can accurately be captured in a survey. Many versions of the technique exist. The main steps in CVM are to: create a hypothetical market for a "good"; communicate the market to the respondent so that he or she can establish a theoretical price in the form of "willingness to pay"; and use the responses to estimate the value of the goods. It is used to estimate consumer surplus, and also option, existence and bequest values.

The USNPS uses the Money Generation Model (MGM) to estimate park economic benefits. This calculates the market benefits that protected areas bring to their surrounding local communities. It is designed for park managers who do not have a substantial background in economics, and is relatively easy to use. A recently developed second generation MGM is more accurate and user-friendly.

Parks Canada developed an economic benefits model in order to show the true value of protected areas. It provides a comprehensive look at all potential economic benefits, including market and non-market. These are separated into three distinct categories: personal benefits (those that accrue to stakeholders, both users and non-users); business benefits (those that bring about a redistribution of commerce from one area to another); and societal benefits. These benefits are additive and not duplicative. The framework can be applied to other resource uses beyond protected areas, allowing for impact comparisons. The approach can be used to establish the total economic value of a protected area. Using the model reveals information gaps and helps establish priorities for economic valuation research.

The IUCN Task Force on Economic Benefits of Protected Areas recommends that a framework for valuing protected areas should have these three steps:

1. Define the audience (for local, regional, national or global use);

2. Determine the scope of the study (time, data, resources and institutional structure); and,

3. Choose the appropriate analytical techniques (contingent valuation, hedonic pricing, travel cost method, change in productivity methods, change in earnings methods, opportunity cost approach or replacement cost approach) (IUCN, 1998).

> **Box 8.1   Montague Island Nature Reserve, Australia: An example of types of information derived from economic impact studies**
>
> Montague Island Nature Reserve is 9km offshore from the south coast of New South Wales. It is ecologically important for marine mammals, and as breeding habitat for Little Penguins, Crested Terns, Silver Gulls, Sooty Oystercatchers, Wedge-tailed, and Short-tailed and Sooty Shearwaters. It also has important historical, archaeological and marine features. The New South Wales National Park and Wildlife Service (NPWS) manages the island for conservation and for local economic development.
>
> The NPWS did an economic impact assessment of the contribution of the nature reserve to the regional economy, using NPWS expenditures on island management, and expenditures of the park visitors. An input-output analysis was conducted.
>
> In total, the NPWS management expenditure resulted in AU$233,000 in gross regional output. This represented a multiplier of 1.92, indicating that for every dollar spent by the NPWS on park management, another AU$0.92 in gross regional output was generated elsewhere in the local economy.
>
> Guided tours cater to 4,300 visitors each year, with an average expenditure of AU$206.05/person/trip. Annual visitors' expenditures contributed an estimated AU$1,400,000 in gross regional output per year to the regional economy. This included AU$468,000 in household income paid to 19 people in the local economy.
>
> The aggregated NPWS and visitor expenditure impacts were estimated to be AU$1.65 million in gross regional output, and AU$857,000 in gross regional product, including AU$588,000 in household incomes, which equates to 26 local jobs. This is an impressive study of the economic impact of ecotourism on one national park. This relatively large impact occurred with quite modest numbers of park visitors suggesting that even small numbers of visitors can have important local economic impacts.
>
> *Source*: IUCN, 1998; Christiansen and Conner, 1999.

Economic impact and economic benefit studies are best done by a specialist with training in business, finance and economics. Some large agencies, such as the USNPS, the New South Wales National Parks and Wildlife Service, and Parks Canada, employ such specialist personnel. Where skills of this kind exist in-house, it may be possible to prepare special economic valuation packages that can be used by field personnel who lack formal training in economics. Less well endowed managing bodies may find it helpful to collaborate with local university departments of economics to secure such expert help. In developing countries, it may also be possible to get some international donor assistance in undertaking such analyses, especially where donors are also involved in supporting the protected areas' work.

The IUCN Task Force provides 16 case studies of economic evaluation in protected areas (IUCN, 1998). One recently completed case study from Australia can serve to illustrate the type of information derived from economic impact studies (Box 8.1).

8.3   Communicating economic impacts

It is important that the findings of economic impact studies should be communicated to interested stakeholders in appropriate levels of detail:

- *Full economic impact* studies are valuable for the managing agency itself, and for officials in government, aid agencies and business, since they need to know the range of economic benefits that protected areas bring to society.

- *Summary figures* are useful for local governments, local tourism interests, local politicians and the local media. Some protected area agencies inform their local officials annually about the economic impact of the park, which gives the protected area an important profile in the decisions of local communities.

- *Brief summaries* of economic impacts may interest park visitors and local citizens.

The understanding of flow and distribution of the economic benefits from tourism is one of the most critical elements of park economics. Policy makers, planners and managers can influence this flow and its distribution, and need to consider their options carefully. International bodies (such as the World Bank), all levels of government, corporations/businesses of all kinds but especially those involved in tourism, and local citizens and visitors to protected areas – all of these make decisions on future investments of money and time which affect protected areas. Economic benefit valuations can inform many of these decisions. Protected area managers, and their supporters, should therefore do all they can to provide such valuations and communicate the results widely.

> Note: For a fuller introduction to this topic, the reader is referred to a recent IUCN publication in this series: ***Economic Values of Protected Areas: Guidelines for Protected Area Managers*** (IUCN, 1998).

9. Financial aspects of tourism in protected areas

9.1 Introduction

The chapter begins with a brief overview of the global trends in protected area finance that shows the extent of the challenge. It then reviews the fund-raising opportunities available to managers, and public/private sector relationships. Later sections consider various ways in which extra finance can be generated and secured from tourism: through parastatals; development assistance; user fees; and corporate contributions. It ends with a discussion of the issue of concessions.

All management depends upon finance. The foundation of many protected areas has been and continues to be public finance. Unfortunately, many protected area management agencies have insufficient funds to respond properly to the demands of tourism and conservation. Currently, most governments do not fund protected areas fully. Globally speaking, protected area budgets in the early 1990s totalled only about 24% of the estimated US$17 billion required to maintain the areas; and the trend is downward with most countries currently experiencing budget decreases (Lindberg, 2001). Even in developed countries with a long history of protected areas, securing adequate finance from government sources is a struggle: in the USA, for example, government appropriations are regarded by many as insufficient for the needs.

The average public support for protected areas in developed countries (US$2,058 per km^2) is much greater than that in developing countries (US$157), where government funds are limited and protected areas come low down in terms of national priorities. Thus while the costs of effective conservation in African protected areas, for example, are estimated to be between US$200 and US$230 per km^2, the agency budgets for many African protected areas in the early 1990s were generally quite inadequate, as revealed in the Table 9.1 below:

Table 9.1 Annual expenditure on protected areas by km^2 in eastern and southern Africa (all figures in US$)

South Africa	$2,129	Uganda	$47
Zimbabwe	$436	Tanzania	$30
Kenya	$409	Zambia	$23
Namibia	$70	Angola	<$1
Botswana	$51		

Source: Lindberg, 2001.

119

In general, protected area staff in developing countries are poorly paid, there is limited funding for protected area investment, and alternative land uses (or destructive activities like poaching) are seen as more lucrative by local people and national politicians. However, developing countries can gain access to funds from international assistance programmes, NGO activities and other donations (see section 9.5 below). As in many parts of the developing world, the capital needed for protected area facilities and equipment in much of eastern and southern Africa comes from such sources; operating funds, though, depend more upon tourism income (and in some cases resource extraction which may prejudice the objectives of the protected area).

However, against a background of generally declining government support for protected areas, managers need to be creative in raising funds – and no source is more promising than through tourism. But even where tourism is a potentially important source of income, it alone cannot generate sufficient funds for all aspects of cultural and natural heritage protection. Also, protected areas provide a range of other vital services to society, whose values should be recognised by some form of public finance. Thus there continues to be a strong case for governments to help fund protected areas **and the emphasis placed here on generating income through tourism is not intended to undermine basic support of this kind**.

9.2 Fund-raising opportunities for protected area managers

Lindberg and Enriquez (1994) illustrate the existing funding sources and how they vary between developed and developing countries (Figure 9.1). Figure 9.1 shows that funds provided to the park agency from government are the most prevalent revenue source.

Figure 9.1   Protected area revenue sources

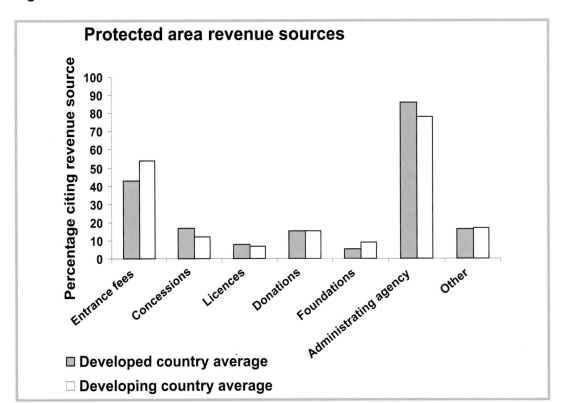

> **Box 9.1   Potential income sources for protected areas**
>
> ▓ Government funding programmes (mandatory or discretionary)
>
> ▓ Park entrance fees
>
> ▓ Recreation service fees, special events and special services
>
> ▓ Accommodation
>
> ▓ Equipment rental
>
> ▓ Food Sales (restaurant and store)
>
> ▓ Merchandise sales (equipment, clothing, souvenirs)
>
> ▓ Donations, foreign aid
>
> ▓ Licensing of intellectual property
>
> ▓ Sale or rental of image rights
>
> ▓ Parking
>
> ▓ Cross product marketing
>
> ▓ Public investments
>
> ▓ Private sector initiatives
>
> *Source*: Eagles, 1997.

Such tax-based income is vulnerable to budget cuts by central government. The second most prevalent source is from entrance fees, a tourism-based income source.

Box 9.1 lists a number of income sources potentially available to protected areas. Many of the income sources shown in Box 9.1 do not appear in Figure 9.1, suggesting that there is considerable potential for park agencies to increase income by utilizing a broader range of revenue sources. Tourism has the potential to provide agencies with many of these income sources. A few examples are provided below and developed later in this chapter.

Visitor fees

Most parks charge some form of entrance fees, either per person or per vehicle, or a combination of both. Some parks provide specialised recreation services, such as guided tours or special events. Frequently a special-use charge is applied to these services, to cover the cost of provision of the service and to earn income for other uses. Parks that allow vehicle entrance must provide parking sites. Charging for parking can be a lucrative source of income. For example, some camp-sites allow one vehicle to be covered per camp-site registration. Any other vehicles are charged a parking fee. Ear-marking revenues for the protected area is important to improve stakeholder acceptance of fees. For example, a recent survey in Tasmania showed that 86% of the public felt fees were good if the income was returned directly to parks, but only 36% support park fees if they go to the national treasury (ANZECC, 2000).

Accommodation

One of the largest expenditure categories for travellers is that of accommodation. Some parks operate camp-sites, cabins, and lodges, and charge visitors accordingly. Accommodation charges can be one of the largest income sources available for protected areas.

The management of accommodation (whether directly or through a concession) is a complicated activity that requires specially trained staff and proper business procedures.

Equipment and food services

Outdoor recreation often requires specialised equipment, much of which is difficult to transport over long distances. Therefore, the provision of such equipment in parks, either for sale or rental, can be a source of revenue. All park visitors require food, either in the form of groceries or prepared in restaurants. The purchase of food is a major expenditure item for travellers, and parks can earn a substantial income from this source. Managers must decide whether it is better to operate these services within the agency structure, or utilise a concessionaire.

Consumer products

Merchandise sales are potentially a very large source of income for parks, but one that is seldom utilised. However, in recent years the sale of tailor-made specialised parks merchandise, such as clothing, equipment and publications, has become quite successful. Major crafting industries develop around parks where the park agency facilitates contact between the craftsmen and the tourists, involving communities living within or around the areas, and bringing jobs and income to the people involved. Box 9.2 lists these (and other) types of local economic activity which were built up in Zimbabwe a few years ago, on the back of wildlife and protected area tourism.

Public/industry donations

Satisfied park visitors are sometimes willing to make donations to protected areas. Such donations are most frequently provided toward specific initiatives, such as a new

---

Box 9.2 Tourism-related, protected area-based rural enterprises in Zimbabwe

- Manufacture and supply of building materials
- Uniform manufacture
- Food and game production
- Game meat retail and distribution
- Furniture manufacture
- Curio manufacture
- Guiding services
- Transport
- Sale and distribution of firewood
- Cultural tourism activities
- Traditional show village
- Community-based wildlife products
- Accommodation

Source: DFID, 1998.

**Box 9.3 KwaZulu-Natal Conservation Trust, South Africa: An innovative
Trust which licences its "brand" to appropriate products for a fee**

The KwaZulu-Natal Conservation Trust (KZNT) is an independently registered
capital fund. This was established in 1989 to allow public and corporate donations to
conservation, due to ongoing reductions in public funding of protected areas. The
Nature Conservation Service works closely with KZNT in fund-raising and conservation.

The Trust has a variety of means of generating revenue including: collections,
donations, sponsored sporting events, and trading in art (donated by artists and
sculptors). The Trust has an emblem, which is licensed for use on a range of clothing,
equipment and accessories, in return for a royalty.

Source: Buckley and Sommer, 2001.

---

facility, research or a special recreation programme. Satisfied and concerned foreign
visitors have been known to return to their home countries and lobby for foreign aid
budgets to be applied to the parks they have visited.

Cross product marketing and image sale

Protected areas represent a valuable "intellectual property", as an image with which
corporations wish to be associated. For example, park names are often very well known
and appreciated. Additionally, their sites are attractive and are highly desired by some
enterprises, such as advertisers and movie producers. A few protected areas earn
substantial income from the sale of licences to use their names and images. Cross
product marketing is a very popular business practice, but is rare in protected areas. This

Arowhon Pines Lodge, Algonquin Provincial Park, Ontario, Canada

The spending of park visitors on accommodation and food is important to regional economic impacts.
©*Paul F. J. Eagles*

occurs when two allied products advertise and sell each other's product. An example in a protected area context might be a shared market programme between a film company and a park. Each gains by co-operation in marketing their product. An interesting protected area example is shown in Box 9.3.

9.3 Public and private sector financial relationships

Tourism management in protected areas requires finance, but most agencies take advantage of only a small portion of potential income sources. The mix of finance sources used and the percentage of finance earned from each source is the result of the public policies applied in each jurisdiction as well as the individual initiative of the manager. The type of financial arrangement used is also strongly influenced by the history and structure of the park agency and its creativity. Also, although government agencies are typically competent providers of tourism services, they often have structural limitations that inhibit efficient and effective functioning. Thus the private sector may be better able to deliver certain services.

Some countries, such as Tanzania, have a history of full cost recovery for agency operations from tourism fees and charges. Others, such as the USA or New Zealand, have a long-held policy of providing access to the national parks with funding from government grants and low levels of fees and charges. In recent decades, there has been a global trend for governments to use park visitation income to provide higher levels of operational finance for parks and protected areas.

Financing protected areas is a thorny question the world over. Even in countries with a long history of protected areas, financing them adequately is a struggle. In the USA, for example, funds are both discretionary and mandatory, yet the latter types of appropriations are limited. An expert panel in the USA considered the question of what strategies could be employed for funding (wilderness areas), and the results are shown in Table 9.2.

Table 9.2 therefore presents examples of a range of optional funding strategies (in the first column). The rows show evaluations of their effectiveness with regard to various criteria: Economic and ecological effectiveness, Institutional and political viability, Equity, Accountability, Predictability, and Flexibility.

Table 9.2 Evaluation of funding strategies

Strategy	Economic and Ecological Effectiveness	Viability	Equity	Accountability	Predictability	Flexibility
Capture ecosystem service values	o	+	+	o	+	o
Public investments and donations	+	—	o	+	—	o
Private sector initiatives	+	o	o	+	—	o
Federal funding programmes/ reforms	+	—	+	+	+	—
General public funding	+	—	+	+	+	—

Key: + = High ; o = Medium; — = Low

Source: Alkire, 2000.

The roles of the public and private sectors in protected area tourism can be both mutually supportive and conflicting. The provision of services to the park visitor, the level of charges for these services and the public/private mix of service provision are public policy issues. Typically, there is a complicated mix of public and private service provision, and the long-term success of protected area tourism requires co-operation between both the public and private sectors.

The public sector has the unique role of resource protection (Table 9.3). Security of the environment and public safety is an overarching government responsibility. In most cases, basic tourism infrastructure is paid for by the public purse.

Table 9.3 Public sector role in park tourism

Roles typically undertaken by the public sector
1   Environmental protection
2   Infrastructure (roads, airports, rail lines, electricity, sanitation)
3   Security and enforcement
4   Monitoring of impacts, evaluation of quality
5   Allocation of access
6   Limits of acceptable change
7   Information (interpretation, visitor centres)
8   Conflict resolution

Source: Eagles, 1997.

Governments may impose taxes, allocating a portion of revenues to protected area management (e.g. by directing appropriated funds, or establishing an endowment and using the interest for management). This is important, since in many places, it is unlikely that tourism alone can provide sufficient funds for all aspects of cultural and natural heritage protection (e.g. land purchase of the Redwoods National Park in the USA cost over US$500 million). Government may also levy taxes (e.g. the US taxes up to 5% of a manufacturer's price on outdoor recreational equipment, including backpacks, binoculars, cameras, field guides and recreational vehicles, which goes to wildlife agencies and yields US$350 million).

For many agencies, it is necessary for all protected area operational finance to be earned from tourism. In such circumstances, the prices must reflect the cost of production of the tourism product, including resource protection. Although the creation of a protected area implies that the benefits of so doing outweigh the costs, often the benefits are non-financial and spread in space and over time (whereas the costs are immediate and financial). So, currently most governments do not fund protected areas fully, and there is a trend to reducing support, as already noted.

Typically, the private sector provides most of the services and consumer products (Table 9.4). Private operators provide accommodation, food, transport, media and advertising. The private sector has the ability to respond quickly to consumer demands and to develop specialised products.

Table 9.4   Private sector role in park tourism

	Roles typically undertaken by the private sector
1	Accommodation and food
2	Transportation (buses, automobiles, airplanes)
3	Information (guides, advertising)
4	Media (films, books, videos)
5	Site promotion and advertising
6	Consumer products (clothes, souvenirs, equipment)
7	Personal services (entertainment)

Source: Eagles, 1997.

Although the private sector operators can respond quickly to new consumer desires for recreation or tourism services, they are not able to respond quickly to changes in fees that they are charged by agencies or governments. The commercial tourism sector generally sells tours well in advance. They cannot, therefore, accommodate sudden fee changes.

Public and private sector co-operation

The current mix of public/private responsibilities is flexible, for example park agencies can provide most of the services that were listed in Table 9.4 (and are sometimes required to do so when it is necessary to earn operational finance from tourism). Moreover the private sector can deliver many of the services in Table 9.3.

Both the public and private sectors in wealthier countries usually provide information. New Zealand is a world leader in the development of a sophisticated, community-based, visitor information system. On the South Island, most towns and national parks have visitor centres, which serve as clearing-houses for all types of information. Through public and private co-operation, this advanced and appreciated information source is made available to all travellers. In poorer countries, such as many of those in Africa, it is the private operators who largely provide information, whereas the public sector provides resource protection, infrastructure and security services.

Public and private co-operation is evident in the provision of information databases on the Internet. Information available in this fashion includes what is typically available in visitor centres, in protected area publications and in guidebooks. It is expected that all major protected areas will provide this type of information in the future, and their tourist industry is well positioned to take advantage of this new technology, since there is an excellent match of computer literacy with ecotourists.

The operation of a protected area tourism industry requires the co-operation of both the public and private sector. Neither can do the job alone. Each is fundamentally dependent upon the other. This situation is not always easy and much time and effort can be wasted in real or apparent conflict situations. The long-term health of the natural environment and the financial condition of all sectors of ecotourism depend upon co-operation.

9.4 Funding of protected areas through parastatals

In many countries all income earned by a government agency goes to central government, (this is true, for example, of the USNPS). Under such arrangements, each year the central government sends out a mandatory and/or discretionary budget amount for operations. The annual budget is typically tied to political considerations in government, not to the level of protected area income or the level of service delivery. This funding structure is very difficult for an agency offering tourism services, the costs of which may consequently vary over time, sometimes quite dramatically. Also, most government agencies do not provide service or competency-based payments to employees. Such institutional arrangements may inhibit protected areas from providing high quality services, charging appropriate fees, or functioning in a positive, proactive fashion; and there is little incentive for the employee to provide high levels of service quality.

Such concerns have been behind the development of protected area agencies which have *parastatal* forms of operation. Examples include Tanzania National Parks (TANAPA) and the Kenya Wildlife Service. Typically, parastatal agencies function like companies within government (often called crown or public corporations). The key components of a parastatal structure are shown in Table 9.5.

Table 9.5   Key components of a parastatal agency (crown or public corporation)

	Components
1	Internal financial management
2	Year over year retention of earnings
3	Flexible staffing policies
4	Competency-based incentives to employees
5	Flexibility in setting fees and charges
6	Flexibility in licensing concessions, properties and services
7	Ability to respond quickly to client demands
8	Board of Directors
9	Higher levels of client service

Thus the main advantages of parastatals are: their ability to retain the money they earn; the incentive this creates to raise additional funds; and their more autonomous and entrepreneurial approach to operations. As a result, parastatals tend to be much more financially successful and better financed than government agency forms of operation. In the Caribbean, parastatal park agencies spent twice as much on conservation activities than did government park agencies (James, 1999). And in Africa, parastatal agencies had 15 times as much funding as did government park agencies – see for example Box 9.4. Clearly, the operational structure of protected agency's operations greatly influences their financial viability.

> **Box 9.4 KwaZulu-Natal Conservation Service, South Africa: A parastatal model for protected area management**
>
> KwaZulu-Natal (KZN) has been involved with protected areas in Africa for over a century. Its Nature Conservation Service (NCS) was established in 1998 for protected area management, and it is able to retain all revenues earned. Its approach is to focus on biodiversity conservation, community involvement and sustainable resource use, particularly through tourism.
>
> KZN NCS has established a system of biosphere reserves and other conservation lands, which are managed under voluntary cooperative agreements with local land-owners (222 such landowner-managed conservancies). These have multiple uses, including farming, and managing part of the land for wildlife. Owners pay the NCS a fee per ha each year, which is used for staffing, equipment, management and moni-toring. This has resulted in increased wildlife habitat. When the wildlife increases too much on the lands, the NCS sells the surplus to private wildlife reserves and reserves. Wildlife sales have earned over US$2.23 million since 1997.
>
> Besides obtaining wildlife at subsidised prices, communities have received dona-tions worth over US$7.75 million with NCS's assistance. Indigenous tribal communi-ties manage through protected area boards, and NCS has allowed communities to harvest meat, fish, thatching and weaving materials, benefiting them to a total of US$1.64 million. NCS trains and employs local people as staff and tourist guides, and have developed small businesses including handicrafts. The tourists pay a community levy of about US$750,000 p.a., which is distributed by local boards.
>
> *Source*: Buckley and Sommer, 2001.

9.5 International sources of assistance

Development assistance

In much of the developing world, support for protected areas comes in part from outside donors. There are *multilateral* donor agencies (e.g. the World Bank, Inter-American Development Bank and Asian Development Bank) and *bilateral* ones (e.g. the European Union, and national programmes such as those of the Danish International Development Agency [DANIDA], the UK Department for International Development [DFID], the Canadian International Development Agency [CIDA] and Japan International Co-operation Agency [JICA]). Together these provide a significant amount of financing for conservation and protected area activities. Funding from these sources may be used to help countries fulfil commitments made under the biodiversity-related conventions. An important addition to multilateral funding has come over the past 10 years with the establishment of the Global Environment Facility, which is channelled through the World Bank, the United Nations Environment Programme and the United Nations Development Programme, *inter alia* to help implement the CBD.

In general, multilateral bank funding is available only to governments or to private-sector projects expressly approved by governments. Therefore, projects submitted to development agencies, especially multilateral banks, must usually have the backing of the appropriate government agencies, and generally be submitted by or with those agencies. Typically a development bank grant or loan for the establishment and maintenance of national parks and protected areas would be provided as support to implement a national conservation plan. Sometimes conservation funding might also be attached to an infrastructure development project, for example, as mitigation for the environmental effects of developing roads, railways, dams, etc. Increasingly international funding is being channelled through NGOs in both the development and conservation sectors.

Although most bilateral and multilateral agencies focus their support mainly on poverty relief and meeting the needs of the rural poor, many see the development of tourism in connection with protected areas as a means to those ends. This has led to the advocacy of "pro-poor" tourism strategies. Such an approach, which has the support of the UN Commission on Sustainable Development, has been defined as "aiming to influence tourism development to unlock opportunities for the poor – whether for economic gain, other livelihood benefits or engagement in decision- making" (Ashley *et al.*, 2001; see also www.propoortourism.org.uk). Though protected area-based tourism will not automatically bring benefits to poor people in rural areas in developing countries, where this can be done it is likely that protected area managers will be able to attract international sources of development funding.

Debt-for-nature swaps

Debt-for-nature swaps are one form of international assistance that can be developed almost exclusively for conservation and protected areas. Under such arrangements, part of the official debt of a government is exchanged for local currency to invest in a domestic environmental protection project (Thapa, 2000). Such projects may include designation and management of protected areas, park personnel training, and environmental education programmes. While debt-for-nature swaps may involve two governments (bilateral-official debt), in many cases a local NGO has been involved (trilateral-official and private debt). Often, governments are aided in this transaction by an international NGO, in which case it must work with a domestic NGO in the debtor country that will be responsible for the administration and facilitation of the swap project (see Box 9.5).

Since this first swap of foreign debt in Bolivia, many other countries have participated in such swaps, and the number is expected to increase in future. Swaps have already generated more than US$100 million for domestic environmental protection projects. Mexico, for example, has converted US$3.7 million via nine different transactions, with Conservation International involved in all cases. Other NGOs active in debt-for-nature swaps in different countries are The Nature Conservancy and the Worldwide Fund for Nature/World Wildlife Fund (WWF).

Box 9.5   Bolivia, Conservation International and the USA: An example of the first debt-for-nature swap

In 1987 the first swap of foreign debt occurred between the US and Bolivia (US$650,000 was exchanged for US$100,000 of local currency to be used towards protection of the Beni Biosphere). The locally-based branch of the NGO, Conservation International, played a key administrative and operational role in the project.

**Figure 9.2   Relationship between debt-for-nature swap and
protected area tourism**

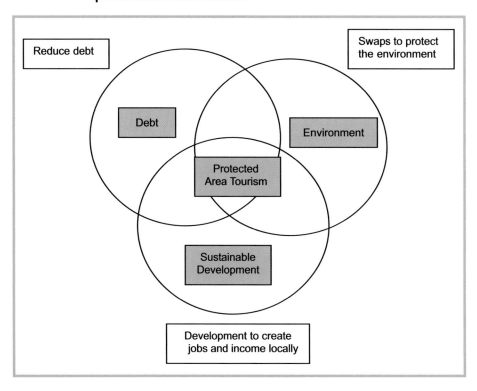

Source: Thapa, 2000.

Debt swaps alleviate the debt burden of developing countries, help with protected area creation or operations, support sustainable development programmes to create local jobs and income, and increase funds for environmental organisations (see Figure 9.2). For example: WWF's debt swap with Ecuador established a fund yield that was twice the size of the parks' and reserves' budget; and although swaps represent a small dent in the national debt of Costa Rica, the interest alone from the swaps is several times greater than the annual budget allocated to the country's park service (Thapa, 2000).

9.6 Tourists' contribution via fees

Table 9.6 shows that there are several types of visitor fees levied on protected area property (they also appear in Box 9.1 with "off-park" sources, such as cross product marketing and licensing of intellectual property). In most protected area systems, tourism fees and charges are an important part of the income of the park and agency. Even in wealthier countries, user fees are charged by protected areas, as government appropriations do not cover all the management costs. In developing countries the fee income is typically critical to the survival of the management agency.

Table 9.6   Types of fees and charges in protected areas

Fee type	Description
Entrance fee	Allows access to points beyond the entry gate.
Recreation fees	Fees for recreation programmes and services.
User fee	Fees for facilities within the protected area; e.g. parking, camping, visitor centres, boat use, shelter use, etc.
Concession fees	Charges or revenue shares paid by concessionaires that provide services to protected area visitors.
Merchandise sales	Monies from sales of products, supplies, and souvenirs.
Food sales	Income from groceries and restaurants.
Accommodation	Income from camping and roofed accommodation operated by park.
Licences and permits	For private firms to operate on protected area property; e.g. tour operators, guides, and other users.
Taxes	Hotel room taxes, airport taxes, and vehicle taxes.
Leases and rent fees	Charges for renting or leasing park property or equipment.
Voluntary donations	Includes cash, 'in-kind' gifts, and labour; often through 'friends of the park' groups.

Sources: Eagles, 2001; Brown, 2001.

The costs associated with managing recreational services provided in a protected area should be reflected in visitor use fees. Many studies have shown that protected area visitors are generally willing to pay much higher fees in parks than are currently charged in developing countries. This willingness is associated with a desire that the fees go directly towards the management of the environment visited and service provided, not to a central government coffer. However, a common problem is that the destinations typically lack the expertise to design effective pricing strategies and financial management structures. Those that do, may reap considerable financial benefits. For example, the following Marine Protected Areas cover most or all of their expenses through entry fees and other tourism-related income: Hol Chan (Belize), Ras Mohammed (Egypt), Bonaire (Netherlands Antilles) and Palau, Micronesia (Lindberg, 2001).

Visitor fees may be quite complex, and multi-dimensional, as shown in Table 9.7. Such complicated fee structures are designed to capture income from the wide diversity of activities and uses that occur in many protected areas.

Table 9.7   Idaho State Park visitors use fee structure, 1999

Type of fee	Fee (US$)
Entrance adult resident and non-resident	0
Passenger vehicles resident and non-resident	2–3
Group bus (resident and non-resident)	20
Annual pass (resident and non-resident)	35
Entrance fee, senior citizen	0
Vessel launchings	3
Overnight boat moorage	5
Cabins, tepees and yurts	30–80
Reservation fee	6
Camp-site, 3 hook-up	18–22
Camp-site, 2 hook-up	16
Camp-site, 1 hook-up	12
Improved camp-site, no hook-up	7–12
Primitive camp-site, no hook-up	7

Source: Brown, 2001 quoting National Association of State Park Directors.

Guidelines on reducing public resistance to fees are these:

- Use fee revenues for quality improvements to trails, toilets, maps, and other facilities;
- Make small fee increases rather than making them in large jumps;
- Use moneys for operational costs rather than as a control mechanism for visitor entry;
- Retain and use money for specific, known, park purposes, rather than for general revenues;
- Use extra money for conservation of the area visited; and
- Provide abundant information to the public about the income earned and the actions funded through it.

Many protected areas are unable to attract large numbers of visitors: and in some cases it would be inappropriate to do so. In setting fee levels in such cases, managers must consider demand for the protected area, the costs of providing the services, and travel costs. It is difficult to pinpoint an appropriate price. Protected areas with low demand and low visitation may not be able to charge sufficiently high fees to cover costs (of course, re-examining marketing strategies may positively impact demand). However, low use may occur because of very high travel costs. For example some Canadian Arctic parks are very expensive to reach. When visitors have invested a great deal to reach a unique destination, it is reasonable to assume that the protected area could charge a premium fee.

Pricing policies

The allocation of prices for the various programmes and services of parks is a key element of park tourism. The main principle underlying park pricing is government policy with regard to public use. In some (typically wealthier) societies, protected areas are seen as a public good that are provided for the benefit of all members of society. In these situations, general government revenue is allocated to the park to fund operations. In other (typically poorer) societies, other public services are deemed to be more deserving of scarce public funds. When this happens, protected areas must gain revenue from tourism or other forms of resource use.

Protected area managers need to answer two important questions when determining how to develop a pricing policy that fits with the values of the area. First, what are the objectives of the protected area's pricing strategy? This question needs to be answered with the users in mind. Secondly, how are the prices established for a specific product or service in accordance with these objectives?

However, each park is unique and, therefore, a variety of pricing objectives may be necessary to describe the inherent values that are attributed to all of the stakeholders. Managers are challenged to develop a comprehensive and focused rationale for fees, and each rationale must be clearly defined in order to defend against scrutiny from park users and political bodies.

In examining pricing schemes for access to protected areas in both developed and developing countries, Brown (2001) concluded that fee prices should be based on visitor demand for access. Managers should choose fee levels that are neither capricious nor inequitable. A range of pricing schemes can be used for protected areas, but flexibility in fee structure is crucial (Table 9.8). Box 9.6 shows how a sophisticated fee structure can work in practice.

Table 9.8   Types of protected area pricing strategies

Pricing scheme	Description
Peak load pricing	Different prices for different times, depending on demand.
Comparable pricing	Prices based on average of user fees charged by other parks for equivalent attractions or services (difficulties may arise when the park is unique and there are not other comparables on which to base a price).
Marginal cost pricing	Prices set where the added costs equal the added benefits derived from the park; prices set at the intersection of the marginal cost and marginal benefit curve.
Multi-tiered pricing	Different prices based on residency, age, location, etc. (these have been found to yield more revenue than a high or low fee alone, but have limits).
Differential pricing	Different prices based on level of service offered (e.g. different prices for camp-sites in different locations of a park may result in a more even distribution of use or increase in revenue).

Source: Brown, 2001.

Box 9.6   Galápagos National Park (GNP) and Marine Reserve: An example of visitor use fees

The GNP has an entrance fee for visitors, on a graduated scale, with foreign visitors charged more than domestic visitors. The fee scale is illustrated below.

Visitor use fees for the Galápagos National Park

Category	Charge in US$
Foreign tourist (non-resident)	100
Foreign tourist <12 years	50
Foreign tourist of a member country of the Andean Community or Mercosur	50
Foreign tourist of a member country of the Andean Community or Mercosur <12 years	25
Citizen or resident of Ecuador	6
Citizen or resident of Ecuador <12 years	3
Foreign tourist non-resident attending a national academic institution	25
National or foreign children <2 years	No fee

Source: Government of Ecuador, 1998.

Prior to the Special Law of 1993, an average of only 30% of visitor use fees went to the budget of the GNP and the rest went to the Ecuadorian Institute of Forests, Protected Areas and Wildlife (INEFAN). Now, fee levels are higher, and the distribution is different. INEFAN only gets 5% of the income, and 45% goes to GNP and the Marine Reserve.

Visitor use fees before the Special Law (US$)

Category	Before 1993	1993–1998
Nationals	0.55	3.00 + 2.50 municipality tax
Foreigners	40.00	80.00 (+ 30.00 municipality tax if enter through San Cristóbal, or + 12.00 if enter through Baltra)

However, these fees still generate only about 25% of the National Park budget, thus making managers unable to manage appropriately the increasing number of visitors to the park and marine reserve. In addition, the under-pricing of fees for tourism operators has been identified as an opportunity, since after the visitor use fee was increased, it did not affect visitor demand for access, and indeed visitor numbers have been increasing steadily.

The visitor use fee increases (as well as the operator licences) are not equivalent to the real recreational value of the islands to the visitors/users. For example the fees were not based on a willingness-to-pay study, nor on the actual cost to the park of providing tourism opportunities. Thus, there is a probability that fees currently charged are below the fair market price. It is suggested that GNP, like other protected areas, should evaluate their current pricing scheme, to set visitor and licence fees that reflect the market demand. There is also an opportunity to collaborate better with local municipalities, to ensure that the 30% of visitor user fees allocated to local governments are appropriately fed back into conservation benefits.

Source: Benitez, 2001.
Web site: http://nature.org/aboutus/travel/ecotourism/resources/

> **Box 9.7   Healthy environments encourage higher willingness to pay**
>
> In two surveyed Marine Protected Areas, it was found that high marine site quality could be used to support higher fees, in a virtuous cycle.
>
> Survey results from the Turks and Caicos Islands indicate that divers would be willing to pay an extra 13% in dive prices for a dive featuring 12 groupers, rather than for a trip featuring one grouper. And they would be willing to pay 5.6% more for a trip with a large grouper, rather than a trip with small grouper.
>
> In the Maldives, divers would be willing to pay US$87 more to visit healthy reefs than others.
>
> In the Red Sea, it has been found that sustaining site quality enables marketing a top-end position for marine tourism destinations, with associated high levels of profitability.
>
> *Source*: Lindberg, 2001.

Very often concerns that increased fees will discourage visitors prove unfounded. For example, at Bonaire Marine Park, where dive operators actively lobbied against the US$10 fee, there was no apparent decline in visitation due to the fee; and in Costa Rica, tour operators were strongly opposed to the introduction of a 2-tiered fee, yet revenues actually went up. Similarly, when fees were doubled in "Crown Jewel" sites, (e.g. Grand Canyon, Yellowstone, or Western Canadian national parks), visitation remained the same. In Ontario Provincial Parks, fee increases of over 40% resulted in substantial increases in visitation: the new income allowed for the provision of better and new recreational services, so attracting more visitors (Moos, 2002).

One lesson can be drawn from these examples: **tourists are ready to pay for quality**. Box 9.7 describes a specific example of this in the marine environment.

Pricing fees is one thing, collecting them is another, particularly if access is not controlled, or in large areas, or in marine areas. Some marine protected areas administer fees directly, for example at Hol Chan Marine Reserve in Belize, staff sell tickets at the dive/snorkel site. At others, revenues from fees barely cover the costs of collecting, especially at sites with low visitation levels. In the USA, collection costs for their national parks service and forest service are about 20% of the fee revenues. Some parks are so remote that it is technically difficult to place staff to collect and manage fees. In some places, tickets or passes may be sold through tourism or other businesses, or by using an honour system, backed up by spot checks by park rangers. Thus entry may be sold though tour operators, as at the Great Barrier Reef (AU$4 per day), or at Bonaire Marine Park (US$10 per day). This is paid when divers arrive at the resort, and they must wear a plastic tag to dive. While spot checks for tags are made on shore, peer pressure is effective enough on dive boats to ensure that all divers pay the fee (Lindberg, 2001).

Willingness to pay

It is important to understand the visitors to the protected areas in order to determine their ability and willingness to pay for services and products (note that 'willingness' and 'ability' are different concepts, since people may demand subsidised services even when they can afford to pay for them). Parks Canada conducts visitor surveys and maintains databases to encourage better management of park programmes and develop new methods of generating revenue. The agency considers market factors such as supply and demand, the price, quality and location of similar services outside the protected area, when setting the rate for the use of services (whether these are controlled by Parks Canada itself, or by private enterprise within the park). Parks Canada has, for example, experimented with a centralised reservation system in the Maritime Provinces. Campers reserved sites over the telephone and paid with a credit card, which went to a contractor. The protected area managers had no administration costs related to camp-site reservations and payments. Public response was high, with 100% reservation during July and August. This on-line reservation system for camp-sites is now being developed nationally. The Provinces of Manitoba and Ontario both introduced centralised camp-site registration systems in the mid-1990s. Initially the system was based on a phone-in approach, and later Internet access became available. The systems became very popular, resulting in increased camp-site utilisation across the province, increased use of remote protected areas which had previously had a low public profile, and much higher public

---

Box 9.8   Costa Rican protected areas: Results of willingness to pay surveys to increase protected area revenues

Costa Rica has an extensively developed system of protected areas, covering over 25% of the country's area. Park entrance fees in the 1980s were US$1 for both nationals and foreigners (generating up to US$1million annually). However, in the 1990s, there was further loss of funding sources and the agency raised national park entrance fees to US$15 (and advance booking fees were US$10 and US$5.25 for bulk booking by travel agents). Although visitation decreased, revenues in the first 9 months of 1995 were four times the amount earned in the entire 12 months of 1994! However, widespread opposition to the increase resulted in a reduction of the increase.

Costa Rica found the revenues still did not cover the costs of park operations. So it moved to a two-tiered fee in 1996, with foreigners paying six times as much as nationals for national park entrance. In addition, budgets are supplemented by:

- Donations
- User and concession fees
- Fees from concessions of operation of radio and television towers and a food concession at the zoo
- Fiscal stamps, which must be purchased for documents such as passports, first-time auto registrations as well as all liquor vendors and places of entertainment
- Contributions from the Costa Rican Tourism Institute

In 1995, a study found that the fee of US$6 for foreigners and US$1 for residents was not the optimal fee for revenue generation. Both nationals and foreigners were willing to pay more. Foreigners were willing to pay more than double their current fee (US$23 for Poás and US$14 for Manuel Antonio). Costa Rica residents expressed willingness to pay for future visits to national parks (US$11 for Poás and US$10 for Manuel Antonio). This willingness to pay is almost 900% more than the current fee for residents. There is an opportunity to use more appropriate ways to set visitor fees in Costa Rica's protected areas, which would both generate more revenues for current levels of visitation, and would contribute better to operations.

Source: Brown, 2001.
Web site: http://nature.org/aboutus/travel/ ecotourism/resources/

satisfaction with the procedures for camp-site allocation. Another example of testing the market, and the willingness of visitors to pay for services, is given in Box 9.8.

9.7 Corporate contributions to protected areas

Corporate funding is becoming more common in protected areas. The motivations behind corporate support for protected areas are several:

- A desire to support, and be seen to be supporting, a worthwhile cause;
- For tourist companies working in a protected area, the need to sustain the basis of their industry;
- The need to access resources in or near the protected area;
- As a kind of compensation for damage done to the protected area (e.g. mining in it, or nearby);
- The need to acquire a greener image for the company or its products; and
- The benefits that protected areas can bring to their staff and customers.

The degree of support that can be expected from the corporate sector will depend on the prevailing traditions of that sector in the country concerned, tax incentives, the wealth at the disposal of business and industry, and often the existence of an enlightened leader within the sector.

Box 9.9   Examples of innovative corporate financing and partnerships

Ecosystem services

- *Annual Payment*: Del Oro S.A., a Costa Rican orange growing corporation, pays Guanacaste Conservation Area (GCA) US$5/hectare/year for water supply and water-shed protection for that part of the catchment area within GCA that also serves as the plantation's water source. The total value of the 20-year contract is US$480,000 (US$24,000/year).

- *Natural Pest Control and Pollination*: Del Oro S.A. also pays GCA a $1/hectare/year for supplying natural pest control services to the orange plantation established adjacent to the conservation area. Again the value of the 20-year contract is US$480,000.

- *Certifiable Tradable Offsets (CTOs)*: Costa Rica has a Greenhouse Gas Fund to promote joint implementation projects under the United Nations Framework Convention on Climate Change. Investors seeking to offset carbon emissions contribute to the fund in exchange for CTOs. The government intends that these CTOs be used as credits against greenhouse gas emissions.

Corporate imaging

- *Corporate sponsorship*: A US bill to amend a National Park act grants the National Park Foundation the authority to licence others to use Foundation trademarks, slogans, etc. to promote or advertise that the individual or company is an official supporter of the National Park Service. This requires that all net income derived from the licences and authorisations be expended on programmes, projects or activities that benefit the National Park Service.

Cont.

> **Box 9.9   Examples of innovative corporate financing and partnerships (cont.)**
>
>   ▓ *Profit sharing*: Grand Teton Alpine Spring Water and Yellowstone Springs Spring Water are owners of a bottled water company that sends profits from natural spring water bottled from west Yellowstone region to two national parks (Grand Teton and Yellowstone). Regional distributors also make a direct contribution to the parks. Payments go to projects, not administration. In 1998, Yellowstone NP received US$1,100 and Grand Tetons US$600.
>
> **Corporate donations**
>
>   ▓ *Corporate Incentives*: Spanish Peaks Brewing Company donated 10¢ for each case of Black Dog Ale sold to Horizon Air, to the Yellowstone Park Foundation, in 1998.
>
> **Scientific research and royalties**
>
>   ▓ Yellowstone National Park made an agreement with Diversa Corporation to share scientific data and royalties from the company's bio-prospecting in the park's geo-thermal pools. Diversa will pay NPS US$100,000 over five years and 0.5%–10% in royalties for any commercial sales of pharmaceuticals it produces. Any revenue gained would be used for research and conservation in Yellowstone.
>
> **Renting equipment**
>
>   ▓ The Ohio State park system offers camping gear such as cooking stoves, tents and cots for rent to its visitors in an effort to increase revenues, attract visitors, and reduce dependence on tax dollars.

Protected area managers should familiarise themselves with the characteristics of the business and industry sector and its potential to help finance the protected area. The scope for innovative partnerships can be considerable as indicated in Box 9.9.

9.8 Managing concessions and contracts within protected areas

9.8.1 Introduction

Park tourism involves the provision of a wide variety of services to visitors. In theory an agency or manager may ensure the provision of a service or facility in several ways:

1. Government ownership and operation;

2. Government ownership and non-profit operation;

3. Private construction, ownership and operation of the facility, (usually on a long lease);

4. Government ownership, with operations normally delivered by the private sector.

Concessions are agreements made between the protected area agency and the operators, and could therefore relate to options 2–4 above. Normally these will be undertaken in the private sector, though concessions can also be let to NGOs and to other not-for-profit enterprises, as well as to community bodies. In every case, the concessionaire provides specified tourism services in the protected area under an agreement. Most agencies require operators to have a licence to operate a business in the park, such as hotel management, or food store operation. The licence may be exclusive, with no other similar licensed operation permitted, or non-exclusive, when other operations are also allowed.

Private sector involvement in protected areas is most commonly related to:

▦ Accommodation	▦ Site maintenance
▦ Tour operations	▦ Camp-site maintenance
▦ Waste collection	▦ Concessions
▦ Transit	▦ Information provision

9.8.2 Whether to use concessions

In deciding whether or not to let out concessions in the first place, the agency will first need to consider the following:

The capacity and legal powers of the protected area agency: Managers themselves may lack skills, economic and organisational resources to manage and develop tourism facilities effectively themselves. However, an agency that has a legal structure comparable to a parastatal or a corporation may be able to operate most facilities itself. For example, the Niagara Parks Commission, Ontario, Canada, operates virtually all the protected area facilities (e.g. stores, restaurants, attractions and financial institutions) that occur on its land (Eagles, 1993). Where there is money to be made, this agency ensures that the profit is used to cover general operating costs.

The strengths of the private sector: There are several reasons why the private sector may be well placed to deliver specialised services and products:

▦ It is more easily able to adapt to changing markets, needs and conditions

▦ It often has more flexibility in labour contracts

▦ It is often freer to innovate and respond quickly

▦ It can more easily raise capital and other funds

▦ It has more freedom in setting price levels

▦ It is not hedged around by the constraints of government policy.

The income foregone: Though concessions can be a powerful revenue-generating tool for protected agencies, all profit made by the concessionaire is potential income foregone by the park agency. An alternative maybe to restructure the park agencies along more business-like lines (see for example the earlier discussion on parastatals).

The suitability of the operation for a concession: The private sector responds promptly when there is the possibility of a profit through offering a service, but it is normally only interested in operations that provide sufficient financial returns. So they may not want to operate during low visitation periods, or to provide services at average prices. The protected area management will therefore need to consider subsidising an unprofitable but essential operation, or running it themselves.

The suitability of non-private sector concessionaires: Concessions can also be let to other groups, such as NGOs. In the case of local communities, this would enable them to derive direct benefit from the economic opportunities created by the existence of the protected area. It may however be necessary for the protected area agency to support the community by helping to build capacity, e.g. by providing training in business skills, in the local community, or to encourage the community to go into partnership with a private sector operator.

9.8.3 Basic considerations in drawing up and letting concessions

The goal of a concession, from the agency's point of view, is to further the goals of the park, to provide access to the heritage resources in a way that is compatible with the legislation, and to provide for certain needs of visitors. Therefore, it is important that the contract detail the services required, their timing and their quality. Concessionaires operate within a special, sensitive natural and cultural environment.

The following are among the more important issues that protected area managers need to take account of in drawing up concessions:

- It is necessary that the staff members be suitably trained for such operation. Company and staff qualifications can be one selection criterion.

- There are many operational details, such as hours of operation, range of services, and level of service, that must be outlined in the contract.

- A fundamental issue is that of pricing policy. In some jurisdictions, it is recognised that the park concession has a monopoly and, therefore, regulation of prices is required. In others, competition is encouraged through the development of multiple concession operators in different locales.

- The arrangements for monitoring are important too, and should be specified in the licence, along with the actions that will follow if the concessionaire fails to meet agreed standards.

The choice of concession companies is a critical element. The choice can become highly political, with scope for political interference or park staff self-serving behaviour.

Craft Shop in Masai Village, Ngorongoro Conservation Area, Tanzania

Park managers can provide opportunities for local people to become involved in park tourism. ©*Paul F. J. Eagles*

Therefore, selection procedures should be fair to all parties, open, transparent and neutral. Wherever possible, competitive tendering procedures should be adopted.

The Madikwe Game Reserve in South Africa (see Box 3.4) is an example of close and successful co-operation between a government protected area agency and private sector tourism operators. It has secured substantial income from tourism, thereby providing jobs and income for local people, and has helped finance a world-class wildlife restoration project (Northwest Parks and Tourism Board, 2000).

9.8.4 Detailed points to be considered in relation to concessions

Concessionaires prefer a longer-length licence period in order to establish the business, earn sufficient return on initial capital expenditures and to earn maximum profits. Park managers often prefer a shorter tenure in order to maintain flexibility. Concessionaires often argue successfully for longer tenures when there are high capital costs associated with the contract. Agencies often consider that shorter timelines increase their ability to maintain controls over service quality and conditions of operation. The length of the contract must be long enough for the company to develop their procedures, explore the market and establish a solid business presence. However, the contract should not be too long, so as to avoid complacency. A term of 5 –10 years is often chosen with annual monitoring and evaluation of the contract performance.

Leasing vs. ownership

Typically, the basic facilities, such as the store or the camp-site, are owned by the protected area, but are leased to the private sector for a period of time, say five years. Sometimes the infrastructure is constructed by the concessionaire, but becomes protected area property after a specified time. The infrastructure may be constructed by the concessionaire, donated to the park upon completion, and then leased back to the concessionaire. Tourism facilities owned by private enterprise under a form of land lease are often disadvantageous to park management, because of the weak ability of the protected area to manage the activities and behaviour of privately-owned facilities in a park.

Rights and responsibilities

The concession or licence contract outlines the rights and responsibilities of each party. Issues covered in the contract include:

1)	Minimum or compulsory trading hours	6)	Infrastructure maintenance responsibilities
2)	Standards for customer service	7)	Signage
3)	Environmental practices	8)	Advertising
4)	Pricing policy	9)	Staff and operations accreditation standards
5)	Public access to facilities	10)	Design of facilities

Box 9.10   Galápagos National Park and Marine Reserve, Ecuador: Example of revenues from boat concession fees

The terrestrial part of the Galápagos Islands National Park became a World Heritage Site in 1979. The park was declared a Biosphere Reserve in 1985. The Galápagos Marine Resources Reserve was created in 1986. It was declared a whale sanctuary in 1990, and in 1998 the Galápagos Marine Reserve was created – the second largest marine reserve in the world. The marine reserve too became part of the World Heritage site in 2001.

High volume tourism began in the Galápagos in 1969 and has been increasing ever since. There were fewer than 5,000 visitors in 1970, but more than 66,000 in 1999, leading to an increase in tourist infrastructure and services, and of the resident population too. Tourism is now mainly on live-aboard boats; since visitors travel largely by boat, and eat and sleep on board, the need for significant tourist infrastructure on outlying islands is greatly reduced (Wallace, 1993). In 1972, there was one ship for overnight passengers, while by 2000 there were 80 ships registered, with a passenger capacity of 1,729.

The Galápagos National Park Service (GNPS) has been managing tourism since the 1970s, and charges an entrance fee for park visitors. Besides this fee, it charges a concession fee to each boat (an operation licence). This fee varies with the category of ship and number of berths.

Annual licence fees for boats per berth (US$)

Type	Category	$ Amount
Cruise	A	250
Cruise	B	200
Cruise	C	150
Day tour	R	250
Day tour	E	50

Source: GNPS Tourism Unit.

Distribution of ships by category

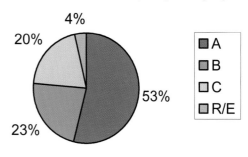

Source: GNPS Tourism Unit.

Ships are classified according to their size, number of berths, and quality of the berths. Category A cruise ships are the most luxurious and C the least. Category R day tour boats are the most luxurious.

Distribution of ships by passenger capacity

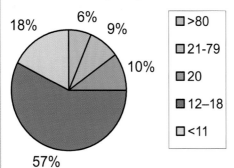

Although the number of ships operating in the Galápagos NP has been reduced from 90 in 1996 to 80 in 2000, the total passenger capacity increased from 1,484 in 1996 to 1,735 in 2000. Concession fees generate about US$400,000, or 8% of the income generated by the park visitor entrance fees.

Source: Benitez, 2001.

Source: GNPS Tourism Unit.

It is important that the financial responsibilities of each partner, the concessionaire and the protected area, are listed in sufficient detail. It is useful to measure performance of the contract at periodic intervals. Penalties for non-compliance must be clearly stated. There must be a procedure outlining the rules for cancellation of the contract due to non-compliance with contract stipulations.

Fees

Typically, the park receives a fee from the concessionaire. This fee can be in many forms. It can be a straight *annual set fee*. It can be a *flat fee* in conjunction with a *royalty* or a percentage of concessionaire gross revenue. It could simply be a *percentage* of all revenue. The fee payable can be gradually increased over times. The fee can be structured to provide *incentives* for the concessionaire to operate at specific times, for example a lower fee in low volume periods. For one example of a fee structure for concessions, see Box 9.10.

Monitoring, incentives and enforcement

Concession management can be a major problem for protected area managers. Concessionaires sometimes ignore contractual requirements, even illegally constructing facilities in the park and operating businesses not allowed in their contract. Their employees may lack training and cause problems, such as theft and environmental damage. It is not uncommon for concessionaires to try to avoid contract rules by going to higher levels of government officials or influential politicians. Private operators may take a very short-sighted view of their interests, and show little desire to support other aspects of park operations, such as providing accurate information, assisting injured visitors or helping in emergency situations. Once a bad operator gets into place, it can be very difficult to terminate the concession. The enforcement of concession contracts and the policing of concessionaires can be very expensive and time-consuming for park managers.

Role of local communities in concessions

Local communities can play a beneficial role in concessions. As already noted, community concessions may be one way of helping to generate income, offset costs of lost access to resources, and thus helping to gain the support of local communities. In addition, local people are often excellent guardians of their resources, since it is *their* livelihoods that are at stake. Local businesses, too, may be used for services (such as certain operation and maintenance services) in a cost-effective manner for the protected area agency. It is also possible to share revenues with the local community, whether derived from concessions or visitor fees. While this is not yet much done in developed countries, it has been quite widely used in parts of Africa for example. It is an important option for protected area management, which can contribute significant funds to the local community.

Concessions: conclusion

Concession management is one of the most important and most time-consuming activities for park managers. Virtually every park agency undertakes such management, but there is a need for more sharing of knowledge and experience in this field. There is a paucity of literature available to help managers in this activity. A concerted effort is needed to analyse the options available, the successes and failure of various approaches, the management skills necessary and the most desirable methods in various circumstances. Such information needs to be made widely available to park managers.

9.9 Summary

This chapter has discussed some of the financial aspects of tourism in protected areas. This discussion reveals the complexity and sophistication of park finance. Clearly protected area agencies require staff members that are specially trained in finance, as well as accounting and marketing. It is generally not desirable for people trained in other areas to transfer into such a field without suitable training. Since so many protected areas and their agencies are becoming more reliant on their income from park tourism, their future depends upon competent financial management.

Note: For a fuller introduction to this topic, the reader is referred to two recent IUCN publications: *Financing Protected Areas: Guidelines for Protected Area Managers* (IUCN, 2000), which is a publication in this series; and *Guidelines for Financing Protected Areas in East Asia* (Athanas *et al.*, 2001).

Lodge in the Village of Monteverde, Costa Rica

Local communities often provide important visitor services, such as for accommodation, food, medical care and transport. ©*Paul F. J. Eagles*

144

10. Human resources planning for tourism in protected areas

10.1 Introduction

This chapter contains a number of general observations about the importance of human resources planning. While these observations are true of the staff of protected areas in general and of all aspects of their work, it is especially relevant to those staff engaged in tourism and recreation management. When tourism is a critical component of park management, it is important for a park and a protected area agency to have staff members who are expert in the field. Therefore, most agencies need to consider the human resources planning needed for this important area.

Human resource management needs to be integrated into existing protected area management plans. Effective human resource management recognises and utilises the human asset of an organisation in order to fulfill short- and long-term goals. In combination with current theories of ecologically based land management, and sustainable sources of income, this will provide an excellent foundation for managing tourism sustainably in protected areas.

10.2 The human asset

All protected area employees and volunteers need to be recognised as its valued ambassadors. They are, possibly, the most important single factor in ensuring the successful management of tourism in protected areas. It is therefore essential that the vital nature of the service that employees provide to visitors be recognised. Front-line workers especially, such as rangers and staff in visitor centres, are the visible public expression of the management philosophy behind the protected area's operation. If the relationship between staff and visitors is positive, the benefits will be many.

In a well-run organisation, management knows about its staff. It should have access to data on its labour force, especially about recruitment and turnover rates, as well as being generally informed about the welfare of its workforce. Good human resource planning and development create a workforce that is more likely to succeed. Therefore protected area authorities that are committed to researching, hiring and developing their personnel by using appropriate human resource development strategies will be better placed to protect the environment, involve local communities and share the conservation message with tourists. If the staff are selected carefully and skilfully trained, protected areas will operate more smoothly and tourists will undoubtedly notice, appreciate and share their appreciation with other potential visitors.

There are general trends in the labour force at large that can be used to improve human resource planning, recruiting and pay. In most countries, statistics on employment participation rates are compiled by national statistics agencies. This index is a measure of the proportion of people eligible for inclusion in the labour force who are actually in it,

---

Box 10.1 Contents of a job analysis

1. Work outcomes – the tasks to be accomplished

2. Work procedures – required job activities

3. Equipment and tools necessary for quality job performance

4. Work environment characteristics

5. Job specifications – the knowledge, skills, attitude and other characteristics necessary for a suitable level of performance

---

and can be used to project labour force availability within different employment sectors. By comparing the participation rate with population demographics, a planner is able to identify which segments of the labour force to target to increase the success of recruitment efforts.

10.3 Job analysis

Each post assigned to a protected area employee should have a specific and detailed job description. The purpose of delineating each work assignment is to ensure job satisfaction for the individual and an efficient and effective organisation overall. This is especially important in protected areas where – in some countries at least – some staff may come into the organisation with strong views as to what their role should be. If false expectations are not dispelled at the hiring stage, disenchantment may follow for staff member and employer.

Job analysis is a commonly used strategy for identifying organisational human needs and is recommended here. It is a systematic process of determining the nature or content of a work assignment through the collection and organisation of relevant information. Managers who plan work assignments in this way can capture and transform the ideals of an organisation into performance specifications for individuals.

The characteristics that are typically analysed in a job analysis are listed in Box 10.1.

Job analyses provide the foundation for most human resource management activities because they are used as reference points for various other functions. Box 10.2 outlines how the job analysis process is used in other human resource management areas.

Box 10.2 Job analysis process

Planning and staffing	**Employee development**	**Employee maintenance**
1. Current and future staffing needs	1. Inform employee about performance standards	1. Determine compensation
2. Recruiting information	2. Training	2. Health and safety
3. Selection criteria	3. Performance appraisal	3. Labour relations – to bargain over job responsibilities
	4. Career planning	

146

Human resource planning must start from the present situation. An understanding of current staffing needs forms a baseline for determining future requirements as changes occur in the management strategy. The information derived from job analyses is the key criterion for recruiting job applicants in a targeted manner. Selecting the ideal applicant should be based upon the measurable criteria determined from the job analysis.

Staff development programmes offer a mutually beneficial strategy for both employer and employee. At the beginning of a work assignment, employees are typically oriented to the organisation by a discussion on work expectations and performance standards. The job analysis should provide the structured framework for such information exchanges. Training seminars are necessary to enhance an employee's performance in specialised areas, such as customer service training or equipment certification. Annual performance appraisals, or employee evaluations, need to be approached in a structured way, using written standards. Employees within an organisation often seek advancement. By clearly communicating the job specifications and desired work outcomes for each position, employees are better placed to measure their own success and plan their own career progression.

Determining an appropriate level of compensation for each position within a protected area can be a difficult task. The information and job criteria provided within the job analysis can aid such decisions by basing compensation rates on the content and qualifications required for each job. This process safeguards equity by standardising pay structures. A job analysis can also be used to identify potential job hazards such as environmental exposure or vulnerable wildlife contact. Managers can then use such information in risk management initiatives by notifying employees of training regimes to minimise such risks. Protected area employers may also find that their responsibilities include dealing with labour union issues. Often these concern job requirements, pay and condition. The existence of a written job analysis and job description will help to facilitate discussions with union representatives.

Although a job analysis can appear to be highly formalised, the benefits that derive from such an organised and practical approach far outweigh the associated costs.

10.4 Recruitment and selection

Recruitment is the process of attracting qualified candidates to apply for vacant positions within an organisation. *Selection* is the final stage of the recruitment process, when decisions are made as to who will be chosen for vacant positions.

Protected areas are mission-driven organisations with management objectives that are often thought to be in conflict. Finding the right people to fit each work assignment is extremely important for an organisation that depends on the skills and attitudes of their staff. But since protected areas need to pursue a special and sensitive combination of goals, the recruitment and selection of the people charged with the delivery of the work of the protected area is particularly important. This applies particularly to those staff who are employed to interface with tourists, since this often calls for a wide range of professional skills and human qualities that are rarely found in combination.

Recruitment always plays an important function in the development of a healthy and motivated staff. It should be thought of as encompassing all the activities which may affect the number or types of individuals applying for a given vacancy. Numerous social and economic factors influence the pool of available talent that might apply. The role of

Park Managers in Kalkalpen National Park, Austria

All park management is ultimately dependent upon dedicated and professional park managers.
©*Paul F. J. Eagles*

recruitment may vary slightly depending on whether the protected area is managed in the private, public or not-for-profit sector, since rather different cultures apply – but in most respects the principles are the same.

The techniques used to recruit and select individuals for various positions differ globally, and the strategies used need to be carefully adapted to, and planned for, the local environment. Examples of culturally specific considerations include reliance upon family-run firms, the traditions of the society in which the protected area is based, and the role and traditions of public sector agencies in the country concerned. Other considerations will be specific to the organisation, such as its size, history, stage of development and geographical location. Many of these factors will need to be considered when planning the right recruitment and selection strategy. It may be useful to conduct a comparative analysis with other related organisations to help choose an appropriate local strategy. It is important, however, never to lose sight of the mission and purpose of the protected area throughout the planning process.

10.5 Human resource development

The purpose of *Human Resource Development* (HRD) is to improve the capacity of the human resource through learning and performance at the individual, process and organisational levels. By applying a well-ordered and professional HRD approach to work in the protected areas field, the skills, knowledge and attitudes of park personnel will be enriched and the overall quality of work performed will improve. The three branches of HRD are training and development, organisational development, and career development.

10.5.1 Training and development

Training is a vital investment in staff. It should be strategically planned in order to provide a meaningful learning experience for new or current employees and volunteers. Training and development should be focused on developing the individual employee's fundamental competencies, so that he or she can perform current and future jobs to the highest standard. Training should result in the development of the knowledge, skills and attitudes of protected area personnel. Training is not only necessary at the beginning of an employment contract, but must accompany the job throughout. Developing employees' skills not only helps to improve performance but it also increases the likelihood that jobs remain interesting and challenging. Training programmes should be designed to cover all aspects of management required in the protected area concerned. However in these guidelines on tourism we emphasise the particular importance of training in:

- visitor and community relations,
- financial planning and business skills,
- environmental education,
- conflict resolution,
- ecological research and monitoring, and
- patrolling and law enforcement.

10.5.2 Organisational development

Organisational development is about improving the energy generated when employees work together. Programmes that contribute to improving the quality of work life, team building and similar objectives produce a loyal and committed employment environment. Again, while the advice given here is general, it is also especially relevant to the challenge of dealing with visitors to protected areas.

10.5.3 Career development

Career development is a facet of human resource development that is focused on individual employees and helps prepare an employee for future positions in the organisation. There are many positive benefits of preparing and developing current employees for advancement within an organisation. The benefits experienced by the employee include job satisfaction, motivation and a desire to contribute and perform well, with direction and purpose. The protected area also benefits from career development, since well-trained staff are more likely to be enthused employees; also the costs of recruitment and selection are reduced.

Career development often involves certification programmes, educational diplomas or degrees, apprenticeships and the use of training courses for continuing professional development. More recently, technology has enabled relatively isolated park employees to improve skills through correspondence programmes and distance learning.

10.6 Performance evaluation

Performance evaluations or *appraisals* provide protected area managers with essential information for making strategic management decisions. The information gained through the collection, analysis and evaluation of employees' performance enables managers to communicate how well staff are doing, and – if necessary – provides the reasons why changes should be made. An effective evaluation system can be used to determine if human resource management is helping to achieve protected area aims. The data collected can also be used to identify current human resource development needs, validate the way that staff are recruited, selected, trained and paid, and generally evaluate the success of human resource programmes.

Since businesses vary, evaluation programmes vary too. Thus each protected area needs to develop a performance evaluation system that reflects its unique values, goals and objectives. The evaluation process enables the employer and employee to assess and discuss performance and, in so doing, facilitates communication. Working together during the evaluation process, managers and employees can develop goals and objectives. This fosters employee motivation and empowerment, and mutual respect between all parties involved.

Surprisingly, few park agencies have effective staff performance evaluation programmes. Even fewer have remuneration schedules that are tied to goal accomplishment, such as the implementation of a management plan. If an agency is serious about implementing its policy, including its management plans, it needs to set up such evaluation-based procedures. Performance evaluation tied to remuneration levels is one way to encourage implementation.

Once all the elements of human resource management are understood and in place, it is important to develop a human resource plan for the protected area system and each individual park.

Art Gallery in Algonquin Provincial Park, Ontario, Canada

Older parks develop their own unique culture. The arts often play an important role in the development of cultural identity for parks and their environments. ©*Paul F. J. Eagles*

11. Monitoring tourism in protected areas

11.1 Why monitor?

Monitoring is an essential component of any planning or management process, for without monitoring, managers know nothing about progress towards the objectives they have been set or have set themselves. Monitoring is the systematic and periodic measurement of key indicators of biophysical and social conditions. The word *systematic* means that an explicit plan should exist to set indicators, chart how and when these should be monitored, and show how the resulting data will be used. *Periodic* means that indicators are measured at predetermined stages. This chapter outlines some considerations involved in developing and implementing a monitoring programme as this relates to tourism in protected areas.

While management experience is an important element of decision-making, the results of systematic monitoring provide a more defensible basis for management actions. Subjective impressions of conditions are not good enough: the public demands to see the data upon which decisions are taken, and to be assured that they were collected in a scientifically reliable manner. Without the data on conditions and trends that monitoring provides, managers cannot respond to many public concerns and criticisms, nor can they properly fulfil their responsibilities, nor judge the effectiveness of actions they take. Moreover, if managers do not undertake the monitoring, someone else will – and such monitoring may well be biased. However, monitoring requires ample funding, trained personnel, access to data and sufficient time to implement programmes. In reality, the resources for monitoring are not always readily available and implementation often falls well short of what is desirable.

There are two particular aspects of monitoring tourism in protected areas:

1 *Monitoring visitor impacts*: Visitors to protected areas have environmental and social impacts. Managers should understand and manage those impacts. Through the appropriate planning process for the park, tourism and related objectives are defined and indicators developed. Through periodic measurement of indicators, data on visitor impacts are collected, analysed and evaluated. Managers should then determine what action is needed to address problems.

2 *Monitoring service quality*: The planning process also determines the kind of experience which it is intended to provide for visitors. Monitoring service quality, therefore, involves collecting, analysing and evaluating information about the fulfilment of the needs of visitors.

11.1.1 What should managers monitor?

Indicators should be identified early on in the planning process. Indicators relate to issues or conditions which are influenced by some action or trend. Monitoring provides managers with essential information about the protection of the values for which the area was established. Indicators need to be selected carefully, because of scarce financial and personnel resources. Also, because the appropriateness of indicators can change over time, their suitability should be reviewed periodically.

Several points should be noted about the use of indicators to monitor tourism in protected areas:

1   They should identify *conditions* or *outputs* of tourism development or protected area management (e.g. the proportion of the park impacted by human activity or annual labour income from tourism) rather than *inputs* (e.g. the money spent on a programme);

2   They should be descriptive rather than evaluative;

3   They should be relatively easy to measure; and

4   Initially only a few key variables should be selected for monitoring.

The Nature Conservancy (TNC) reviewed monitoring methods for protected area programmes in Latin America (Rome, 1999). They found monitoring programmes were most effective when they addressed impacts and threats, and dealt with issues that affected both the full range of stakeholders, and the protected area.

TNC listed the impacts for which indicators should be developed for monitoring purposes as follows:

1   Environmental impacts – on the protected areas and surrounding lands, both physical and biological (usually measured through quantitative methods);

2   Experiential or psychological impacts – on visitors (usually qualitative methods);

3   Economic impacts – on communities and protected areas (usually quantitative methods);

4   Socio-cultural impacts – on communities (usually qualitative methods); and

5   Managerial or infrastructure impacts – on protected areas and surrounding lands.

Box 11.1 Makira, Solomon Islands and Irian Jaya/Papua, Indonesia: Biodiversity Conservation Network (BCN) monitoring of ecotourism activities

The BCN supports biodiversity conservation activities. In these ecotourism projects, environmental indicators were selected as dependent variables, affected by ecotourism as well as other income-generating activities (e.g. nut gathering in the Solomon Islands).

In Makira, Solomon Islands, the indicators were:

1.   Fruit dove frequency measured by a range of surveyors, including tourists and guides, and

2.   Annual socio-economic surveys.

In Irian Jaya/Papua, the indicators of the biological conditions of coral reef include:

1.   Numbers of butterfly fish, live coral, and other fish caught at designated sites, and

2.   Beach trash and a range of socio-economic indicators in the community.

Cont.

> **Box 11.1 Makira, Solomon Islands and Irian Jaya/Papua, Indonesia:**
> **Biodiversity Conservation Network (BCN) monitoring of**
> **ecotourism activities (cont.)**
>
> Measurement programmes in Makira resulted in changed management actions, including seasonal restrictions on pigeon hunting, and bans on pesticides.
>
> Those in Irian Jaya/Papua led to experimental transplanting of coral, and pressure on government agencies to discontinue practices damaging coral reefs.
>
> These examples demonstrate how monitoring stimulated community concern and remedial management activities.
>
> *Source*: Rome, 1999.
> Web site: http://nature.org/aboutus/travel/ecotourism/ resources/

An example of a monitoring programme dealing with ecotourism impacts, which was taken from the TNC study, is shown in Box 11.1.

11.1.2 Where should managers monitor?

Monitoring should be focused on:

1. Areas where problems are most acute, and/or where staff or visitors have indicated concerns. These are likely to include:

  ▪ places where conditions are at the limit, or violate existing standards (e.g. a slight change in camp-site conditions that results in camp-site impacts becoming unacceptable and thus may lead to a closure);

  ▪ places where specific and important values are threatened; and

  ▪ places where conditions are changing rapidly (Cole, 1983).

2. Areas where new management actions are taking place (e.g. if the management plan introduces a wilderness zone, with the aim of reducing visitor numbers or modifying visitor behaviour, managers should consider monitoring in that area to determine how the policy is working);

3. Areas where the effects of management are unknown. For example, while there has been much research on the effects of recreation on soil, vegetation, and camp-site conditions, there has been little research on the effectiveness of rehabilitation techniques, and how recreation variables influence rehabilitation;

4. Areas where information is lacking, and a monitoring programme will provide data on tourism and protected area conditions and trends.

11.1.3 When should monitoring occur?

Frequently asked questions include: "At what season should camp-site impacts be measured"? or "When should trail encounters be measured (on the "average" day, on peak days, on randomly selected days in the season)?". Timing depends on the indicator being monitored. Research on visitor impacts can be used to identify the most appropriate frequency for re-measurement.

By the time that environmental impacts are clearly evident – for example, erosion has taken hold on an over-used trail – management options may be reduced. It then becomes a choice of reducing numbers or limiting visitors' activities (politically difficult, though often necessary), or making the environment more resistant to impacts through hardening (financially difficult to find budgets for infrastructure and maintenance). But if impacts had been measured earlier, and remedial action taken promptly, there would be less impact and lower management costs.

The establishment of a monitoring programme at the outset of project development, and the gathering of baseline information allows for early warning of impending changes, enabling timely management action to take place. It is therefore critically important to develop baseline data on initial conditions. The values placed on all subsequent monitoring data will depend upon the changes observed compared to the baseline data.

11.1.4 Who should monitor?

It might be thought that trained staff would be required for monitoring, and for some specialised aspects of the programme that is true. But other groups can also be involved:

- field staff and rangers;
- the local community;
- local schools and universities;
- specialist tourist programmes that support protected area research, such as Raleigh International and Earthwatch;
- tourism operators; and
- visitors (e.g. visitors to Itala Nature Reserve, KwaZulu/Natal, are issued with observation cards to help locate movements of wildlife).

Box 11.2 summarises a monitoring programme where staff, guards and scientists collaborated.

Box 11.2 A protected area monitoring programme. Noel Kempff Mercardo National Park, Bolivia: A collaboration of efforts

At this national park, an ecotourism site, simple biological monitoring occurs between a Nature Conservancy partner, Fundacion Amigos de la Naturaleza (FAN) and the Bolivian national park system.

What? They monitored megafauna and endangered species for some years. There is no monitoring of cultural and socio-economic impacts because there are no communities in the park.

Who? Park guards and FAN staff are responsible. Nature guides have been involved recently.

How? They use data collection procedures recommended by visiting scientists. The nature guides collect information on bird and animal sightings.

Results? Information collected helped staff to plan and manage more effectively. They now know better when river turtles are nesting, when they hatch, when they are in most demand by locals, when fish are migrating, etc. Also, they have baseline data from which to assess future impacts, particularly if ecotourism should grow more.

Source: Rome, 1999
Web site: http://nature.org/aboutus/travel/ecotourism/resources/

11.2 The characteristics of a monitoring system

Monitoring should be approached in an organised, systematic manner. The following are the ideal characteristics of a monitoring system:

- *Meaningful variables* – the variables measured should provide information that is useful in leading to management change;
- *Accurate results* – the results should reflect actual conditions;
- *Reliable system* – the monitoring should lead to repeatable results, from which reliable conclusions can be drawn;
- *Able to detect change* – the system must be able to detect change resulting from human activity and environmental fluctuations;
- *Affordable* – the monitoring design must consider the ability of the agency to fund and carry out the recommended procedures;
- *Easy to implement* – procedures should be as simple and straightforward as possible; and
- *Appropriate to management capability* – the monitoring protocol must be capable of implementation within the capacity of the protected area management (if it calls for additional resources, this must be made explicit).

TNC has developed **Guidelines** for monitoring programmes, see Box 11.3.

Box 11.3 The Nature Conservancy guidelines for monitoring programmes

1. Monitoring should be incorporated into general planning and management.

2. Monitoring must be grounded in protected area management and community development objectives.

3. The complex causes of impacts must be recognised and analysed.

4. Indicators and methods for measuring them must be selected carefully.

   A number of criteria are recommended for selecting good indicators:

Measurability	Accuracy
Precision	Utility
Consistency	Availability of data
Sensitivity	Cost to collect and analyse
Degree of relationship with actual tourism activity	

5. When selecting standards or acceptable ranges for measuring indicators, several factors must be considered (for biological indicators, it is important to ensure that minimum levels are sufficient to maintain population numbers and genetic diversity; when considering visitor reactions, it is important to realise that visitors generally recognise physical and experiential impacts more accurately than biological ones).

Cont.

> **Box 11.3 The Nature Conservancy guidelines for monitoring programmes (cont.)**
>
> 6. Local stakeholder participation is critical. In developing areas, local communities are demanding increasingly larger roles in the establishment, planning and management of protected areas. Therefore, impact monitoring must go beyond what happens in the protected area itself.
>
> 7. Monitoring methodology and analysis of findings must be user-friendly and minimally demanding in time or budget.
>
> 8. Monitoring results must be carefully analysed to determine appropriate management options.
>
> 9. Monitoring must lead to specific management and awareness-building actions.
>
> *Source*: Rome, 1999.
> Web site: http://nature.org/aboutus/travel/ecotourism/resources/

11.3   Developing a monitoring programme

A formal monitoring plan is needed to give effect to a monitoring programme in a scientific and professionally responsible way. This should be a formal exercise for several reasons. The process of writing a plan requires considerable thought, demands that planners evaluate what the plan is designed to achieve, reveals to others intended actions, and thus encourages professional critique. Also, from time to time protected area managers are re-assigned from one area to another. When this happens, the existence of a formal monitoring plan helps maintain monitoring procedures, an important consideration because the effects of many management actions may not be visible for years.

To be effective, a *monitoring plan* should be developed with these features:

1. *Objectives and rationale* – the goals of the monitoring plan relate directly to the goals outlined in the protected area management plan;

2. *Indicators* – the chosen indicators are those that best indicate the conditions to be monitored;

3. *Monitoring procedures* – the frequency, timing and location of measurement activity, as well as specific instructions on methods used;

4. *Analysis and display of monitoring data* – procedures for data analysis and for the presentation of results; and

5. *Personnel* – explicit indication of responsibility for monitoring, effectively integrating the monitoring task into the overall management of the protected area.

TNC recommends the steps appropriate for developing and implementing a tourism impact monitoring plan (Box 11.4).

Box 11.4 Steps to develop and implement a tourism impact monitoring plan

A) Planning for monitoring

    1)   Formation of a steering committee.

    2)   Holding a community meeting.

B) Developing a monitoring programme

    3)   Identifying impacts and indicators to be monitored.

    4)   Selecting methods of measurement.

    5)   Identifying limits or ranges of acceptable change.

    6)   Developing an operational monitoring plan.

C) Conducting monitoring and applying results

    7)   Training staff, managers and community representatives.

    8)   Carrying out monitoring and examining data.

    9)   Presenting monitoring results.

D) Evaluating and Advancing Monitoring

    10)   Evaluating the monitoring programme and conducting outreach.

Source: Rome, 1999.
Web site: http://nature.org/aboutus/travel/ecotourism/resources/

11.4 Research

Research can provide new knowledge, insight and procedures for tourism management. Ongoing research programmes frequently reveal trends and patterns that are valuable for planning and management. All stakeholders can benefit from research. The benefits are most apparent when protected area management involves tourism providers in research, and when all protected area staff and all private tourism operators are informed of research findings, so that they can use these in their work.

There are several key **Guidelines** to be considered in the stimulation and management of park tourism research:

Consider involving a wide range of researchers: Research may be done by agency or company employees, consultants, university teachers and students. Much valuable research can be obtained for a very low cost through the creation of a supportive and encouraging environment. Harmon (1994) provides additional guidelines to assist park managers in co-ordinating and managing research in protected areas.

Adopt an open attitude to research: It is important that park managers encourage potential research. Some agencies do this by maintaining an inventory of potential research topics that would be of use for park management. To be useful, the inventory should include a title for the research, a description of the topic, a contact name within the agency, possible research sites and information on the availability of funding. Ideally the inventory should be made widely available to potential research partners in hard copy and electronic format.

Set up a research permit process: Many protected area agencies maintain a research permit process in order to screen topics for suitability, to assist with the maintenance of a research record, and to set conditions for the conduct of the research. It is common to request all researchers to provide a copy of their research publications to the protected area. Those who do not fulfil the permit requirements may be penalised, such as having their research privileges denied at a future date.

Give practical help to researchers and institutes: Some park agencies take special steps to encourage directed park research. These can include:

- sharing employment costs for a research leader between a university and a park agency;
- maintaining research facilities and accommodation for researchers;
- maintaining a library of all studies undertaken in the protected area;
- maintaining a database of past research data sets;
- providing transport for researchers within the protected area; and
- generally fostering a positive attitude by park staff towards research and researchers.

Conduct tourism research using protected area staff or consultants: Where this is done, the studies should be made available to the larger research community outside the park and the agency. Many protected areas do a poor job of making their own research findings available to the larger community, yet stakeholders will be interested in research findings. When an agency makes its data available for secondary research by outside researchers, it is considered an act of responsible goodwill, since the data can be mined for secondary analysis.

Involve private sector tourism operators: These are often willing and useful partners in a park tourism research programme, helping to fund the research and provide assistance in its conduct. They may make their own research findings available to the park. Private-public partnerships can be positive vehicles in encouraging tourism research in parks.

Communicate the results of research: This is crucial. In some countries protected area personnel actively encourage research dissemination, through conferences, special lectures and the direct mailing of research findings. It is often useful to compile books of research findings for a park or for a subject area. Research findings should be made available to field staff in a form and language that they understand. Many park interpretive programmes explain park research findings to visitors, which in turn can improve tourism management efforts. For protected areas with specialised ecotourism programmes, it is very important that the private sector operators and their staff are kept informed of the most recent research findings: some managers do this when they hold regular information meetings with their private sector operators.

Stimulate research with awards: Some agencies provide awards to tourism researchers. These encourage and support good research work and stimulate further interest in the field. Ongoing research effort requires constant encouragement and support efforts by senior managers of the protected area agency.

Note: For a fuller introduction to this topic, the reader is referred to a recent IUCN publication in this series: ***Evaluating Effectiveness: A framework for assessing the management of protected areas*** (Hockings *et al.*, 2000).

12. Conclusions

Protected areas normally achieve recognition and enhanced protection when sufficient numbers of people visit them, appreciate them, and take political action to assure their survival. Park tourism is a critical component of protected area establishment and management.

These guidelines provide a conceptual background for understanding park tourism and its management. They provide a theoretical basis for management, and they include practical advice to planners and managers.

Sustainable tourism practice within protected areas is a long-term commitment. But while it is important to think long-term, it is also necessary to set realistic short and mid-term goals. Individuals, businesses and organisations must be aware that benefits are long-term, and should not expect to experience them immediately after sustainable practices are implemented. In practice, only a small portion of benefits will arise quickly; most will depend upon many years of continued effort.

It is important for protected area planners to develop incentive measures that will influence decision-making processes within society. It is necessary to create inducements to incite or motivate government, local people, and international organisations to conserve biological and cultural diversity. All existing legislation and economic policies need to be reviewed in order to identify and promote incentives for the conservation and sustainable use of the resources, and to remove or modify those that threaten biological diversity and cultural integrity.

Protected area managers need to make ongoing efforts to communicate with all stakeholders. Only with the broad support of the community will management be successful in the long term. These guidelines suggest that national and international organisations need to encourage governments to make improvements in the following critical areas:

1. Support for effective legislation, with adequate resources for implementation;

2. Creation of national policies on protected areas and the management of tourism (as well as education about the environment and conservation); and

3. Development of a management plan for each protected area, covering all activities, including tourism, to ensure that objectives are achieved and resources are well-used.

At present, the cash flow from tourism often returns largely to urban areas, well away from the protected areas themselves. It is always advantageous to invest and assign some tourism revenue to local communities, so that local people see direct financial benefits from park tourism. Planners and managers should therefore be active in stimulating maximum local economic benefit.

Appendix A
Definitions of tourism

It is important for measurement, statistics and reporting that standardized definitions of tourism be used. This appendix contains the World Tourism Organization definitions for tourism.

Tourist: a person travelling to and staying in places outside his or her usual environment for not more than one consecutive year for leisure, business, and other purposes.

Tourism: the activities of persons travelling to and staying in places outside their usual environment for not more than one consecutive year for leisure, business, and other purposes.

Domestic tourism: involving residents of the given country travelling only within this country.

Inbound tourism: involving non-residents travelling in the given country. It is often useful to classify visitors by country of residence, rather than by nationality.

Nationality: the government issuing the passport (or other identification document), even if the person normally resides in another country.

Outbound tourism: involving residents travelling in another country.

Internal tourism: comprises domestic and inbound tourism.

National tourism: comprises domestic tourism and outbound tourism.

International tourism: consists of inbound and outbound tourism.

International visitor: any person who travels to a country other than that in which he has his usual residence but outside his usual environment for a period not exceeding 12 months and whose main purpose of visit is other than the exercise of an activity remunerated from within the country visited.

Domestic visitors: any person who resides in a country, who travels to a place within the country, outside his usual environment for a period not exceeding 12 months, and whose main purpose of visit is other than the exercise of an activity remunerated from within the place visited.

Overnight visitors: visitors who stay at least one night in collective or private accommodation in the place visited.

This definition includes cruise passengers who arrive in a country on a cruise ship and return to the ship each night to sleep on board, even though the ship remains in port for several days. Also included in this group are owners or passengers of yachts and passengers on a group tour accommodated in a train.

Sameday visitors: visitors who do not spend the night in collective or private accommodation in the place visited.

Tourism expenditure: the total consumption expenditure made by a visitor or on behalf of a visitor for and during his trip and stay at a destination.

Appendix B
Park tourism definitions

For the measurement and reporting of park tourism it is important that standardized approaches and terminology be used. This appendix contains the definitions of the World Commission on Protected Areas (Hornback and Eagles, 1999).

Visit: a measurement unit involving a person going onto the lands and waters of a park or protected area for the purposes mandated for the area.

Each visitor who enters a park for the purpose mandated for the area creates a visit statistic. Typically, the visit statistic has no length of stay data associated with it. However, the collection of additional data on the length of stay of a visit allows for the calculation of visit-hour and visit-day figures.

Visitation: the sum of visits during a time period.

Visitation is usually expressed as the summation of use for periods, such as daily, monthly, quarterly, or annually.

Visitor: a person who visits the land and waters of a park or protected area for purposes mandated for the area. A visitor is not paid to be in the park and does not live permanently in the park.

Typically, the mandated purpose for the visit is outdoor recreation for natural parks and cultural appreciation for historic sites.

Entrant: a person going onto lands and waters of a park or protected area for any purpose.

The entry figure for a park is typically larger than the visitor figure. The entry figure includes data for all recreational or cultural visits as well as data for people who are in the park for activities not related to the purposes mandated for the area. For example, the entry figure may include park visitors, plus those just driving through, local people who may pass through a corner of the park, or the daily activities of park workers. These non-visitors are usually not there for recreational or cultural purposes, but their use of park resources, such as roads, do have an impact and, therefore, their activities are worthy of note.

Ecotourists: Individuals who travel to relatively undisturbed or uncontaminated natural areas with the specific objective of studying, admiring, and enjoying the scenery and its wild plants and animals, as well as any existing cultural manifestations. (Ceballos Lascurain, 1996).

Wilderness travellers: Those who travel to areas where management objectives feature protection of the natural processes that have shaped the physical-biological character of the setting. Mechanized access is prohibited or greatly restricted, as are resource exploitation activities. Recreation is a legitimate use, yet subordinated to the goal of environmental preservation (Eagles, 1995).

Adventure tourists: Travellers who participate in strenuous, outdoor vacation travel, typically to remote places renowned for their natural beauty and physical attributes, involving hazardous activities (Eagles, 1995).

Car campers: Travellers who travel for social motives, with both friends and family, in both urban and wild settings. While the primary focus is social gratification within a natural setting, learning, instruction, levels of solitude, and interests and activities are other focal points (Eagles, 1995).

Cultural heritage contains:

> **Monuments:** architectural works, works of monumental sculpture and painting, elements or structures of an archaeological nature, inscriptions, cave dwellings, and combinations of features, which are of outstanding universal value from the point of view of history, art, or science;

> **Groups of buildings:** groups of separate or connected buildings, which because of their architecture, their homogeneity or their place in the landscape, are of outstanding universal value from the point of history, art, or science;

> **Sites:** works of man or the combined works of nature and man, and areas including archaeological sites which are of outstanding universal value from the point of history, art, or science.

Cultural tourist: Travellers who immerse themselves in the natural history, human history, the arts and philosophy, and the institutions of another region or country.

Heritage tourist: Travellers who visit from outside the host community, motivated wholly or in part by interest in the historical or lifestyle/heritage offerings of a community, region, group, or institution.

Appendix C

Operational policies for tourism for the National Park Service of the United States of America

The 1995 White House Conference on Travel and Tourism established a basis and framework for closer co-operation and mutual understanding between land-managing agencies and the tourism industry. Regional and state tourism conferences have brought park managers and tourism operators together. This dialogue has fostered many of the principles incorporated in the following operational policies:

It is National Park Service policy to:

4.1 Develop and maintain a constructive dialogue and outreach effort with state tourism and travel offices, and other public and private organizations and businesses, using a variety of strategies, including but not limited to memberships in organizations, participation in conferences and symposia, and internet-based information resources.

4.2 Collaborate with industry professionals to promote sustainable and informed tourism that incorporates socio-cultural, economic, and ecological concerns, and supports long-term preservation of park resources and quality visitor experiences. This collaboration will be used as an opportunity to encourage and showcase environmental leadership by the Service and by the tourism industry, including park concessionaires.

4.3 Encourage practices that highlight America's diversity and welcome park visitation by people of all cultural and ethnic backgrounds, ages, physical abilities, and economic and educational means.

4.4 Foster good relationships with park neighbours by promoting visitor and industry understanding of, and sensitivity toward, local cultures, customs, and concerns.

4.5 Provide cost-effective park visitor orientation and information services to visitors in parks and, as funding and partnerships allow, at the visit planning stage, at park gateway communities, and at appropriate threshold locations within park units. As part of this effort, the Service will work to ensure that all who provide information to visitors are well informed and provide accurate information about park activities and resources, including current conditions and seasonal variations.

4.6 Pursue practices, such as the use of universal design and the inclusion of metric measures on signs and printed media, that will contribute to the safety and friendly accommodation of all visitors.

4.7 Encourage visitor use of lesser-known parks and under-utilized areas; use during non-peak seasons, days of the week, and times of the day; and visitation to related sites beyond park boundaries, as appropriate, to enhance overall visitor experiences and protection of resources.

4.8   Specifically address long term tourism-related trends and issues, and their implications for park plans and management decisions.

4.9   Represent park needs and realities during the preparation of plans and proposals for gateway community services and park tour operations that could impact park visitation, resources, visitor services, and infrastructure support.

4.10   Promote positive and effective working relationships between park concessionaires and others in the tourism industry to ensure a high quality of service to park visitors.

4.11   Identify desired resource conditions and visitor experiences, and work to establish supportable, science-based park carrying capacities, as the basis for communicating acceptable levels and types of visitor use, recreation equipment use, tours, and services. Carrying capacities are defined for each park as an outcome of the National Park Service planning process.

4.12   Participate in and monitor travel industry research, data gathering, and marketing initiatives to ensure that the Service is fully informed of demographic changes and visitor trends.

4.13   Work with partners to provide timely, accurate, and effective park information, and to ensure that realistic situations and safe, resource-sensitive recreational practices are depicted in promotional materials and advertising. This includes providing appropriate information as early as possible to the tourism industry regarding changes in operations and fees.

4.14   When feasible, and consistent with park resource protection and budgetary needs, schedule construction, repairs, and resource management practices, such as prescribed burns, in ways and at times which keep key visitor attractions and services accessible for public use during peak visitation periods. This will help to minimise adverse impacts on visitors, as well as on park-visitor-dependent businesses.

4.15   Establish and maintain lines of communication and protocols to handle the impact of park emergencies and temporary closures so that state tourism offices and the public, including tourism communities and tourism-related businesses, have the best and most current information on when park services will be restored.

4.16   Inform visitors, state tourism offices, gateway communities and tourism-related businesses about current conditions of key park resources and current protection and recovery/restoration measures. Establish a common understanding on what is needed to ensure adequate protection of those resources for present and future enjoyment and how this can contribute to sustainable park-related businesses and economies.

4.17   Develop new partnerships to help implement Service-wide priorities, and seek partnership opportunities with the industry to fund products and programmes mutually beneficial to accomplish National Park Service mission goals.

Director's Order #17: National Park Service Tourism
Approved: Robert Stanton. Director, National Park Service
Effective Date: September 28, 1999
Sunset Date: September 28, 2003

Appendix D
A comparison of five visitor management frameworks[1]

As noted in Section 6.3.1, several visitor management frameworks have been developed. This appendix gives further information on the following:

- Limits of Acceptable Change (LAC)
- Visitor Impact Management (VIM)
- Visitor Experience and Resource Protection (VERP)
- Visitor Activity Management Process (VAMP)
- The Recreation Opportunity Spectrum (ROS)

Limits of Acceptable Change (LAC – see also Table 6.3)

Developed by researchers working for the U.S. Forest Service in response to concerns about the management of recreation impacts. The process identifies appropriate and acceptable resource and social conditions and the actions needed to protect or achieve those conditions.

Steps of the process: A nine-step process, normally illustrated as a circle of steps:

1. Identify area concerns and issues.

2. Define and describe opportunity classes (based on the concept of ROS).

3. Select indicators of resource and social conditions.

4. Inventory existing resource and social conditions.

5. Specify standards for resource and social indicators for each opportunity class.

6. Identify alternative opportunity class allocations.

7. Identify management actions for each alternative.

8. Evaluate and select preferred alternatives.

9. Implement actions and monitor conditions.

Applications best suited for: The process is a good vehicle for deciding the most appropriate and acceptable resource and social conditions in wilderness areas. It has been applied to wild and scenic rivers, historic sites and tourism development areas.

Relationships: The process incorporates opportunity classes based on concepts of ROS and a means of analysis and synthesis. It is built into the USNPS VERP framework.

---

[1] Adapted with permission from Nilsen and Tayler, 1998.

Strengths: The final product is a strategic and tactical plan for the area based on defined limits of acceptable change for each opportunity class, with indicators of change that can be used to monitor ecological and social conditions.

Weaknesses: The process focuses on issues and concerns that guide subsequent data collection and analysis. Strategic and tactical direction may not be provided on management topics where there are no current issues or concerns.

Process for Visitor Impact Management (VIM)

Developed by researchers working for the USNPS and Conservation Association, and for use by the USNPS. The process addresses three basic issues relating to impact: problem conditions; potential causal factors; and potential management strategies.

Steps of the process:

1. Conduct pre-assessment database review.

2. Review management objectives.

3. Select key indicators.

4. Select standards for key impact indicators.

5. Compare standards and existing conditions.

6. Identify probable causes of impacts.

7. Identify management strategies.

8. Implement.

Standards are established for each indicator based on the management objectives that specify acceptable limits or appropriate levels for the impact.

Applications best suited for: This is a flexible process parallel to LAC that can be applied in a wide variety of settings. It employs a similar methodology to assess and identify existing impacts and particularly the causes.

Relationships: Like LAC, this process has been incorporated into the VERP system (see below).

Strengths: Process provides for a balanced use of scientific and judgmental considerations. It places heavy emphasis on understanding causal factors to identify management strategies. The process also provides a classification of management strategies and a matrix for evaluating them.

Weaknesses: The process does not make use of ROS, although it could. It is written to address current conditions of impact, rather than to assess potential impacts.

Visitor Experience Resource Protection (VERP)

Created by the USNPS. It is a new process dealing with carrying capacity in terms of the quality of the resources and the quality of the visitor experience. It contains a prescription for desired future resource and social conditions, defining what levels of use are appropriate, where, when and why.

Steps of the process:

1. Assemble an interdisciplinary project team.

2. Develop a public involvement strategy.

3. Develop statements of park purpose, significance and primary interpretive themes; identify planning mandates and constraints.

4. Analyse park resources and existing visitor use.

5. Describe a potential range of visitor experiences and resource conditions (potential prescriptive zones).

6. Allocate the potential zones to specific locations within the park (prescriptive management zoning).

7. Select indicators and specify standards for each zone; develop a monitoring plan.

8. Monitor resource and social indicators.

9. Take management actions.

Factors, indicators and standards: The following **factors** are considered in the planning process:

- park purpose statements
- statements of park significance
- primary interpretation themes
- resource values, constraints and sensitivities
- visitor experience opportunities
- resource attributes for visitor use
- management zones

Resource and social indicators, as well as associated standards, were developed for each zone at Arches National Park, where the process was first tested.

Applications best suited for: The VERP framework was conceived and designed to be part of the USNPS's general management planning process. This analytical, iterative process attempts to bring both management planning and operational planning together as one exercise. The emphasis is on strategic decisions pertaining to carrying capacity based on quality resource values and quality visitor experiences. The product is a series of prescriptive management zones defining desired future conditions with indicators and standards.

Relationships: This process refers specifically to both LAC and VIM. No mention is made of ROS or VAMP. VERP parallels the basic processes of VAMP and ROS, and is seen as a component of LAC (see Table 6.3).

Strengths: Like VAMP, VERP is a thought process that draws on the talents of a team and is guided by policy and the park purpose statement. It guides resource analysis through the use of statements of significance and sensitivity, and visitor opportunity analysis is guided by statements defining important elements of the visitor experience. Zoning is the focus for management.

Weaknesses: Additional work is required to pilot the approach in different environments. "Experience" is not defined and the indicators for it are absent beyond the examples for Arches National Park. The will and ability to monitor sufficiently to provide information to guide management actions must also be tested.

Management Process for Visitor Activities (VAMP)

Created by Parks Canada as a companion process to the Natural Resources Management Process within the Parks Canada Management Planning System. The process provides guidance for planning and management of new parks, developing parks and established parks.

Steps of the process: The process uses a model based on a hierarchy of decisions within the management programme. Management plan decisions relate to the selection and creation of opportunities for visitors to experience the park's heritage settings through appropriate educational and recreational activities. Decisions about managing and delivering support services for each activity are reflected in the service plan. The basic principles of VAMP are within three Parks Canada documents:

- Guiding Principles and Operational Policies;
- Management Planning Manual; and
- Visitor Activity Concept Manual.

General steps of the management plan process are:

1. Produce a project terms of reference.

2. Confirm existing park purpose and objectives statements.

3. Organize a database describing park ecosystems and settings, potential visitor educational and recreational opportunities, existing visitor activities and services, and the regional context.

4. Analyse the existing situation to identify heritage themes, resource capability and suitability, appropriate visitor activities, the park's role in the region and the role of the private sector.

5. Produce alternative visitor activity concepts for these settings, experiences to be supported, visitor market segments, levels of service guidelines, and roles of the region and the private sector.

6. Create a park management plan, including the park's purpose and role, management objectives and guidelines, regional relationships, and the role of the private sector.

7. Implementation – set priorities for park conservation and park service planning.

Factors, indicators and standards: *Factors* that are considered in developing indicators and standards include:

- visitor activity profiles
- kind
- quantity, diversity, location
- experiences/benefits sought
- support services and facilities required at all stages of trip cycle

- stakeholder profiles
- interpretation theme presentation
- resource values, constraints and sensitivities
- existing legislation, policy, management direction, plans
- current offer of services and facilities at all stages of trip cycle
- regional activity/service offer
- satisfaction with service offer

Applications best suited for: The detailed process is specific to the planning programme of Parks Canada and is paralleled by the Natural Resources Management Process. The basic VAMP concept incorporates the principles of ROS. The framework will benefit from and can easily incorporate the principles of VIM, LAC and VERP. The focus is assessment of opportunity, while the more precise impact question is left to the Natural Resources Management Process.

Relationships: The overall process provides a comprehensive framework for the creation and management of opportunities for visitors within the Parks Canada Management Planning Program.

Strengths: Comprehensive decision-making process based on a hierarchy. It benefits from the structured thinking required to analyse both opportunity and impact. It combines social science principles with those of marketing to focus on visitor opportunities.

Weaknesses: Although well-developed at the service planning level, VAMP does not yet have the clout it should have at the management planning level, mainly because the "opportunities for experience" definition has not been built into management plans or into the zoning.

Recreation Opportunity Spectrum (ROS)

Developed by researchers working for the U.S. Forest Service and Bureau of Land Management in response to concerns about growing recreational demands and increasing conflict over use of scarce resources, and a series of legislative directives that called for an integrated and comprehensive approach to natural resource planning. The process comprises six land classes to aid in understanding physical, biological, social and managerial relationships, and to set parameters and guidelines for management of recreation opportunities.

Steps of the process:

1. Inventory and map the three perspectives that affect the experience of the visitor, namely the physical, social and managerial components.

2. Complete analysis:

   a) identify setting inconsistencies;

   b) define recreation opportunity classes;

   c) integrate with forest management activities; and

   d) identify conflicts and recommend mitigation.

3. Schedule.

4. Design.

5. Execute projects.

6. Monitor.

The end product is a definition of the opportunity for experience expected in each setting (six land classes—primitive to urban), the indicators of the experience, and the parameters and guidelines for management.

Factors, indicators and standards: Seven *setting indicators* have been identified. They represent aspects of recreation settings that facilitate a range of experiences that can be influenced by managers:

1. Access

2. Remoteness

3. Visual characteristics

4. Site management

5. Visitor management

6. Social encounters

7. Visitor impacts

Criteria have been developed by the U.S. Forest Service for each of the indicators and for each of the six land classes; for example, distance guidelines, remoteness, user density in terms of capacity and frequency of contact, and degree of managerial oversight required.

Applications best suited for: This process can be employed in almost all landscape planning exercises. However, the nature of the spectrum, the indicators and their criteria depend on the purpose of the area, the mandate of the organization and the responsibilities of management.

Relationships: This management matrix approach has been incorporated into the LAC system (see above and Table 6.3), and can be used with VIM (see above). It has been recognised within VAMP (ditto), but is hindered by the current use of zoning in Parks Canada.

Strengths: It is a practical process with principles that force managers to rationalise management from three perspectives:

- protection of the resource;
- opportunities for public use; and
- the organization's ability to meet preset conditions.

It links supply with demand and can be readily integrated with other processes. It ensures that a range of recreation opportunities are provided to the public.

Weaknesses: The recreation opportunity spectrum, its setting indicators and their criteria must be accepted in total by managers before any options or decisions can be made. Disagreement will affect the rest of the planning programme. ROS maps need to be related to the physical and biophysical characteristics of each area.

Appendix E
European Charter for Sustainable Tourism in Protected Areas

The importance of Europe's protected areas as destinations for tourism underlined the need for sound management. One way to promote sound management is to establish a model of good practice and identify and acknowledge areas that follow it. The European Charter for Sustainable Tourism in Protected Areas was developed with the support of the European Commission and the EUROPARC Federation by the Parcs naturels régionaux de France. A parallel initiative of the Worldwide Fund for Nature, the Pan Parks programme (Box 7.4) focuses on larger parks that follow similar principles but are able to offer a particular wilderness experience. These two programmes are recognised by the European Commission as providing a basis for extending good practice throughout the whole of its *Natura 2000* protected area network.

The European Charter was developed over five years, initially using information from 10 pilot parks and input from an advisory group of 25 sustainable tourism experts and representatives of tourism operators. The Charter is about recognising parks that have set up the right structures and processes for the development and management of sustainable tourism, accepting that there will be wide differences in the actual experience offered by individual parks. A central requirement is that each park should have a sustainable tourism strategy and action plan elaborated in close consultation with local stakeholders representing tourism, conservation and local community interests.

The first round of applications in 2001 led to seven parks being recognised under the Charter. An ongoing programme to promote further applications is being developed. Each applicant park is asked to agree formally to the principles and to submit a report on the actions taken to address these. This report is assessed by an external verifier, appointed by EUROPARC, who visits the protected area and holds interviews with relevant stakeholders and with the park management.

Some issues and lessons arising from developing the Charter include:

■ *The need to make the process relevant to, and valued by, protected areas themselves*
A problem facing any process of accreditation of this kind is how to sustain it over time. Ideally, there needs to be support and funding from external agencies such as the European Union. However, there also needs to be commitment by the actual bodies affected, in this case the protected areas themselves. They must see the value of accreditation; otherwise it is not worth undertaking and will remain largely an academic exercise that will eventually wither.

■ *The importance of clarity and simplicity.*
With hindsight, the development phase was too long. Protected area requirements and materials concerning the Charter were too complicated. Protected area managers, including some in the pilot parks, were reluctant to use them. The message and the medium had to be simplified and clarified.

■ *The value of benchmarking actions amongst parks*
The Charter provides a very useful way for each park to measure its actions against agreed good practice. Verifiers report to the protected areas themselves as well as to an evaluation committee. This process can also help directly in raising management standards. In all cases where protected areas have been recognised under the Charter, this has been subject to compliance with recommendations for addressing certain identified weaknesses.

■ *The value of an external stimulus in raising local interest*
One of the Charter's greatest benefits has been its role in providing an incentive for bringing local interests together. For example, in the Spanish park Zona Volcanica de la Garrotxa, a well-established network of tourism sector groups has been considerably strengthened by working together towards the goal of Charter recognition. Publicity surrounding accreditation can also be used locally to raise the profile of sustainable tourism and the role of the park.

EUROPEAN CHARTER FOR SUSTAINABLE TOURISM IN PROTECTED AREAS

Basic aims and requirements

Underlying aims

1. To recognise Europe's protected areas as a fundamental part of our heritage, which should be preserved for (and enjoyed by) current and future generations.

2. To develop and manage tourism in protected areas in a sustainable way, taking account of the needs of the environment, local residents, local businesses and visitors.

Working in partnership

3. To involve all those directly implicated by tourism in its development and management, in and around the protected area.

Preparing and implementing a strategy

4. To prepare and implement a sustainable tourism strategy and action plan for the protected area.

Addressing key issues

5. To provide all visitors with a high quality experience in all aspects of their visit.

6. To encourage specific tourism products which enable discovery and understanding of the area.

7. To communicate effectively to visitors about the area's special qualities.

8. To increase knowledge of the protected area and sustainability issues among all those involved in tourism.

9. To ensure that tourism supports and does not reduce the quality of life of local residents.

10. To protect and enhance the area's natural and cultural heritage, for and through tourism.

11. To increase benefits from tourism to the local economy.

12. To monitor and influence visitor flows to reduce negative impact.

The above aims and requirements form the framework for the Charter. Under issues 3 to 12, there is a list of required actions against which adherence to the Charter can be checked.

Web site: www.parcs-naturels-regionaux.tm.fr

References

Alkire, C. (2000). Funding Strategies for Wilderness Management. In McCool, S. F., Cole, D. N., Borrie, W. T. and O'Loughlin, J. (compilers) *Wilderness Science In A Time Of Change* Conference, Missoula, Montana, May 23–27, 1999. Proceedings. USDA, Forest Service, Ogden, UT, USA. [Online]
Available: www.wilderness.net/pubs/science1999/index.htm [2002, January 14]

Ashley C., Roe D. and Goodwin H. (2001). *Pro-Poor Tourism Strategies: Making Tourism Work for the Poor.* Overseas Development Institute, International Institute for Environment and Development, and Centre for Responsible Tourism, London, UK.

Ashor, J.L. and McCool, S. F. (1984). Politics and rivers: Creating effective citizen involvement in management decisions. *Proceedings of the National River Recreation Symposium.* College of Design, Louisiana State University, Baton Rouge, LA, USA.

Athanas, A., Vorhies, F., Ghersi, F., Shadie, P. and Sheppard, D. (2001). *Financing Protected Areas in East Asia.* IUCN, Gland, Switzerland and Cambridge, UK.

Australian and New Zealand Environment and Conservation Council (ANZECC). (2000). "Benchmarking and Best Practice Program: User-Pays Revenue". Report of the ANZECC Working Group on National Parks and Protected Area management. [Homepage of Environment Australia] [Online] Available: www.ea.gov.au/parks/ [2002, January 14]

Australian and New Zealand Environment and Conservation Council (ANZECC). (2001). "Visitor Risk Management and Public Liability". [Homepage of ANZECC Working Group on National Parks and Protected Area Management] [On-line] Available: www.ea.gov.au/parks/anzecc/reports/risk-management/index.html [2002, January 15]

Baez, A.L. (2001) "Costa Rica Como Destino Turistico". Unpublished Conference Paper, Rio De Janeiro, Brazil.

Baez, A.L. and Fernandez, L. (1992). "Ecotourism as an Economic Activity: The Case of Tortuguero in Costa Rica". Unpublished paper presented at the First World Congress of Tourism and the Environment, Belize.

Bell-Edwards, N. (1999). Making a commitment to HRD: a challenge for protected area authorities. In F. Analoui (Ed.), *Effective human resource development: A challenge for developing countries* (pp.167–192). Ashgate Publishing Ltd, Brookfield, VT, USA.

Beltran, J. (2000). *Indigenous and Traditional Peoples and Protected Areas: Principles, Guidelines and Case Studies.* IUCN, Gland, Switzerland and Cambridge, UK.

Benimadhu, P. (1995). *Adding value: The role of the human resource function.* The Conference Board of Canada, Ottawa, ON, Canada.

Benitez, P. S. (2001). *Visitor Use Fees and Concession Systems in Protected Areas: Galápagos National Park Case Study.* The Nature Conservancy Report Series Number 3. [Homepage of the Nature Conservancy] [Online]
Available: nature.org/aboutus/travel/ecotourism/ resources/ [2002, January 14]

Biosis Research. (1997). "Best Practice in Performance Reporting in Natural Resource Management". Prepared for ANZECC Working Group on National Parks and Protected Area Management – Benchmarking and Best Practice Program. [Homepage of Environment Australia] [Online] Available: www.ea.gov.au/parks/ [2002, January 14]

Bosselman, F.P., Peterson, C.A. and McCarthy, C. (1999). *Managing Tourism Growth: Issues and Applications.* Island Press, Washington, DC, USA.

Brown, C.R. (2001). "Visitor Use Fees in Protected Area: Synthesis of the North American, Costa Rican and Belizean Experience". The Nature Conservancy Report Series Number 2. [Homepage of the Nature Conservancy] [Online] Available: nature.org/aboutus/travel/ecotourism/resources/ [2002, January 14]

Buckley, R. and Pannell, J. (1990). Environmental impacts of tourism and recreation in national parks and conservation reserves. *Journal of Tourism Studies* **1(1)**: 24–32.

Buckley, R. and Sommer, M.. (2001). *Tourism and Protected Areas: Partnerships in Principle and Practice.* CRC for Sustainable Tourism Pty Ltd. and Tourism Council Australia, Sydney, Australia.

Byers, B. A. (nd). *Understanding and Influencing Behaviours in Conservation and Natural Resources Management.* Africa Biodiversity Series, No. 4. Biodiversity Support Program. World Wildlife Fund, The Nature Conservancy, and World Resources Institute, USA.

Ceballos-Lascurain, H. (1996). *Tourism, Ecotourism and Protected Areas.* IUCN, Gland, Switzerland and Cambridge, UK.

Center for Strategic and International Studies. (2002). Global Aging Initiative. [Homepage of CSIS] [Online] Available: www.csis.org/gai. [2002, April 11]

Christiansen, G. and Conner, N. (1999). *The contribution of Montague Island Nature Reserve to regional economic development.* New South Wales National Parks and Wildlife Service, Hurstville, NSW, Australia.

Church, P. and Brandon, K. (1995). *Strategic Approaches to Stemming the Loss of Biological Diversity. Center for Development Information and Evaluation*, US Agency for International Development, Washington, DC, USA.

Cole, David N. (1983). Monitoring the condition of wilderness campsites. Research Paper INT-304. 10pp. USDA Forest Service, Intermountain Forest and Range Exper. Station, Ogden, UT, USA.

Cole, D. N. (1987). Research on soil and vegetation in wilderness: A state-of-knowledge review. *Proceedings of the National Wilderness Research Conference: Issues, State-of-Knowledge, Future Directions, USA*, pp.135–177.

Cole, D. N., Petersen, M. E., and Lucas, R. C. (1987). Managing wilderness recreation use: common problems and potential solutions. Gen. Tech. Rep. INT-GTR-230. USDA Forest Service, Intermountain Research Station, Ogden, UT, USA.

Davey, A. (1998). *National System Planning for Protected Areas.* IUCN, Gland, Switzerland and Cambridge, UK.

DFID (UK Department for International Development). (1998). *Changing the Nature of Tourism.* DFID, London, UK.

Dixon, J. and Sherman, P. (1990). *Economics of protected areas: A new look at benefits and costs.* Island Press, Washington, DC, USA.

Dowling, R.K. (1993). Tourism Planning, People and the Environment in Western Australia. *Journal of Travel Research* **31(4)**: 52–58.

Driml, S. and Common, M. (1995). Economic and Financial Benefits of Tourism in Major Protected Areas. *Australian Journal of Environmental Management* **2(2)**: 19–39.

Driver, B. L. (1990). The Recreation Opportunity Spectrum: Basic Concepts and Use in Land Management Planning. *Proceedings of a North American Workshop on Visitor Management: Perspectives of Several Canadian and United States Park, Protected Area and Natural Resource Management Agencies: Towards Serving Visitors and Managing Our Resources* (pp.159–183). Tourism Research and Education Centre, University of Waterloo, Waterloo, ON, Canada.

Eagles, P. F. J. (1993). Parks Legislation in Canada. Pages 57–74 in P. Dearden and R. Rollins, *Parks and Protected Areas in Canada: Planning and Management.* Oxford University Press, Toronto, ON, Canada.

Eagles, P. F. J. (1995). Understanding the Market for Sustainable Tourism. Pages 25–33 in S. F. McCool and A. E. Watson (Compilers), *Linking tourism, the environment and sustainability.* Proceedings of a special session of the annual meeting of the National Recreation and Parks Association; 1994 October 12–14; Minneapolis, MN, Gen. Tech. Rep. INT-GTR-323. U. S. Department of Agriculture, Forest Service, Intermountain Research Station, Ogden, UT, USA.

Eagles, P. F. J. (1998). International Ecotourism Management: Using Australia and Africa as Case Studies. Albany, WA, Australia: Paper presented at Protected Areas in the 21st Century: From Islands to Networks, World Commission on Protected Areas.

Eagles, P. F. J. (2001) Nature-based Tourism Management. Pages 181–232 in G. Wall (Ed.), *Contemporary Perspectives on Tourism*, Occasional Paper Number 17. Department of Geography Publication Series, University of Waterloo, Waterloo, Ontario, Canada.

Eagles, P. F. J. and Higgins, B. R. (1998). Ecotourism Market and Industry Structure. Pages 11–43 in Kreg Lindberg, Megan Epler-Wood and David Engeldrum (Eds.), *Ecotourism: A Guide for Planners and Managers*, 2nd ed. The Ecotourism Society, North Bennington, VE, USA.

Eagles, P. F. J. and Martens, J. (1997). Wilderness Tourism and Forestry: The Possible Dream in Algonquin Provincial Park. *Journal of Applied Recreation Research* **22(1)**: 79–97.

Eagles, P., McLean, D. and Stabler, M. (2000). Estimating the Tourism Volume and Value in Parks and Protected Areas in Canada and the USA. *George Wright Forum* **17(3)**: 62–76.

Eagles, P. F. J., Bowman, M. E., and Chang-Hung Tao, T. (2001). *Guidelines for Tourism in Parks and Protected Areas of East Asia.* IUCN, Gland, Switzerland and Cambridge, UK in collaboration with University of Waterloo, Waterloo, ON, Canada.

Falkenberg, L., Meltz, N. and Stone, T. (1999). *Human resource management in Canada.* Harcourt Brace & Company, Toronto, ON, Canada.

Farrell, T.A. and Marion, J.L. (2002). The Protected Area Visitor Impact Management (PAVIM) Framework: A Simplified Process for Making Management Decisions. *Journal of Sustainable Tourism* **10(1)**: [in press].

Federation of Nature and National Parks of Europe (the EUROPARC Federation). (1993). *Loving them to death? Sustainable Tourism in Europe's Nature and National Parks.* EUROPARC, Grafenau, Germany.

Fry, F., Hattwick, R. and Stoner, C. (1998). *Business an integrative framework.* Irwin McGraw-Hill, New York, NY, USA.

Georgiou, S., Moran, D., Pearce, D. and Whittington, D. (UNEP) (1997). *Economic values and the environment in the developing world.* Edward Elgar Publishing, Inc., Lyme, NH, USA.

GoNorthwest. (2000). "Guide to the Bob Marshall Wilderness". [Homepage of the Bob Marshall Wilderness] [On-line]
Available: www.gonorthwest.com/Montana/northwest/bobmw.htm [2002, January 14]

Graefe, A. R. (1990). Visitor Impact Management. In Graham, R. and Lawrence, P. (Eds.) *Towards Serving Our Visitors and Managing Our Resources.* Proceedings of the First Canada/U.S. Workshop on Visitor Management in Parks and Protected Areas, Waterloo, Ontario. Tourism and Research and Education Centre, University of Waterloo and Canadian Parks Service. pp.213–234.

Green, M. J. B. and Paine, J. (1997). State of the World's Protected Areas at the End of the Twentieth Century. Albany, WA, Australia: Unpublished paper presented at Protected Areas in the 21st Century: From Islands to Networks, World Commission on Protected Areas.

Hall, C.M. and McArthur, S. (1998). *Integrated Heritage Management: Principles and Practice.* The Stationery Office, London, UK.

Haas, G.E., Driver, B.L., Brown, P.J. and Lucas, R.C. (1987). Wilderness management zoning. *Journal of Forestry* **85 (1)**: 17–21.

Harmon, D. (1994). *Coordinating Research and Management to Enhance Protected Areas.* George Wright Society, Hancock, MI, USA.

Heath, E. and Wall, G. (1991). *Marketing tourism destinations: A strategic planning approach.* John Wiley and Sons, New York, NY, USA.

Hockings, M., Stolton, S. and Dudley, N. (2000). *Evaluating Effectiveness: A Framework for Assessing the Management of Protected Areas.* IUCN, Gland, Switzerland and Cambridge, UK.

Hogan, C. (2000). *PAN Parks: A Synergy between Nature Conservation and Tourism in Europe's Protected Areas.* PAN Parks Communications office. 13 July.

Holdgate, M. (1999). *The Green Web – A Union for World Conservation.* Earthscan, London, UK.

Honey, M. (1999). *Ecotourism and Sustainable Development: Who Owns Paradise?* Island Press, Washington, DC, USA.

Hornback, K. and Eagles, P. (1999). *Guidelines for Public Use Measurement and Reporting at Parks and Protected Areas.* First Edition. IUCN, Gland, Switzerland and Cambridge, UK; Parks Canada; Cooperative Research Centre for Sustainable Tourism for Australia. [On-line]
Available: www.ahs.uwaterloo.ca/rec/worldww.html [2002, January 14]

Horwich, R.H., Murray, D., Saqui, E., Lyan, J. and Godfrey, D. (1992). Ecotourism and Community Development: A View from Belize. pp.152–168. In Lindberg, K and. Hawkins, D. E., *Ecotourism: A Guide for Planners and Managers.* The Ecotourism Society, Bennington, VT, USA.

Huber, R.M. and Park, W. (1991). *Development plan and Financial Analysis for the Enhancement of the Sulphur Springs Natural Landmark.* OAS/St. Lucia Tourist Board, Voice Press, St. Lucia.

ICOMOS. (1999). "International Cultural Tourism Charter: Managing tourism at places of heritage significance". [Homepage of ICOMOS] [On-line] Available: www.icomos.org/tourism/charter.html [2002, January 14]

Industry, Science and Technology Canada, International Working Group on Indicators of Sustainable Tourism, International Institute for Sustainable Development, and World Tourism Organization. (1993). *Indicators for the sustainable management of tourism.* International Institute for Sustainable Development, Winnipeg, MN, Canada.

IUCN. (1998). *1997 United Nations List of Protected Areas.* IUCN, Gland, Switzerland and Cambridge, UK.

IUCN. (1994). *Guidelines for Protected Area Management Categories.* IUCN, Gland, Switzerland and Cambridge, UK.

IUCN. (1998). *Economic Values of Protected Areas: Guidelines for Protected Area Managers.* IUCN, Gland, Switzerland and Cambridge, UK.

IUCN. (1999). *Parks for Biodiversity – Policy Guidance based on experience in ACP Countries.* For the European Commission by IUCN, Gland, Switzerland and Cambridge, UK.

IUCN. (2000). *Financing Protected Areas: Guidelines for Protected Area Managers.* IUCN, Gland, Switzerland and Cambridge, UK.

James, A. N. (1999). Institutional constraints to protected area funding. *PARKS* **9(2):** 15–26.

Kelleher G. (1999). *Guidelines for Marine Protected Areas.* IUCN, Gland, Switzerland and Cambridge, UK.

Langholtz, J., and Brandon, K. (2001). Privately Owned Protected Areas. pp.303–314. In D.B. Weaver (Ed.). *The Encyclopedia of Ecotourism.* CABI Publishing, Wallingford, UK.

Langholz, J. (1999). Conservation Cowboys: Privately-Owned Parks and the Protection of Tropical Biodiversity. Unpublished PhD Dissertation, Cornell University, Ithaca, NY, USA.

Leung, Y. and Marion, J. (2000). Recreation impacts and management in wilderness: A state-of-knowledge review. In Cole, D. N., McCool, S., Borrie, W. T. and O'Loughlin, J. *Wilderness science in a time of change: Vol. 5, Wilderness ecosystems, threats, and management.* pp.23–48. USDA Forest Service, Rocky Mountain Research Station, Ogden, UT, USA.

Lindberg, K. (1998). Economic Aspects of Ecotourism. In Lindberg, K., Wood, M E. and Engeldrum, D. (Eds.). *Ecotourism: A Guide for Planners and Managers. Volume 2.* The Ecotourism Society, Bennington, Vermont, USA.

Lindberg, K. (2001). *Protected Area Visitor Fees: Overview.* Cooperative Research Centre for Sustainable Tourism, Griffith University, August. [Homepage of The International Ecotourism Society] [Online] Available: www.ecotourism.org/retiesselfr.html [2002, January 21]

Lindberg, K. and Enriquez, J. (1994). *Summary Report: An Analysis of Ecotourism's Contribution to Conservation and Development in Belize.* Vol. 1. WWF, Washington, DC, USA.

Lucas, R. (1964). *The recreational capacity of the Quetico-Superior area.* USDA Forest Service Lake States Forest and Experiment Station, St. Paul, MN, USA.

Manidis Roberts Consultants. (1997). *Developing a Tourism Optimisation Management Model (TOMM): A model to monitor and manage tourism on Kangaroo Island.* Manidis Roberts Consultants, Sydney, NSW, Australia.

Manfredo, M., McCool, S. and Brown, P. (1987). Evolving concepts and tools for recreation user management in wilderness. *Proceedings of the National Wilderness Research Conference: Issues, State-of-Knowledge, Future Directions, USA.* pp.320–346.

Manning, R. (1986). *Studies in outdoor recreation: A review and synthesis of the social science literature in outdoor recreation.* Oregon State University Press, Corvallis, OR, USA.

Manning, R. E., Lime, D. W., Hof, M. and Freimund, W. A. (1995). The Visitor Experience and Resource Protection (VERP) Process. *The George Wright Forum* **12(3)**: 41–55.

Manning, R.E. and Lime, D.W. (2000). Defining and Managing the Quality of Wilderness Recreation Experiences. In McCool, S. F., Cole, D. N., Borrie, W. T. and O'Loughlin, J. (compilers), *Wilderness Science In A Time Of Change* Conference, Missoula, Montana, May 23–27, 1999. Proceedings. USDA, Forest Service, Ogden, UT, USA. [Online]
Available: www.wilderness.net/pubs/ science1999/index.htm [2002, January 14]

Martin, S. (1989). A framework for monitoring experiential conditions in wilderness. In Lime, D. W. (Ed.), *Managing America's enduring wilderness resource* (pp.170–175). University of Minnesota Tourism Center, St. Paul, MN, USA.

Marty, S. (1984). *A Grand and Fabulous Notion: The First Century of Canada's Parks.* NC Press Limited, Toronto, ON, Canada.

McCool, S.F. and Stankey, G.H. (1984). Carrying capacity in recreational settings: Evolution, appraisal and application. *Leisure Sciences* **6(4)**: 453–473.

McCool, S. F. (1990). Limits of Acceptable Change: Evolution and Future. R. Graham, and R. Lawrence (Eds.), *Towards Serving Visitors and Managing Our Resources: Proceedings of a North America Workshop on Visitor Management in Parks and Protected Areas* (pp.185–193). Tourism Research and Education Centre, Waterloo, ON, Canada.

McNeely, J. A. (Ed.).(1993). *Parks for life: Report of the IVth World Congress on National Parks and Protected Areas.* IUCN, Gland, Switzerland.

McNeely, J. A. and Thorsell, J. W. (1989). Jungles, Mountains, and Islands: How Tourism can Help Conserve the Natural Heritage. *World Leisure and Recreation* **31(4)**: 29–39.

Moos, R. (2002). Ontario parks – a successful business operating model. *PARKS* [In press]

National Wilderness Preservation System. (2000). "Bob Marshall Wilderness". [Homepage of the National Wilderness Preservation System] [On-line]
Available: www.wilderness.net/nwps/ [2002, January 14]

National Park Service. (1993). *Guiding principles for sustainable design.* National Park Service, Denver Service Centre, Denver, CO, USA.

National Parks and Wildlife Services. (2000). "New South Wales Parks and Reserves Montague Island Nature Reserve" [Homepage of Montague Island Nature Reserve] [On-line] Available: www.npws.nsw.gov.au/parks/south/sou018.html [2002, January 14]

Nilsen, P. and Tayler, G. (1998). A Comparative Analysis of Protected Area Planning and Management Frameworks. Pages 49–57 in McCool, S. F. and Cole, D. N. (Compilers), *Limits of Acceptable Change and Related Processes: Programs and Future Directions*. Proceedings of conference, 1997 May 20–22, Missoula, MN. Gen. Tech. Rep. INT-GTR-371. U. S. Department of Agriculture, Forest Service, Rocky Mountains Research Station, Ogden, UT, USA.

Northwest Parks and Tourism Board. (2000). "Madikwe Game Reserve". [Homepage of the North West Parks and Tourism Board] [On-line]
Available: www.parks-nw.co.za/madikwe/index.html [2002, January 14]

Operation Wallacea. (2000). "What is Operation Wallacea?" [Homepage of Operation Wallacea] [On-line] Available: www.opwall.com/ [2002, January 14]

Pam Wight and Associates. (2001). *Best Practices in Natural Heritage Collaborations: Parks Agencies and Eco-Adventure Operators*. Canadian Tourism Commission, Ottawa, Canada.

Parks Canada. (1985). *Management process for visitor activities.* Parks Canada, National Parks Directorate, Hull, PQ, Canada.

Parks Canada. (1986). *Visitor risk management handbook.* Department of Canadian Heritage, National Parks Directorate, Hull, PQ, Canada.

Parks Canada. (1988). *Getting started: A guide to service planning.* Parks Canada, National Parks Directorate, Hull, PQ, Canada.

Parks Canada. (1991). *Visitor activity concept.* Parks Canada, VAMP Technical group, Hull, PQ, Canada.

Parks Canada. (1992).*Camping manual.* Parks Canada, National Parks Directorate, Hull, PQ, Canada.

Parks Canada. (1994a). *Guiding Principles and Operational Policies.* Parks Canada, National Parks Directorate, Hull, PQ, Canada.

Parks Canada. (1994b). *St. Lawrence Islands National Park Management Plan.* Parks Canada, National Parks Directorate, Hull, PQ, Canada.

Parks Canada. (2002). "Parks Canada Visitor Risk Management Handbook". [Homepage of Parks Canada] [On-line]
Available: parkscanada.pch.gc.ca/library/risk/english/intro3_e.htm [2002, January 14]

Pynes, J. (1997). *Human resources management for public and non-profit organizations* Jossey-Bass Inc., San Francisco, California.

Rome, A. (1999). *Ecotourism Impacts Monitoring: A Review of Methodologies and Recommendations for Developing Monitoring Programs in Latin America.* The Nature Conservancy Report Series Number 2. [Online]
Available: nature.org/aboutus/travel/ecotourism/resources/ [2002, January 14]

Sandwith, T., Shine, C., Hamilton, L. and Sheppard, D. (2001). *Transboundary Protected Areas for Peace and Co-operation.* IUCN, Gland, Switzerland and Cambridge, UK.

Schoemaker, J. (1984). Writing quantifiable river recreation management objectives. *Proceedings of the National River Recreation Symposium*, pp.249–253.

Sharp, G. W. (1976). *Interpreting the Environment.* John Wiley and Sons, New York, NY, USA.

Soufrière Marine Management Area (SMMA). (2000). "Soufrière Marine Management Area Site Map". [Homepage of the Soufrière Marine Management Association] [On-line] Available: www.smma.org.lc/ [2002, January 14]

Stankey, G. H., Cole, D. N., Lucas, R. C., Petersen, M. E. and Frissell, S. S. (1985). *The Limits of Acceptable Change (LAC) System for Wilderness Planning.* USDA Forest Service, Intermountain Forest and Range Experiment Station, Ogden, UT, USA.

Swanson, T. (UNEP-1996). *The economics of environmental degradation.* Edward Elgar Publishing, Inc., Cheltenham, UK.

Tasmania Parks and Wildlife Service. (2000). "Best Practice in Protected Area Planning and Management". ANZECC Working Group on National Parks and Protected Areas Management Benchmarking and Best Practice Program [On-line] Available: www.ea.gov.au/parks/anzecc/reports/management-planning/index.html

Taylor, G. E. (1990). The Visitor Management Process. *Proceedings of a North American Workshop on Visitor Management: Perspectives of Several Canadian and United States Park, Protected Area and Natural Resource Management Agencies: Towards Serving Visitors and Managing Our Resources* (pp.235–247). Tourism Research and Education Centre, University of Waterloo, Waterloo, ON, Canada.

Thapa, B. (2000). The Relationship Between Debt-for-Nature Swaps and Protected Area Tourism: A Plausible Strategy for Developing Countries. In McCool, S. F., Cole, D. N., Borrie, W. T. and O'Loughlin, J. (Compilers), *Wilderness Science In A Time Of Change* Conference, Missoula, Montana, May 23–27, 1999. Proceedings. USDA, Forest Service, Ogden, UT, USA. [Online] Available: www.wilderness.net/pubs/ science1999/index.htm [2002, January 14]

The Interorganizational Committee on Guidelines and Principles for Social Impact Assessment. (1994). "Guidelines and principles for social impact assessment". [On-line]. Available: www.gsa.gov/pbs/pt/call-in/siagide.htm (Dead)

Tiegland, J. (2000). The Effects on Travel and Tourism Demand from Three Mega-trends: Democratization, Market Ideology and Post-materialism as Cultural Wave. In Gartner, W.C. and Lime, D. W. (Eds.), *Trends in Outdoor Recreation, Leisure and Tourism,* pp.37–46. CABI Publishing, Wallingford, UK.

The Outspan Group. (1996). *Benefits of protected areas.* Parks Canada, Hull, PQ, Canada.

Tourism Canada (1995). *Adventure Travel in Canada: An Overview of Product, Market and Business Potential* Industry Canada, Ottawa, Canada.

Tourism Council Australia, and CRC Tourism. (1998). *Being green keeps you out of the red* Tourism Council Australia, Woolloomooloo, NSW, Australia.

UNESCO. (1999). "Enrolment ratios by level of education". [Homepage of UNESCO Institute for Statistics] [Online]. Available: www.uis.unesco.org/ [2002, January 14]

UNESCO. (2000). "World Education Report 2000". [Homepage of UNESCO] [On-line]. Available: www.unesco.org/education/information/wer [2002, January 14]

UNESCO. (2002). "Recommendation concerning the safeguarding and contemporary role of historic areas". [Homepage of UNESCO] [On-line] Available: www.unesco.org/culture/laws/historic/html_eng/page1.shtml [2002, January 14]

United Nations. (1993). Report of the United Nations conference of environment and development. Volumes 1–3. United Nations, New York, NY, USA.

United Nations Environment Programme. (1997). *Global environment outlook*. United Nations Environment Programme and Oxford University Press, New York, NY, USA.

Van Sickle, K. and Eagles, P. F. J. (1998). User Fees and Pricing Policies in Canadian Senior Park Agencies. *Tourism Management* **19(3)**: 225–235.

Wakatobi Dive Resort. (2000). "Wakatobi Research". [Homepage of Wakatobi Dive Resort] [On-line] Available: www.wakatobi.com/homepage.html [2002, January 14]

Wells, M. P. (1997). *Economic perspectives on nature tourism, conservation and development*. Pollution and Environmental Economics Division, Environmental Economics Series, World Bank, Washington, DC, USA.

Wes, H. (1998). HRM issues and implications of the process of localisation. In Analoui, F. (Ed.), *Human resource management issues in developing countries*, pp.61–69. Ashgate Publishing Ltd, Brookfield, VT, USA.

Western Australia Conservation and Land Management. (2001). "Visitor Risk Management and Public Liability". Prepared for ANZECC Working Group on National Parks and Protected Areas Management. [Homepage of ANZECC Working Group on National Parks and Protected Areas Management] [Online]
Available: www.ea.gov.au/parks/anzecc/reports/index.html [2002, January 14]

Wight, P.A. (1996). Planning for Success in Sustainable Tourism. Invited paper presented to "*Plan for Success*" Canadian Institute of Planners National Conference, Saskatoon, Saskatchewan, June 2–5.

Wight, P. (1997). North American ecotourists: Market profile and trip characteristics. *Journal of Travel Research* **24(4)**: 2–10.

Wight, P. (2001). Integration of Biodiversity and Tourism: Canada Case Study. Paper presented at the International Workshop Integrating Biodiversity and Tourism, UNEP/UNDP/BPSP/GEF, Mexico City, March 29–31.

Wight, P. (2002a). Planning for Resource Protection and Tourism Management in Protected Areas: a Practical Perspective. In Wall, G. (Ed.), *Tourism: People, Places, Products*. Department of Geography, University of Waterloo, Waterloo, ON, Canada.

Wight, P. (2002b) Practical Management tools for resource protection in tourism destinations. In Diamantis, D. and Geldenhuys, S. (Eds.), *Ecotourism: Management and Assessment* Continuum, London, UK and New York, USA. [in press]

World Tourism Organization and World Travel and Tourism Council. (1992). *Agenda 21 for the travel and tourism industry: Towards environmentally sustainable development*. World Tourism Organization, World Travel and Tourism Council, London, UK.

World Tourism Organization. (1994). *Global tourism forecasts to the year 2000 and beyond*. Volumes 1-7. World Tourism Organization, Madrid, Spain.

World Tourism Organization. (1997). *Tourism market trends: The world*. World Tourism Organization, Madrid, Spain.

World Tourism Organization. (1999). *Tourism satellite account: The conceptual framework*. World Tourism Organization, Madrid, Spain.

World Tourism Organization. (2001). *Sustainable Development of Tourism: A Compilation of Good Practices*. World Tourism Organization, Madrid, Spain.